DISABILITY
AND *SPORT*

Karen P. DePauw, PhD
Washington State University

Susan J. Gavron, PED
Bowling Green State University

Human Kinetics

Library of Congress Cataloging-in-Publication Data

DePauw, Karen P.
  Disability and sport / Karen P. DePauw, Susan J. Gavron.
    p. cm.
  Includes bibliographical references and index.
  ISBN 0-87322-848-0
  1. Sports for the handicapped. I. Gavron, Susan J., 1947-
  II. Title.
GV709.3.D47 1995   94-25215
796'.1'96--dc20   CIP

ISBN: 0-87322-848-0

Acquisitions Editor: Richard D. Frey, PhD; **Developmental Editors:** Ann Brodsky and Julia Anderson; **Assistant Editors:** Jacqueline Blakley, Kirby Mittelmeier, and Rebecca Ewert; **Editorial Assistant:** Karen Grieves; **Copyeditor:** Elaine Otto; **Proofreader:** Kirsten Kite; **Indexer:** Kathy Bennett; **Typesetting and Text Layout:** Yvonne Winsor; **Text and Cover Designer:** Stuart Cartwright; **Photographer (cover):** Chris Hamilton; **Illustrators:** Beth Young and Gretchen Walters; **Printer:** Edwards Brothers

Printed in the United States of America   10 9 8 7 6 5 4 3

Human Kinetics
Web site: www.humankinetics.com

United States: Human Kinetics, P.O. Box 5076, Champaign, IL 61825-5076
800-747-4457
e-mail: humank@hkusa.com

Canada: Human Kinetics, 475 Devonshire Road, Unit 100, Windsor, ON N8Y 2L5
800-465-7301 (in Canada only)
e-mail: humank@hkcanada.com

Europe: Human Kinetics, P.O. Box IW14, Leeds LS16 6TR, United Kingdom
+44 (0)113-278 1708
e-mail: humank@hkeurope.com

Australia: Human Kinetics, 57A Price Avenue, Lower Mitcham, South Australia 5062
(08) 82771555
e-mail: liahka@senet.com.au

New Zealand: Human Kinetics, P.O. Box 105-231, Auckland Central
09-309-1890
e-mail: humank@hknewz.com

Contents

Preface

The sport movement for individuals with disabilities has changed dramatically over the last 40 years with even more changes ahead. Public awareness has increased. More and more individuals with disabilities of all ages (especially youth) find interest in sport. Sport programs and opportunities worldwide have increased in scope and number as well. In short, sport has become a viable option for individuals with disabilities.

It's now up to professionals to assist in the further development of sport for and including individuals with disabilities. Thus, it is important that professionals be knowledgeable about sport and disability and its complexity.

This book has been written primarily for physical educators, coaches, sport administrators/managers, adapted physical education specialists, and therapeutic recreation specialists who would provide or administer sport programs that include individuals with disabilities. *Disability and Sport* should not only be used as a textbook for undergraduate and graduate courses in sport and disability but also in conjunction with courses offered to those seeking degrees (or advanced training) in physical education, recreation, coaching, sport administration/sport management, and other related fields of study.

Disability and Sport will also serve as a valuable resource book for public school personnel, community organizations, sport associations and agencies, including disability sport organizations, and individuals with disabilities and their family members wishing to obtain information regarding sport opportunities for aspiring athletes with disabilities. Everyone connected with sport (public school, community recreation, competitive sport, and even professional sport) will work with individuals with disabilities in some capacity. Thus, appropriate background and training are important.

In this book, we have attempted to provide readers with an understanding of the historical context for sport today and trends for the future, an awareness of sport modifications and the multitude of sport opportunities available, as well as knowledge of the issues and complexity of sport and disability. Scattered throughout the chapters are sport biographies of selected athletes with disabilities as examples of excellence in athletic performance around the world. Even as we have attempted to reflect an international perspective as much as possible, available resources are limited and therefore prevent a thorough discussion of sport and disability worldwide. Thus, the book tends to reflect more of the status of sport and disability in North America, especially the United States.

This is not a "how to" book, but we have included some introductory material on coaching, sports medicine, classification, sport and adapted equipment, and event management. In addition, we have provided a brief overview of research on sport and athletes with disabilities for the readers. Currently, there is no other book on sport and disability that is as comprehensive in nature. *Disability and Sport* includes a number of valuable resources: names and addresses for sport organizations serving individuals with disabilities in nations around the world, listings of major international sport federations for athletes with disabilities, and sport organizations and federations in the United States. In addition, lists of sport videos and films, periodicals on sport and physical activity, and scholarships for athletes with disabilities are included.

Disability and Sport is a comprehensive view of sport and disability. Although this sport world continues to evolve, *Disability and Sport* will provide readers with a synthesis of information about sport for and including individuals with disabilities. We enjoyed compiling the information and writing the book; we hope you enjoy reading it.

Acknowledgments

A book of this magnitude and complexity could not have been written without the efforts of many. A number of people throughout the world contributed to its completion.

We extend our heartfelt thanks to everyone at Human Kinetics for their expert direction in nurturing the development and completion of this project. In particular, we thank our developmental editors, Ann Brodsky and Julia Anderson, who were patient and forthcoming in their comments and suggestions.

We are grateful to all the people who reviewed our manuscript in its various stages. Their critiques and suggestions improved the book.

To our friends and colleagues, Ron Davis and Mike Ferrara, thanks for writing a chapter for the book. Thanks to Gudrun Doll-Tepper, Free University of Berlin, whose thorough critique made vast improvements in the overall quality of the book, and who tirelessly contacted individuals for the sport bios. Our sincere thanks to Diane Smerdon, who typed chapter after chapter as well as a multitude of appendixes, figures, tables, and seemingly endless references. We also wish to thank our students, colleagues, and administrators at our respective universities for their support and understanding as this book evolved. When professional endeavors and personal lives overlap, it is reassuring to have continual support and encouragement from friends and family—thank you!

Finally, there are two other groups of people we wish to acknowledge: the individuals with disabilities who participate in sport and the individuals who have volunteered over the years as coaches and administrators of disability sport. We are indebted to these people and their efforts.

The idea for this book about sport and disability was generated during a plane ride 8 years ago. We are delighted that the project is completed so that others can have access to information on this very important topic.

Credits

FIGURES

Page 66: From *1993 USOC Fact Book* (p. 14) by the United States Olympic Committee, 1993, Colorado Springs: Author. Adapted with permission.

Page 70: From *1993 USOC Fact Book* (p. 11) by the United States Olympic Committee, 1993, Colorado Springs: Author. Adapted with permission.

Pages 80-82: Adapted from *COSD Minutes* (May 1991) with permission of the USOC, Colorado Springs, CO.

Pages 169-170: From "Factors Influencing the Learning Process" (pp. 121-130) and "Teaching Styles and Approaches" (pp. 131-150) by S.M. Rich. In *Adapted Physical Education* by J.P. Winnick (Ed.), 1990, Champaign: Human Kinetics. Copyright 1990 by Joseph P. Winnick. Reprinted by permission.

Page 171: From "Coaching Individuals With Disabilities," 1989, *Sports Coach*, **12**(4), pp. 6-8. Copyright 1989 by the Australian Coaching Council. Adapted with permission.

Page 180: From *Special Events Inside and Out* (pp. 8-10) by R. Jackson and S.W. Schmader, 1990, Champaign, IL: Sagamore Publishing. Copyright 1990 by Sagamore Publishing, Inc. Adapted with permission.

Page 182: From *Special Events Inside and Out* (p. 26) by R. Jackson and S.W. Schmader, 1990, Champaign, IL: Sagamore Publishing. Copyright 1990 by Sagamore Publishing, Inc. Adapted with permission.

Pages 183-184: From *Special Events Inside and Out* (pp. 27-31) by R. Jackson and S.W. Schmader, 1990, Champaign, IL: Sagamore Publishing. Copyright 1990 by Sagamore Publishing, Inc. Adapted with permission.

Pages 231-232: Information on accessible camping in national parks available from "Accessible Camping in the National Parks" by W.K. Ellis, 1992, *Sports 'n Spokes*, **17**(5), pp. 47-50.

PHOTOS

Opening photos for chapters 2, 3, 4, 8, 9, 11, and 13 courtesy of Karen P. DePauw.

Part I Opening Photo: Courtesy of Michael Gobran.

Chapter 1 Opening Photo: Courtesy of Ron Davis/Ball State University.

Page 7: Courtesy of Kai Schrameyer.

Page 13: Courtesy of Errol Marklein.

Page 45: Courtesy of Robert Steadward.

Page 47: Courtesy of Katie Herrmann.

Page 49: Courtesy of Diana Golden.

Page 51: Courtesy of Special Olympics International.

Page 53: Courtesy of Duncan Wyeth.

Page 58: Courtesy of Brenda Gilmore.

Page 67: Courtesy of Hugo Storer.

Page 77: Courtesy of Rodney Hernley.

Page 81: Courtesy of Jan Wilson.

Chapter 5 Opening Photo: Courtesy of Ron Davis/Ball State University.

Page 87: Courtesy of Gunther Belitz.

Page 88: Courtesy of Tanni Grey.

Page 95: Courtesy of Mitchell Seidenfeld.

Chapter 6 Opening Photo: Courtesy of Gudrun Doll-Tepper.

Page 104: Courtesy of Manuel Robles Aguila.

Page 110: Courtesy of Corina Robitjcho.

Part II Opening Photo: Courtesy of Ron Davis/Ball State University.

Chapter 7 Opening Photo: Courtesy of Ron Davis/Ball State University.

Page 156: Figure 9.1a courtesy of BioSculptor.

Pages 156-158: Figures 9.1b-g courtesy of Flex-Foot, Inc.

Page 158: Figure 9.1h courtesy of Stuart Spencer and Payam Sadat.

Pages 160-163: Figures 9.2a-h courtesy of Quickie Designs, Inc.

Pages 164-165: Figures 9.3a and b courtesy of Jim Cowart.

Chapter 10 Opening Photo: Courtesy of Ron Davis/Ball State University.

Page 177: Courtesy of Sue Moucha.

Part III Opening Photo: Courtesy of The Daily Illini.

Page 213: Courtesy of Karen Farmer-Lewis.

Page 215: Courtesy of Jean Driscoll.

Chapter 14 Opening Photo: Courtesy of Curt Beamer, PVA Publications/ *Sports 'n Spokes.*

P A R T   I

Overview of Sport and Individuals With Disabilities

CHAPTER 1

Introduction to Sport and Individuals With Disabilities

Individuals with disabilities have always been present in society, although they are more prevalent in the twentieth century than in previous centuries. For at least 100 years, individuals with selected disabilities have participated in the sporting world. However, these athletes are just now beginning to receive the recognition they deserve and, more importantly, acceptance as athletes.

The twentieth century saw the confluence of sport and disability into disability sport; it is now a movement whose time has come. As athletic opportunities have expanded and disability sport has matured, so have the individual accomplishments of athletes with disabilities.

Outstanding performances by elite athletes with disabilities are merely seconds or tenths of seconds behind those of elite able-bodied athletes in such sports as downhill skiing and swimming. Athletes with double leg amputations have finished the 100m race in 11.34 seconds; others with less severe impairments finish in less than 11 seconds. Male wheelchair marathoners frequently average 3.5 minutes per mile and complete marathons in approximately 90 minutes. Athletes with cerebral palsy bench press 400 pounds; athletes with other physical impairments bench press over 600 pounds in competition. In field events, athletes with single leg amputations have jumped 6 feet, 8 inches (Atlanta Paralympic Organizing Committee, n.d.). See Appendix A for a listing of selected paralympic records. Thus, there should no longer be a question as to the athletic ability of elite athletes with disabilities.

INDIVIDUALS WITH DISABILITIES AS ATHLETES

Over the years, a number of individuals with disabilities have demonstrated their athletic ability in the sporting arena. Some have achieved in the able-bodied sport world, while others have achieved in disability sport. A few of the many examples follow and others are featured throughout the book.

- Dr. Donalda Ammons excelled in basketball and swimming as a young woman. Her academic interests led her to pursue doctoral studies in foreign language, and she ultimately became director of foreign study programs at Gallaudet University. As a strong advocate for Deaf sport, she has served the American Athletic Association of the Deaf in many capacities, and she was the first woman to chair the U.S. World Games for the Deaf Team Committee.

- Camille Waddell Black competed in the 1992 Paralympics in Barcelona and was the first U.S. dwarf athlete to win a Paralympic gold medal. Camille set a world record in the 100m breaststroke.

- Distance runner Loretta Clairborne was inducted into the National Girls and Women in Sport Symposium Hall of Fame in February 1993. She has competed for a number of years with Special Olympics International.

- Running with a sighted partner, Harry Cordellos (who is blind) has run over 100 marathons; his best finish at the Boston Marathon was 2:57.42. In addition, he has competed in the Iron Man Triathlon in Hawaii and the grueling 100-mile survival run outside San Francisco.

- Dr. Brad Hedrick is not only an elite athlete with a disability but an active professional and researcher in the field of disability sport. He has competed in wheelchair sports, including basketball and athletics (marathon time of 1 hour and 54 minutes; 10K time of 26:49). In addition, he has coached men's and women's wheelchair basketball; he now coaches the U.S. wheelchair basketball team.

- Sharon Hedrick was the first to enter the women's wheelchair division of the Boston Marathon. She won the Olympic Gold medal for the 800m exhibition event in the 1984 Los Angeles Olympic Games and for the 1988 Olympics in Seoul. She graduated with honors completing B.S. and M.S. degrees in health education. She is a registered dietitian and works as a diabetic nutrition education specialist in Illinois.

- Duncan Wyeth, ambulatory cerebral palsy athlete, competed for the first time at the age of 32, in 1978 at the Michigan Regional Cerebral Palsy Games, in cycling and athletics. He has won gold and silver medals in regional, national, and international competitions including cerebral palsy athletes. He served as athlete and coach for the 1988 U.S. Disabled Sport Team for the Seoul Paralympics and received the Male Athlete of the Year (Cerebral Palsy) Award from the United States Olympic Committee. (See feature on page 53.)

DEFINITIONS

Before continuing, it is important to proceed with a common base of knowledge. Many organizations in this field are referred to by their abbreviations. See Appendix B for a list of abbreviations found in this book. Here we have defined a few key terms.

Disability

Various terms have been used to describe individuals with disabilities over the years. Currently, the preferred terminology is one in which the person is first, such as *person with a disability* or *individual with a physical impairment*. Throughout this text, we have attempted to use "people first" language, such as *athletes with disabilities* or *athlete with visual impairment*.

Before proceeding, three terms to describe the population discussed in this book should be clarified: impairment, disability, handicap. *Impairment* is a limiting condition that exists with a person (e.g., less than 20/20 vision, amputated limb, Downs syndrome). When an impairment adversely affects one's performance, the appropriate term is *disability*. The terms *handicap* and *handicapped*, although used to describe individuals with disabilities, tend to imply devaluation or stigma associated with an impairment and thus are not preferable.

Disability Sport

As individuals with impairments (or disabilities) have entered the sport world, various terms have evolved to represent their involvement. Among the more prevalent of these are *handicapped sports, sport for the disabled, adapted sport, disabled sport, wheelchair sport,* and *Deaf sport.* These terms generally imply a sport context designed for individuals with disabilities, and specify, in some instances, the type of disability. These terms do not adequately describe the broader entity of sport in which athletes with disabilities can be found: sport for athletes with disabilities specifically and sport that includes both athletes with disabilities and athletes without disabilities.

Throughout the book, when used alone, *sport* refers to the broadest context of sport; in most instances, we use the term to mean competitive sport (as conceptualized in the United States). The term *sport* as used in other countries (discussed in chapter 6) encompasses much more than competitive sport, but its use here is intended to delimit the scope of the book.

This book is written about sport for and including individuals with disabilities (impairments); thus, the title of *Disability and Sport.* Much of the focus, however, is upon sport for athletes with disabilities (physical, sensory, and mental impairments)—what we call disability sport. We have adopted the term *disability sport* to refer to sport that has been designed for or specifically practiced by athletes with disabilities. Disability sports might include sports that were designed for a selected disability group: goalball for blind athletes, wheelchair basketball for athletes with physical impairments who use a wheelchair, or sitting volleyball for athletes with lower-limb impairments. Disability sport also includes those sports practiced by able-bodied individuals (e.g., athletics, volleyball, swimming, etc.) that have been modified or adapted to include athletes with disabilities (e.g., wheelchair tennis, tandem cycling) as well as those that require little or no modification to allow individuals with disabilities to participate (e.g., athletics, wrestling, swimming).

Disabled sport or *sport for the disabled* are the terms that have been used, and are still prevalent in the literature, to describe that which we call disability sport. *Disability sport* is preferred because sport cannot be disabled and "for the disabled" does not utilize "person first" language.

Deaf Sport

"Deaf sport is a social institution within which Deaf people exercise their right to self-determination through organization, competition, and

KAI SCHRAMEYER

At a glance:

Wheelchair tennis

Involved 5 years in competitive sport

Olympic medal winner

World champion

Tennis anyone? This is a phrase heard around the world. To Kai Schrameyer, a 26-year-old athlete from Bonn, Germany, this is her call to action. This elite wheelchair tennis player is an above-the-knee amputee who has been involved in the sport for just 5 years. In this short time she has earned a silver medal at the 1992 Barcelona Paralympics and won the French Open, Swiss Open, and the Dutch Open in 1993. Her crowning achievement was to win the world championship in 1993. Her energy level was extraordinary: she would train four to six times a week for several hours. Nowadays, Kai is putting this same energy into her studies and finds tennis more of a recreational outlet. Her advice for young people: "Have fun, get involved in different kinds of sports, try everything." Game, set, and match!

socialization surrounding Deaf sport activities" (Stewart, 1991, p. 2). On one level, Deaf sport can be defined as sport in which Deaf athletes compete, a parallel entity to able-bodied (hearing) sport in which individuals with hearing impairments participate.

On another level, Deaf sport should be viewed from a cultural perspective. Not only is Deaf sport a celebration of community among Deaf people but it is a microcosm of the Deaf community (Stewart, 1991).

Although athletes with hearing impairments and deafness typically have not considered themselves a part of disability sport, we see that they do fit within the broader context of sport for and including athletes with disabilities. As such, we acknowledge fully and concur with the argument put forth by Stewart (1991) that "disability leaves the impression that a person [with a disability] has more liabilities than assets" (p. 99), and we also acknowledge the severe limitations of our language. Without wishing to offend, we include Deaf athletes and Deaf sport in this book and shall discuss both not only as part of sport and disability but also within the context of disability sport.

IN THE CONTEXT OF SPORT

Sport is a cultural phenomenon that is often viewed as a product and a reflection of society (Giddens, 1977; Sage, 1987). Sport is a microcosm of the larger society; it is defined and described within the sociocultural and sociohistorical framework of the values, mores, norms, and standards of a specific society or culture.

Historically, sport has tended to be an exclusive club for the white, middle- and upper-class, Protestant, heterosexual, able-bodied male "majority" within a capitalistic society (Bonace, Karwas, & DePauw, 1992). Thus, not all persons who desired access were allowed into the sporting arena.

Women, members of ethnic minorities, and persons with disabilities have been excluded or allowed limited access to sport. Given the similarity in the patterns of exclusion or limited acceptance because of culture, gender, ethnicity, class, or disability affiliation (Karwas & DePauw, 1990), individuals from these groupings can be considered to be "outside" of a particular culture or society, or marginalized (e.g., Hughes, 1949; Park, 1928).

Ours is a social world, "constituted and reproduced through and in human action" (Giddens, 1977, p. 166). Sport is a significant part of this world—a social construction. Not only is sport highly visible but it touches almost everyone as a participant, spectator, or consumer. Sport permeates the very fabric of society. Because sport is so pervasive in society and it has been perceived by society as an equalizer and as a means of gaining acceptance, individuals with disabilities have sought access to sport.

Attitudes Toward Persons With Disabilities in Sport

As a minority (or marginalized) group, individuals with disabilities have limitations placed upon their participation in society. As sport is an integral part of society, similar sanctions and limitations have been imposed for inclusion within the sporting world.

Throughout the history of sport, individuals with disabilities have experienced exclusion and disenfranchisement. Although the progress is slow, it has been positive (Mastro, Hall, & Canabal, 1988). Progress, both past and future, is related directly to the attitudes held by society about sport and disability.

ABU YILLA

At a glance:

Involved 19 years with disability sport

National and international participant, medal winner

Wheelchair basketball and quad rugby player

Abu Yilla was born in Sierra Leone, West Africa, and reared in England. Abu has postpolio syndrome, and is a doctoral student in adapted physical education. In Great Britain, Abu Yilla was involved in eight national championships and was a member of the Great Britain National Team, which won numerous Paralympics, European, and world championships in wheelchair basketball. Since coming to the United States eight years ago, Abu has been a member of the U.S. National Team to Stoke Mandeville Games (gold medal) and a track participant in various dashes from 100 meters to 1,500 meters and relay teams. Recently, Abu's passion for sport has turned to founding and organizing the U.S. Quad Rugby Association and becoming its first president. In 1990 Abu coached the U.S. team to the Stoke Mandeville Games, in which he won a gold medal.

This accomplished academic and athlete talks about sport as "impacting all of my life. It is my raison d'etre for my academic life, and influences my social life." Yet Abu also informs us that one should have interests outside of disability sport: "unidimensional people are boring." Abu Yilla is anything but boring!

As will be discussed in some detail in chapter 2, the historical treatment of individuals with disabilities was focused on difference and based on fear and superstition. This provided the basis for exclusion from society and lies at the heart of "exclusion" from sport. The perception of individuals with disabilities was that they were frail and thus not physically capable. As logic would have it, sport, being representative of physical prowess, could not include those who were weak or physically impaired. The traditional model of sport persisted, and those who were not "physical" or perceived as physically capable were not allowed to participate.

Medical restrictions have always been imposed upon the sport participation of individuals with disabilities. Although there are still some contraindications for full, unrestricted participation, they are decreasing as a result of changing attitudes about the frailty of persons with disabilities and new acceptance of their abilities.

Socialization is a process whereby individuals assimilate, or adopt, the values of a given society. Socialization is an important process of childhood in that it allows for determination of interests, aspirations, and activity selection in the future. Socialization into sport, let alone socialization via sport, is often not a part of the socialization of youth with disabilities. Although sport roles and expectations tend to be socialized early in one's life, different roles (e.g., spectator) and expectations (e.g., participation only, no competition) are socialized for youth with disabilities. Disabled youth who deviate from these social roles and/or expectations have often received negative reinforcement.

Often the attitudes of significant individuals (socializing agents) in the life of a child with a disability provide the reinforcement and modeling of appropriate sport behavior. Inasmuch as teachers, parents, schools, and community agencies are socializing agents or settings, their attitudes, behaviors, and practices serve to model and/or reinforce sporting behavior as is perceived to be appropriate for individuals with disabilities. Many of the socializing agents have just begun to reflect the value of sport participation for individuals with disabilities.

Social attitudes toward sport competition by individuals with disabilities have been mixed. Because of perceived frailty and negative experience resulting from defeat, individuals with disabilities have often been discouraged from competing. Even though participation has finally been deemed acceptable, competition has not yet been fully accepted as appropriate for individuals with disabilities. This mixed response to sport competition appears to be dependent upon the perception of the type and extent of one's disability and one's perceived understanding of competition. Individuals with disabilities have most often been perceived as physically and mentally inferior and therefore as having no cultural need for competition beyond sport for rehabilitation or therapeutic reasons (Lewko, 1979; Orr, 1979; Snyder, 1984).

Disability sport has not been viewed as legitimate sport but rather as something less. Concomitantly, opportunities, rewards, public recognition, and the like have not been afforded athletes with disabilities. Segregated events and competitions have been somewhat acceptable but are still viewed as being of less value than sport competitions for able-bodied individuals.

Integrated participation in sporting events is slowly becoming accepted, but it is far from acceptable sport practice. Individuals with disabilities who compete, or are able to compete, alongside nondisabled individuals are considered the exception rather than the rule. Attitudes are changing and perhaps so is the definition of sport.

Barriers to Inclusion in Sport

Society's attitudes about individuals with disabilities in sport have led to specific barriers to participation. These barriers result from persistent social myths and alarming stereotypes held by the greater society. Many of these stem from the labels that have been created to identify the "problems" or "impairments" that characterize selected individuals in our society.

Many detrimental effects of labeling exist. Categorization allows for overgeneralization and underexpectation, which have plagued persons with disabilities throughout history and have been evident in the limitations placed upon those who wish to enter sport. Mentally retarded persons were not thought to understand or enjoy competition or to be capable of outstanding physical performance. Blind individuals certainly couldn't downhill ski or run marathons. Wheelchair marathoners were never expected to complete the race in under two hours. Differences within a given category were thought not to vary except within a small range. In addition to promoting overgeneralization and underexpectation, labels tend to be permanent, to relieve one from responsibility for change, and to emphasize status quo and not allow for change.

Although labeling persists, the trend within disability sport is now to place greater emphasis upon classifying by *ability* rather than disability. Disability classifications have not been completely erased, but greater attention is being paid to functioning classification (see chapter 7). In general, it is the performances of athletes with disabilities in the 1980s and 1990s that have done much to dispel, but not yet eliminate, the effects of labeling and the persistence of classification.

Many of the barriers to sport that exist for individuals with disabilities are similar to those experienced by women (Grimes & French, 1987) and other marginalized groups (Karwas & DePauw, 1990). These include the

- lack of organized sport programs,
- lack of informal early experiences in sport,
- lack of role models,
- lack of access to coaches and training programs,
- economics,
- lack of accessible sport facilities, and
- psychological and sociological factors.

The increase in the number and variety of available sport opportunities, the increasing visibility of disability sport, and specific role models of athletes with disabilities have facilitated the lowering of some of these barriers.

Among the specific barriers is the lack of organized sport programs. Although increasing, sport opportunities for individuals with disabilities within school physical education or after-school sport programs are inadequate. Community-based recreation and sport programs have increased dramatically over the years, but they remain inadequate to fulfill the needs of the existing, let alone the potential, population. Greater numbers of trained sport and recreation professionals and physical educators (including adapted physical education teachers) are needed.

Like women, athletes with disabilities have suffered from the lack of coaches available to help them train. Most of these athletes have been self-coached. They need trained coaches.

Facilities that are accessible to all disability groups are in short supply, even though laws have been passed that require accessibility. Emphasis must be placed on the local level as well as the state and federal levels to provide the physical accommodation and accessibility to those individuals with disabilities who wish to participate in sport.

Economic, psychological, and sociological factors often remain as barriers to sport participation by individuals with disabilities. The cost of necessary equipment can be especially prohibitive. Many individuals with disabilities do require some additional apparatus or assistive device (e.g., wheelchair, especially designed prosthesis, sighted guide, and visual cues). Because of the numerous barriers to sport participation, individuals with disabilities can face enormous psychological problems—women more so than men (Grimes & French, 1987).

Visible role models are valuable to the development of disability sport and the encouragement of sport participation by individuals with disabilities of all ages. In the 1980s and 1990s, athletes with disabilities have been featured in commercials (e.g., Nike) and on the cover of the Wheaties box. These, along with television coverage of selected events, have helped the disability sport movement become increasingly more visible.

CONCLUDING COMMENTS

Sport is a social institution, a "system of social relationships or a network of positions and roles embodying the values people hold in common" (Leonard, 1980, p. 45). As a social institution and a microcosm of society, sport cannot remain unaffected by political, social, and cultural changes. In the 1990s and beyond, sport will be redefined by and in the new order of the world.

Disability sport has made its mark upon society. Individuals with disabilities have fought for inclusion in sport. Although not complete, the trend is toward progressive inclusion and acceptance (DePauw, 1986c). Well into the 21st century, sport opportunities for and including individuals with disabilities will continue to increase.

ERROL MARKLEIN

At a glance:

100-400m racer

World champion, track, 1981-1983

Paralympic participant in Arnhem, NY, Seoul, and Barcelona

Numerous medal finishes

This now retired racer from Germany was involved in competitive sport for 17 years. From 1980 until 1992, he was a top contender. Errol won three gold medals and one bronze in Seoul as an individual and three gold medals as a member of the German relay team in the 100, 200, and 400m.

This elite athlete says he was primarily "self-motivated to work hard and always challenge myself. The motivation is always not to know if it is possible, [but] to try the impossible." As he reflects on the role of sport in his life, Errol states, "Today I take advantage from all the years of competition. I learned how to treat and get along with other people. I have learned about honesty, kindness, trust, and other basic things of life." Errol sums up his experiences with this reflective note: "Today I realize how rich the sport environment can be if you look left and right of the road." Words of a true champion in sport and life.

CHAPTER 2

Historical Perspectives on Disability and Sport

The rights of individuals with disabilities have been at issue throughout history, but they have been contested particularly during the twentieth century. The acknowledgment of the civil rights of individuals with disabilities evolved in response to changes in social attitudes and behaviors. Although there is now greater inclusion and acceptance of individuals with disabilities in society (DePauw, 1986c), this hasn't always been the case.

HISTORICAL TREATMENT OF PERSONS WITH DISABILITIES

Individuals who did not conform to the prescribed norm of the time in either appearance or behavior have always experienced differential treatment. This treatment varied from cruel to humane and even revered. Historically, those who were perceived as "different" were destroyed, tortured, exorcised, sterilized, ignored, exiled, exploited, pitied, cared for, categorized, educated, and even considered divine (Hewett & Forness, 1974). The treatment was dependent upon the individual, the perception of the nature of the disability, and the cultural values and norms of the time. Throughout most of history, differences in treatment have been based on a categorical distinction between those with physical impairments and those with mental impairments.

Survival and Superstition

The primitive and ancient periods (3000 B.C. to 500 B.C.) were characterized by an organized society in which survival and superstition were the key elements. This society practiced the concept of survival of the fittest. When individuals were found to be obviously "physically deformed" and/or not physically capable of hunting for food or defending themselves, they were left to face the consequences of the harsh environment, which was death usually by starvation or predators (Davies, 1975). Often, these individuals born with physical deformities were considered evil and were therefore isolated from the family unit. This attitude often resulted in the death of those with impairments, and their demise was not looked upon as a loss to the functioning of the unit (Davies, 1975). This survival of the fittest concept permeated the early societies; for example, Indian and Oriental societies often allowed the unfit to die to improve the "quality" of the unit.

During this primitive and ancient period, superstition also tended to guide social responses to persons who behaved differently. These individuals were either feared or considered possessed. Those possessed with "good spirits" were revered; those with "bad spirits" were indulged to prevent revenge. Also practiced during this period were exorcism and trephining, a crude skull operation whereby the evil spirits were released through a small hole drilled in the skull (Hewett & Forness, 1974).

Humanitarian Reform

In the Greek and Roman period (500 B.C. to 400 A.D.), persons born with impairments were faced with a harsh physical environment, infanticide, and eugenics (protection and further development of the species). Many physically disabled and female children were actually abandoned or exiled—literally left to die. The doctrine of the survival of the fittest was applied not only to the environmental conditions but to the harsh discipline and punishment often inflicted upon children. The weakest were not to survive this treatment.

The Greeks and the Romans were concerned about the physical capability of their citizens, but their reasons were biased toward the safety of the state and protection from external enemies. Thus, war was the catalyst for building strong bodies and developing advanced skills for the taking of life. In this environment, those with disabilities were not valued and often were put to death. In contrast, those who became physically impaired (e.g., amputated arm) in battle were honored as heroes (Davies, 1975; Rothschild, 1968).

During this period, the treatment of those with mental impairments was based upon superstition. Inasmuch as mental illness was thought to be caused by the "gods taking away one's mind," the treatments included purification, exorcism, and other demonological practices. These practices were a continuation of early treatment of those with mental impairments.

Later in the Greek and Roman period, different conceptualizations of mental illness evolved, thanks to the efforts of such individuals as Hippocrates and Plato. Hippocrates described mental illness as a disease of natural causes and not the result of possession by demons or the wrath of the gods. Plato advocated care, not exile, exorcism, or demonology, for those with mental impairments. For a brief period, this care included physical activity or exercise, hydrotherapy, massage, and exposure to sunshine. Although survival and superstition remained the key components of this period, the development of limited tolerance for individuals with disabilities was first realized, albeit for a brief moment of humanitarian reform (Hewett & Forness, 1974).

Onset of Judeo-Christian Influence

In respect for the Laws of Moses, the Hebrews did not purposely put to death those who were deformed. Even though individuals with disabilities were not allowed to pray in the Temple or to assume skilled jobs, they were accorded some civility in that they were housed and fed and generally protected from outright death (Davies, 1975).

The early Christians (A.D. 400-1500) had even a greater impact on individuals with disabilities because of the strong emphasis placed on the concept that taking a life was a sinful act. Infanticide was no longer an accepted practice. This live-and-let-live attitude allowed such individuals to be treated with compassion, and it represented a significant change because of the large numbers of Christians (Davies, 1975). Despite the fact that infants born impaired were allowed to live, many were still not able to survive in their harsh physical and social environments.

During the Middle Ages, individuals with disabilities, both physical and mental, were able to survive in the protective environment of monasteries and royal courts. Their status was limited, but their quality of life was much improved over previous periods. The religious influences of the period did much to foster acceptance, understanding, and humanitarian treatment of individuals with disabilities.

The onset of Christianity affected treatment. Those with mental retardation were thought to be "children of God," while those with mental illness were believed to be possessed by the devil (Lilly, 1983). The mentally retarded individuals, the "blessed," were often employed in the courts of kings and queens as court jesters. Although protected and tolerated, they were denied access to the craft guilds and other forms of skilled living because they were deemed incapable (Davies, 1975). For those considered mentally ill, occasionally exorcism, torture, witch burning, and other demonological practices persisted (Hewett & Forness, 1974).

Influence of Science and Medicine

Although science and medicine were to influence the treatment of individuals with disabilities during the sixteenth and seventeenth centuries, individuals with noticeable differences were still persecuted. The demonological tradition persisted; individuals with mental illness were still tortured and/or burned at the stake.

In contrast, those with hearing impairments and mental retardation received more humanitarian treatment. Deaf children of noble birth received education afforded only to a privileged few. Primarily in institutions designed specifically for them, Deaf children were taught reading, writing, arithmetic, astronomy, Greek, and other subjects. Both oral language and finger spelling were used to educate these individuals. Due to their privileged status, children with hearing impairments were provided with a high standard of living.

Individuals with mental retardation were still considered idiots and simpletons, but attempts were made to understand them from psychological and educational perspectives. They were often segregated from society, and although some were employed in workhouses, most remained unemployed and were perceived as a burden on society.

Initial Acceptance

During the 18th century, the society that had been significantly influenced by belief in demons and "evil spirits" finally became overshadowed by the movement toward the rights (and dignity) of humans. The 18th century witnessed a transition from fear, superstition, and hostility toward individuals with disabilities to compassion and a decision to educate these same individuals. Rationalism and enlightenment continued to coexist with the harsh environmental conditions and violent revolution.

In general, children were treated in a more humane manner. Although the average longevity was only 22 years when the environment and physical treatment were harsh, some babies were rescued, nursed at public expense, and placed in workhouses when old enough (Hewett & Forness, 1974). During the industrial revolution, women and children were found among the labor force; because they were unskilled, this situation often led to accidents and even death.

The French Revolution awakened the sense of individual responsibility and led to humane treatment of individuals considered to be mentally ill. They were considered "sick people" and deserving of treatment afforded to "suffering humanity." They were warehoused in large institutions with limited intervention or vocational education. Although cared for, housed, fed, and clothed, additional treatment was not necessarily appropriate to the impairments of these individuals. Inasmuch as these institutions were usually located in the countryside, people with severe disabilities were often "out of sight and out of mind." Thus, it appears that society still was not able to accept such an individual as a functioning part of its existence (Carter, Van Andel, & Robb, 1985).

The treatment during this period involved the use of asylums, hospitals, or schools as residential institutions and even included the establishment of a humanitarian teacher. Schools for blind and Deaf children also appeared by the end of the 18th century. However, very little systematic effort was extended on behalf of those with physical disabilities or mental retardation.

In the later years of the Age of Enlightenment, there was some movement toward accepting those who were different. This progress was achieved through the contributions of educators and philosophers. And, although their quality of life remained marginal, individuals with disabilities were no longer viewed as the work of Satan, and they were allowed to survive (Davies, 1975).

Beginnings of Educational Treatment

Among the major events of the 19th century was the work of Jean Marc Itard with the "wild boy" named Victor. Itard was the first to show that severely retarded individuals could be taught and that improved functioning could result. Normal development and functioning were the goals of this training. Inasmuch as normal functioning was not to be achieved for those with severe mental retardation, as was originally hoped, the view of residential schools as training institutions ultimately gave way to custodial facilities at the end of the 19th century.

Itard is credited with developing an individualized and clinical (medical) methodology as well as an initial understanding of the value of the child-teacher relationship. The work of Eduoard Sequin, Itard's protégé, led to a unique educational system in which the physical, intellectual, and moral development of the child was stressed. In the 1890s, Maria

Montessori built upon the theoretical basis provided by Itard and Sequin and extended this education and training to "normal" children.

Starting in the early 1800s, the notion of the residential institutions found in Europe crossed the Atlantic. From 1818 to 1894, residential institutions for mentally retarded (feeble-minded) persons as well as for Deaf and blind persons were established throughout the United States. Institutional segregation tended to be viewed as the most effective treatment for those individuals with disabilities. Severely retarded persons were thought to need lifetime custodial care, but others less impaired were considered possible candidates for some level of employment. Except for the movement toward "special class" treatment that began in Germany in the late 19th century, this period was characterized as one that promoted individualized education but in a segregated setting.

Social Reform

The 20th century can be viewed as a period of social reform, war, increased governmental concern for individuals with disabilities, and the emergence of concern about disability, especially in the fields of education, psychology, and medicine. The educational approach developed by Itard, Sequin, and Montessori provided the basis for the developmental, individualized, and special education prevalent throughout the 20th century. The quest for quantification of disability and classification of individuals led to the analysis of intellectual potential and psychological testing. Greater understanding of mental illness was brought to light by Freud, Pavlov, and Leo Kanner. And finally, the field of medicine began its investigation and treatment of brain injury and neurological functioning in the 1920s and 1930s.

Although the primary treatment of individuals with disabilities was in residential institutions, in the late 19th and early 20th centuries special class education developed in Europe and spread to the United States. As a result of World War I and the Depression, special programs and classes for individuals with disabilities declined in the United States. After World War II, the programs and services not only resumed but increased.

Overall, the world wars had a positive effect upon attitudes about and programs for persons with disabilities. First, during the course of U.S. compulsory military physical examinations, numerous men were identified who were actually physically impaired but who had led "normal" lives. This discovery contributed to a greater understanding and acceptance of physical impairments. Second, veterans who had been previously accepted in their communities and who became disabled during the war were to enjoy continued acceptance despite their physical impairments. The increased knowledge of physical impairments and acceptance of disability as found among veterans were extended unconsciously to physically disabled children.

Three significant events that occurred during the 20th century in the United States were to influence societal treatment of individuals with disabilities (DePauw, 1986b; Lilly, 1983). First, with the passage of child labor laws and compulsory school attendance laws, many more children entered the classroom.

Second, children entering school late often had difficulty grasping classroom concepts. The IQ test was conveniently administered to them. Thought to be a measure of intelligence and therefore a predictor of academic success, the IQ test was used with many different types of individuals. This resulted in new classifications and special classes in which a watered-down curriculum was taught. The third major event was the court ruling (in *Brown v. Topeka, Kansas Board of Education*) that the schools would be integrated because separate education for black children was illegal. Many of the black children previously educated in lesser quality schools also experienced difficulty with education, especially with the curriculum of the time. As a result, many of these children were tested for IQ and placed in special education classes. The social movement for integration created new problems in the schools, as a result of which many black children were to be labeled as "retarded."

Collectively, these events perpetuated the earlier notion that the problem of those "handicapped" children requiring special education was "in the child." Although most of these children had not been previously "handicapped in society," they became "handicapped in school" and to some extent "handicapped" *by* society (Lilly, 1983). Classification of the individuals by their impairments became common practice.

In response to the outcry for equality by parents of disabled children and by individuals with disabilities, federal and state legislation was enacted during the 1970s to address the issues of education, nondiscrimination, accessibility, and equal opportunity. The legislative mandates for the civil rights of individuals with disabilities reflected a change in social response to and attitudes about individuals with disabilities. Relative to legislative behavior, a change in attitude and response could be seen not only in the United States but in other western nations as well.

Trends

Full participation by individuals with disabilities in most societies is still far from a reality. From a historical perspective, the trend has been one of progressive inclusion and acceptance (DePauw, 1986c). Where individuals with disabilities were once excluded from society, there is now at least partial inclusion.

In addition, different trends can be identified with those with severe and mild impairments (DePauw, 1990a; Lilly, 1983). For those whose impairment is more obvious and severe, the treatment began with isolation, moved toward remediation, and is now focused less on remediation and more on age-appropriate functionality. For those with less obvious and mild impairments, what began as neglect and misunderstanding has progressed to understanding and challenge. In this trend toward inclusion and acceptance, emphasis upon categorization and (over) identification has decreased while focus on the individual rather than on the label has increased. At some point in time, individuals with disabilities will not be considered a "surplus population" (Braginsky & Braginsky, 1971) but, rather, individuals who can and will contribute to the betterment of society.

True inclusion can only come when all persons are able to exercise their right of choice in an accessible society. Examples of such choice are to have the option to participate or not; to select one's friends, workplace, and living conditions; to choose to isolate oneself; to have access to numerous alternatives and not be restricted in these alternatives because of one's culture, ethnicity, sex, disability, class, and so on.

HISTORICAL PERSPECTIVES ON PHYSICAL ACTIVITY AND SPORT

The roots of sport can be traced through a historical perspective of physical activity. Throughout the years, physical activity has taken many forms, including exercise, recreation, therapy, and sport. As it is conceptualized and practiced today, sport is but the outcome of the years of change. Disability sport also finds its roots among the rich history of physical activity and human movement.

Physical activity has been an important component of human life throughout most of history. The roots can be traced back to antiquity, when primitive humans needed strength and endurance for basic survival, hunting, fishing, and fighting. Training one's body was simply part of one's education (see Table 2.1).

A curative use of physical activity was found in records and drawings representing life in China approximately 2700 B.C. Additionally, exercise, massage, and baths were used by early Egyptians, Hindus, Greeks, and Romans. People exercised to prevent and alleviate physical disorders and illnesses. Specific exercises were developed for the sick, convalescent, and sedentary.

Physical activity for the development of a beautiful and well-proportioned body was prevalent in the fifth century B.C. when Athenian education was contrasted with the Spartan brutality (Clarke & Clarke, 1963).

Table 2.1 Historical Periods and Physical Activity

Selected time periods	Uses of physical activity
Antiquity	Strength and endurance for survival
2700 B.C. (China)	Curative period for prevention and alleviation of physical disorders
5th century B.C. (Greek society)	Development of beautiful and well-proportioned body—balance of mental, social, and physical training
Reformation (16th- and 17th-century Europe)	Sound mind and sound body through medical gymnastics
1850s (U.S.)	Medical gymnastics used by U.S. physicians
Early 1900s (U.S.)	Physical education to improve physical condition of youth
After World Wars I and II	Rehabilitation through physical activity Educational model for physical education

Greek society emphasized balance among mental, social, and physical forms of training.

After this early emphasis upon physical activity, it wasn't until the Reformation of the 16th and 17th centuries that physical activity received serious attention again. The development of a sound mind in a sound body was promoted by English philosopher John Locke during this time.

The European influences were many and varied, and they have had a lasting effect upon physical activity today. Specifically, two particular systems of medical gymnastics emerged. The German system and the Swedish system of physical education were both aimed at developing the body, mind, and character of youth using gymnastics, mass drills, and games of skill. Accordingly, exercise was thought to be the best medicine, and physicians were the main advocates for medical gymnastics.

These physical educational systems, also referred to as medical gymnastics, were transported to the United States during the 19th century. By the 1850s, American physicians had begun to use these programs. As a result, specialized programs and facilities were developed to correct postural defects, alleviate organic conditions, and improve physical strength and stamina.

Physical education evolved before, and emerged more prominently after, the world wars. The growth was experienced because many of the youth were unfit for war; thus, physical education programs were developed to address their physical condition. Physicians, who had been long involved with physical activity, became involved in physical education programs prior to World War I and remained so long after World War II. Their involvement after the wars included remedial applications of physical activity, specifically rehabilitation. Physical education continued to flourish and came more under the educational model. On the other hand, rehabilitation and therapy (recreation, physical, corrective) remained under the medical model.

Recreation

Ancient or prehistoric times saw the use of physical activity and recreation as means of treatment to eliminate the evil spirits and thus was part of the religious beliefs (Carter, Van Andel, & Robb, 1985). The Greeks and Romans utilized recreation along with medical care and religion in the healing process. These same cultures also used people as a means of recreation or personal diversion such as in gladiator fights and contests against animals.

During the Middle Ages, the Church was the determining factor in deciding treatment for those who were different. This treatment usually consisted of confinement without the benefit of any rehabilitative services (Carter, Van Andel, & Robb, 1985).

With the advent of the industrial revolution in the 1800s, there were many uses for recreation. Nurses in hospitals utilized bowling greens, music, and rocking horses. Those with disabilities were housed in large state institutions and were afforded some recreational opportunities.

The social and moral fabric of society was severely tested by the advent of war in the early 1900s. The returning veterans heightened society's sense of obligation to those perceived as heroes. For example, in the 1930s, President Roosevelt's New Deal concept fostered and promoted taking care of individuals who were less fortunate. As a result, recreation became a vital aspect within military hospitals again in the 1940s and 1950s because of war. It was during the 1950s that the term *therapeutic recreation* was first found in the literature. Although the term is primarily American, programs of this nature are found throughout the western world.

Since the 1960s, there has been a tremendous growth in the recognition of the needs of individuals for recreation and outdoor pursuits. Today, it is common to find therapeutic recreation programs in hospital settings, rehabilitation centers, mental health settings, adjudicated youth environments, nursing homes, and retirement communities.

Outdoor Recreation

The use of the outdoors as a therapeutic modality was initiated in the late 1800s (Gibson, 1979). Both environmental education and outdoor recreation were employed by the Europeans long before the concept reached the United States (Donaldson & Swan, 1979). One of the earliest uses of the outdoors for therapeutic purposes in the United States began in 1901, when psychiatric patients at the Manhattan State Hospital were placed in tents on the ground to relieve overcrowding. What was originally an administrative decision resulted in observations by the staff members of an improvement in the physical and mental health status of the patients (Gibson, 1979). Some 10 years later another state hospital started a summer camp program.

Formalized camping for children with disabilities can be traced back to 1888 (Vinton, Hawkins, Pantzer, & Farley, 1978). In the 1930s, school camping and wilderness programs for adjudicated youth developed rapidly (AAHPERD, 1976). Today, we see a variety of camping and wilderness programs that specialize in meeting the unique needs of individuals with disabilities. Examples include Bradford Woods, McDonald's Camp Good Times for terminally ill youth, and Easter Seals Camps across the United States for individuals who are physically impaired. Wilderness camping and adventure recreation are also available through Outward Bound, Wilderness Inquiry and Mobility International, and Cooperative Wilderness Handicapped Outdoor Group (C.W. HOG). (See Appendix C for a listing of outdoor recreation opportunities for individuals with disabilities.)

Therapeutic Horseback Riding

Horseback riding was first used by the early Greeks to improve the spirits of individuals considered incurable (Mayberry, 1978). During the 18th and 19th centuries, the medical profession recommended horseback riding to prevent and treat tuberculosis and neurological conditions. Improvement of posture, balance, and muscle control were reported through the active movement of the rider and the passive movement provided by the horse (DePauw, 1986a).

Specific programs of therapeutic horseback riding did not emerge until the 1950s. As with physical education and recreation, the medical profession became instrumental in developing therapeutic horseback riding programs, first in England, then in Europe, and shortly thereafter in the United States. Therapeutic horseback riding programs can be found throughout the world today. That which started more as therapy (medicine) has now expanded into riding as sport (riding for the disabled) and for education (remedial riding and riding as therapy) (DePauw, 1986a). For a detailed overview of therapeutic horseback riding, see Engel (1992).

Sport

The Olympic Games are one of the most visible examples of sport in today's society. Although the Greek Olympic Games were instituted in

776 B.C. (the modern Olympics were revived in 1896), athletic contests were held earlier. The earliest forms were found among the peoples of the East in the second and third millennia B.C. As depicted by wall paintings of the time, wrestling, ball games, weight lifting, and other forms of exercises were found in Egypt. The Herean Games, in which only women competed, preceded the ancient Olympics, but they soon became extinct due to the emphasis on males in athletic contests.

In Greece, sport was found in the context of man's life as a whole and formed an integral part of his education. The cultivation of the whole man included both mental and physical education. The Greeks believed that the mind could not exist without the body and that the body had no meaning without the mind. In these early years of sport, physical beauty and strength were admired and the spirit of competition remained central to the event. Since those early years, sport has been committed to the ideals of physical beauty and strength as well as to the spirit of competition and fair play.

As in early Greek culture, sport permeates all levels of modern society. McPherson, Curtis, & Loy (1989) view sport as a social institution that reflects culture. They define sport as "structured, goal-oriented, competitive, contest-based, ludic physical activity" (p. 15). It is this context of sport into which individuals with disabilities have attempted to enter.

CONCLUDING COMMENTS

A historical review of the treatment and social status of individuals with disabilities reveals a pattern of neglect, followed by benign tolerance and limited acceptance. It can be argued that social status may be situational and may reflect the unique aspects of a given environment, conditions of the time, specific activity, the individual, and the interaction among these factors. In general, one may encounter these same or similar patterns of exclusion or limited acceptance because of culture, gender, ethnicity, class, or disability affiliation (Karwas & DePauw, 1990). As such, these individuals are considered to be "outside" of a particular society. This view comes from the sociological concept of marginality (e.g., Hughes, 1949; Park, 1928).

In addition to the historical inclination of humans to be physically active and to seek sport as an outlet, sport has been perceived as an equalizer and as a means of gaining social acceptance. Due to the visibility of sport and the social acceptance of athletes, groups of individuals have sought entry into sport. Those with disabilities are among the last groups to seek access to the sport world.

CHAPTER 3

Organizations for Sport and Disability

This chapter introduces a number of the disability sport organizations in existence today within the historical context. Included are the major international sport organizations serving individuals with disabilities and the primary U.S. disability sport organizations. Discussion of each organization includes an overview of its history, purposes, programs, membership, and sports within the limits of available literature. (Other national sport organizations around the world are discussed briefly in chapter 6. For a comprehensive listing of sport organizations serving individuals with disabilities, see Appendixes D, E, and F.)

INTERNATIONAL DISABILITY SPORT ORGANIZATIONS

Over the years, a number of international sport organizations for athletes with disabilities have emerged. The major sport federations are highlighted here.

International Committee of Sports for the Deaf

A Deaf Frenchman, E. Rubens-Alcais, is credited with initiating the first International Silent Games. These were held in Paris in August 1924, with the support of the six national sport federations for the Deaf and athletes from nine countries.

Representatives from these nine countries met at the conclusion of the games to establish a union among all Deaf sporting federations and to draft the statutes for the official sanctioning of this organization. Originally called the Comité International des Sports des Sourds (CISS), the organization became known as the International Committee of Sports for the Deaf. From this beginning, the CISS established the following three purposes (adapted from CISS constitution, p. 124):

> Develop and control the physical education in general and the practice of sports in particular among the Deaf of the world,
>
> Promote relations among countries practicing sports for the Deaf and using its influence to initiate and then give guidance to the practice of these sports in countries where it is unknown, and
>
> Supervise the regular celebration of the World Games for the Deaf, World Championships, and Regional Championships.

As specified in its constitution, the CISS has sole responsibility for sports for the Deaf throughout the world. In exercising this responsibility, the CISS sponsors the Summer and Winter World Games for the Deaf, World Championships, and Regional Championships. The sports included in the summer games are athletics, badminton, basketball, cycling, marathon, shooting, soccer, swimming, table tennis, team handball, tennis, volleyball, and water polo. Winter sports include Nordic skiing, speed skating, Alpine skiing, and hockey. The technical regulations of the international federations (IFs) are utilized for competition.

The World Games for the Deaf, exclusive property of the CISS, are offered every two years, alternating summer and winter. These games usually occur the year following the Olympics.

As the oldest disability sport organization, the CISS has enjoyed a long and vibrant history. Hundreds of thousands of athletes have competed under the CISS flag, its emblem, and its motto of "equal through sports." Recognition by the International Olympic Committee came on June 15, 1955. A few years later, in 1968, the CISS was awarded the Olympic Cup (created by Baron Pierre de Courbertin in 1906) for its service to sport for the Deaf.

Although the CISS has always been an autonomous organization, it once was a member of the International Coordinating Committee (ICC) of the World Sports Organizations for the Disabled, and it currently holds membership in the International Paralympic Committee (IPC).

International Stoke Mandeville Wheelchair Sports Federation

The history of the International Stoke Mandeville Wheelchair Sports Federation (ISMWSF) is synonymous with the history of wheelchair sport. Sir Ludwig Guttmann is credited with the initiation of the Stoke Mandeville Games in 1948 and the establishment of the International Stoke Mandeville Games Committee (the forerunner of ISMWSF) in 1960.

Although initially serving athletes with spinal cord injuries, ISMWSF now sanctions all international competition for those who use a wheelchair in competition. The ISMWSF's official sports include archery, athletics, basketball, bowls, fencing, racquetball, rugby, shooting, swimming, table tennis, tennis, weight lifting, and winter sports. Athletes wishing to compete at the International Stoke Mandeville Games must adhere to the ISMWSF classification system (see chapter 7 for more information).

International Sports Organization for the Disabled

Although the ISMWSF existed in the 1960s, it only provided sport programs for those with spinal cord injuries. This left individuals with other disabilities underserved. The International War Veterans Association undertook the challenge to create alternative sport programs, and it founded the International Sports Organization for the Disabled (ISOD) in Paris in 1964.

ISOD historically served as the international governing body for sport programs for amputees, individuals with other locomotor disabilities, and les autres ("the others"—other physically impaired individuals). In this capacity, ISOD worked with the ICC. Although primarily responsible for sport programs for those with locomotor impairments and les autres,

ISOD is also dedicated to developing sports and uniting sports organizations for individuals with disabilities around the world. Specifically, the purposes of ISOD are as follows (adapted from ISOD pamphlet, n.d.):

1. Provide an international forum for the exchange of opinion, experiences, and resources related to sport for individuals with disabilities.

2. Prepare and disseminate international principles and standards recommended for application in all programs of sports for individuals with disabilities.

3. Plan, promote, and coordinate international events and activities designed to stimulate and assist the further development of sport programs for individuals with disabilities in all nations, including specifically

   a. international sports meetings,

   b. technical and education seminars and conferences,

   c. dissemination of relevant information, and

   d. international exchange of technicians and athletes with disabilities.

4. Provide appropriate assistance to individuals and organizations in developing sports for individuals with disabilities.

National sport organizations serving persons with disabilities in each country can apply for ISOD membership.

ISOD participates in sanctioning winter and summer quadrennial games, world championships, continental championships, and invitational tournaments. The summer and winter games were originally called the Olympics for the Disabled and were cosponsored with the ICC. These games are now called the Paralympics (see Table 3.1).

The world championships are held every fourth even year between the quadrennial games and are organized by single sport or multisport. In the odd years between the quadrennial games, continental championships can be held dependent upon requests by continental committees for sports for the disabled. Invitational tournaments are offered by request from the member associations. ISOD summer sports include archery, athletics, badminton, basketball, boccie, cycling, fencing, kayaking, lawn bowling, riding, sailing, shooting, swimming, table tennis, tennis, volleyball, water polo, weight lifting, and wheelchair dancing. ISOD winter sports include Alpine skiing, Nordic skiing, biathlon, cross-country sledge, sledge tobogganing, ice-sledge racing, and sledge hockey.

To date, ISOD continues to represent amputee, les autres, and dwarf athletes in international competition. Although once associated with the ICC, ISOD is a current member of the International Paralympic Committee (IPC).

Table 3.1   Chronology of Paralympic Games

Year	Paralympics Summer	Impairment	Paralympics Winter
1960	Rome (Italy)	Spinal cord injuries	
1964	Tokyo (Japan)	Spinal cord injuries	
1968	Tel Aviv (Israel)	Spinal cord injuries	
1972	Heidelberg (GDR)	Spinal cord injuries	
1976	Toronto (Canada)	Spinal cord injuries, amputees and blind	Ornskoldvik (Sweden)
1980	Arnhem (The Netherlands)	Spinal cord injuries, amputees, blind, cerebral palsy	Geilo (Norway)
1984	Aylesbury (UK)	Spinal cord injuries	Innsbruck (Austria)
1984	New York (USA)	Amputee, blind, cerebral palsy	
1988	Seoul (South Korea)	Spinal cord injuries, cerebral palsy, amputee, blind, les autres	Innsbruck
1992	Barcelona (Spain)	Physical and visual	Albertville, Tignes (France)
1992	Madrid (Spain)	Mental handicaps	
1994		Physical and visual impairments	Lillehammer (Norway)
1996	Atlanta (USA)	Physical and visual impairments	

Cerebral Palsy–International Sport and Recreation Association

Sport for individuals with cerebral palsy was initiated as a separate entity under the auspices of the sport and leisure subcommittee of the International Cerebral Palsy Society (ICPS). This subcommittee sponsored the first international athletic competition for athletes with cerebral palsy in France in 1968. The activities continued, and in 1978, the subcommittee became an independent association: Cerebral Palsy–International Sport and Recreation Association (CP–ISRA).

CP–ISRA promotes and develops competitive sports and recreational sports for persons with cerebral palsy and related conditions. Over the years, it has provided sport competitions, seminars, films, demonstrations, courses and workshops, coaches' training, and recreation programs.

In 1978, ISOD officially recognized the CP–ISRA as the international governing body for cerebral palsy sports. In that capacity, CP–ISRA soon became a member of the ICC and is currently a member of the IPC.

International Blind Sports Association

The International Blind Sports Association (IBSA) was formed in 1981. It is an autonomous organization with "supreme authority in all matters of sports for blind people" (*IBSA Handbook*, pp. 1-1, 1-2). Its purposes include

- planning, promoting, and coordinating international events designed to stimulate the development of sport programs for the blind,
- providing an international forum for the exchange of experience, opinions, aid, and resources related to sports for the blind,
- assisting organizations, institutions, and individuals working in the area of blind sport,
- upholding the Olympic ideal and acting in accordance with its principles, and
- promoting the purposes and ideas of IBSA in schools for the blind and among blind youth in general.

IBSA was the last "disability" specific sport organization to attain recognition by ISOD and compete under its sanction. IBSA is recognized as the international governing body for blind sports and is a current member of the IPC.

International Fund Sports Disabled

In 1983, an international fundraising body for disability sport was founded. The International Fund Sports Disabled (IFSD) was started as a result of a gift from The Netherlands. The monies were used to support not only individual international sport organizations for individuals with disabilities but also the projects of the ICC. In addition, the IFSD subsidized research projects on integrated classification. Although the ICC no longer exists, the IFSD continues to support international sports. Its purpose is to provide financial assistance for the following:

- recreational sport projects,
- training of sports personnel,

- medical examination and sport research,
- adapted sport equipment,
- world conferences and seminars on disability sport,
- educational projects in developing countries,
- publicity and promotion and organizational assistance, and
- Olympic and world events for athletes with disabilities.

Recreational Sports Development and Stimulation Disabled International

In 1986, Dr. Arie Klapwijk organized an international conference, held in Arnhem, The Netherlands, on sport for individuals with disabilities. RESPO '86 focused on recreational sports in developing countries for individuals with severe impairments and disabilities. The success of RESPO '86 indicated the need for continued international cooperation. Although the IFSD had previously supported developmental sport programs in developing countries, in 1991 the IFSD was forced to limit its activities to raising money. As a result, a new organization was needed.

In 1991, Recreational Sports Development and Stimulation Disabled International (RESPO DS–DI) was formed. Its initiation was made possible by financial support from the International Olympic Committee (IOC) in Lausanne, Switzerland. The purposes of RESPO DS–DI are as follows:

1. To promote and support sports with a particular recreational value for persons with a disability, and
2. To develop new forms of sport for persons with a disability.

To meet these objectives, RESPO DS–DI organizes workshops and conferences for coaches and trainers emphasizing recreational as well as elite sports for individuals with disabilities. In addition, RESPO DS–DI has prepared promotional materials, rule books, manuals, and videos.

International Coordinating Committee of the World Sports Organizations for the Disabled

As early as March 1982, discussions were under way about the formation of a committee to coordinate the existing efforts for disability sport on the international level. Finally, in June 1984, an official agreement was signed by the four founding organizations: International Blind Sport Association (IBSA), International Stoke Mandeville Wheelchair Sports Federation (ISMWSF), International Sports Organization for the Disabled (ISOD), and Cerebral Palsy–International Sport and Recreation Association (CP–ISRA). The secretariat for this coordinating committee was located in The Netherlands with funds allocated from the International Fund Sports Disabled (IFSD).

Perhaps one of the ICC's most important functions during its short tenure was the negotiation with the International Olympic Committee (IOC). In January 1985, a small ICC delegation was invited to meet with IOC president Juan Antonio Samaranch in Lausanne, Switzerland. At this meeting, the IOC stipulated that the ICC and disability sport organizations must refrain from using the word *Olympics*. The alternative terminology selected was *Paralympics, para* meaning "attached to" and not representing paraplegic. At that time, the term *Paralympics* was officially adopted for use by the IOC and national Olympic committees. Since 1985, only the United States Olympic Committee (USOC) has expressed reluctance to recognize the term *Paralympics*.

The ICC served officially as the coordinating body for international sport for individuals with disabilities from June 1984 until the establishment of the International Paralympic Committee in 1989. The ICC remained in existence through the 1992 Summer Paralympic Games held in Barcelona.

International Sports Federation for Persons With Mental Handicap

The most recent disability-specific international sport organization is the International Sports Federation for Persons With Mental Handicap (INAS–FMH). This group was formed in The Netherlands in 1986. Since its inception in 1986, INAS–FMH has sponsored two international competitions: the first World Championships in Athletics and Swimming held in July 1989 in Sweden and the Paralympics for the Mentally Handicapped held in September 1992 in Madrid.

The general aims of this organization are to enable access to international events and promote participation of all people with a mental handicap/intellectual disability to sport and recreation activities. The specific purposes of INAS–FMH include the following:

1. promoting sport activities for persons with mental handicaps,
2. training coaches, trainers, officials, etc.,
3. promoting technical and medical research, and
4. disseminating information about sport for those with mental handicaps.

The INAS–FMH philosophy calls for the inclusion of athletes with a mental handicap/intellectual disability in the sport of their choice at their individual levels of ability from local recreational activities to international elite competition.

INAS–FMH is a member of the International Paralympic Committee. As such, INAS–FMH is recognized as the international governing body for sport for mentally retarded or mentally handicapped individuals.

International Paralympic Committee

The International Paralympic Committee (IPC) was established on September 22, 1989, in Dusseldorf, Germany. The IPC currently serves as the coordinating body for international sport for individuals with disabilities. Its purposes include the following (taken from the IPC constitution printed in the *IPC Newsletter*, Spring 1991, p. 4):

> To organize Paralympic and Multidisability World Games and World Championships (the IPC has sole authority to do so),
>
> To liaise with the IOC and all other relevant international sport bodies,
>
> To seek integration of sports for individuals with disabilities into the international sports movement for able-bodied individuals,
>
> To supervise and coordinate the conduct of the Paralympics and other Multidisability World and Regional Games, and to coordinate the calendar of international and regional competitions,
>
> To assist and encourage educational programs, research, and promotional activities to achieve the purposes of the IPC,
>
> To promote, without discrimination, the practice of sports for disabled people for political, religious, economic, sex, or racial reasons, and
>
> To seek expansion of opportunities for disabled persons to participate in sports and of their access to training programs designed to improve their proficiency.

The IPC welcomes full and associate memberships. Full members include the international organizations of sport for individuals with disabilities (CISS, CP–ISRA, IBSA, INAS–FMH, and ISOD), recognized national coordinating or umbrella organizations of sport for individuals with disabilities (national Paralympic committees), and national organizations of sport for individuals with disabilities present as founding members in the Inaugural Assembly or admitted to membership by the General

Assembly. Only one national organization per disability grouping may join the IPC. No country can have more than one full member. Full members have full voting rights and are entitled to participate in all IPC events.

SIGNIFICANT EVENTS IN DISABILITY SPORT CHRONOLOGY: INTERNATIONAL PERSPECTIVES

Prior to the world wars, athletes with disabilities had virtually no opportunities for organized sport competition with the exception of Deaf individuals, single-arm amputee golfers, and selected self-initiating individuals. There were some individuals who were, or became, disabled for which Olympic competition was a reality. Examples include Karoly Tacazs, a two-time Hungarian Olympian who competed in Olympic shooting events left-handed after losing his right arm, and Liz Hartel from Denmark, who won a silver medal in dressage at the Olympic Games in 1952 after being confined to a wheelchair as a result of polio contracted in 1943.

As for Deaf individuals, their involvement in sport can be traced to the Sports Club for the Deaf, which was founded in Berlin in 1888 (see Table 3.2). Between the years of 1888 and 1924, six national sport federations for the Deaf emerged: Belgium, Czechoslovakia, France, Great Britain, Holland, and Poland. These six federations came together for the first International Silent Games held August 10-17, 1924, in France. Competitors from Hungary, Italy, and Romania also participated. In conjunction with these first games, the International Committee of Sports for the Deaf (CISS) became the first international organization to provide sport competition for any disability group (see Table 3.2).

The British Society of One-Armed Golfers was founded in 1932, and annual golf tournaments for amputees have since been held throughout England.

World War II significantly influenced the treatment of individuals with disabilities, especially in terms of rehabilitation (Huber, 1984). Before the war, individuals with disabilities were considered a burden to society. Inasmuch as disabled veterans were previously able-bodied individuals and accepted by society, they were still considered normal even though they had become physically impaired. This acceptance fostered the need for rehabilitation. Because numerous veterans returned home with physical impairments and psychological needs which could not be accommodated by traditional techniques, rehabilitation programs were modified.

The British government is credited with being the first to recognize these needs by opening the Spinal Injuries Centre at Stoke Mandeville Hospital in Aylesbury, England in 1944. Sir Ludwig Guttmann, director of this center, first introduced competitive sports as an integral part of

Table 3.2 Chronology of Disability Sport

Year	Event
1888	First Sports Club for the Deaf (Berlin).
1924	First International Silent Games (Paris—founded by CISS).
1932	British Society of One-Armed Golfers founded.
1935	First U.S. participation in 4th World Games for the Deaf.
1939	George Stafford published *Sports for the Handicapped*.
1944	Sir Ludwig Guttmann established the Spinal Injuries Centre of the Stoke Mandeville Hospital (Aylesbury, England).
1945	American Athletic Association of the Deaf (AAAD) founded.
	First wheelchair basketball game played by war veterans (Corona Naval Station, CA).
1948	First Stoke Mandeville Games for the Paralyzed (Aylesbury, England).
1949	First Annual Wheelchair Basketball Tournament.
	First World Winter Games for the Deaf (Austria). NWBA founded.
1952	Liz Hartel (postpolio) won silver medal in dressage at Summer Olympics, representing Denmark.
	First international wheelchair athlete tournament (Stoke Mandeville).
1956	First athletic scholarships in U.S. for athletes with disabilities (blind wrestlers).
1957	First U.S. National Wheelchair Games (Adelphi College, New York).
1960	First International Games for Disabled (Paralympics) in Rome.
	British Sport Association for All founded by Guttmann.
1963	International Sports Organization for the Disabled founded.

(continued)

Table 3.2   *(continued)*

Year	Event
1967	First Pan American Games for spinal cord injured athletes.
	National Handicapped Sports and Recreation Association formed to govern U.S. winter sports for disabled.
1968	International Cerebral Palsy Society formed.
1968	International Special Olympics founded by Eunice Kennedy Shriver, first competition held in Chicago.
1974	First women's National Wheelchair Basketball Tournament held.
	First National Wheelchair Marathon held in Ohio.
1975	First wheelchair entrant, Bob Hall (postpolio), in Boston Marathon; finished in 2:58.
	First meeting of U.S. Cerebral Palsied athletes at Springfield College, MA.
1976	The Olympiad for the Physically Disabled (Toronto) included blind and amputee athletes.
	United States Association for Blind Athletes formed.
	UNESCO conference established right of individuals with disabilities to participate in physical education and sport.
1977	First female wheelchair entrant to the women's division of Boston Marathon (3:48:51).
	First national championships of USABA held in Macomb, IL.
1978	PL 95-606, the Amateur Sports Act of 1978, passed by Congress.
	George Murray became the first person in a wheelchair to finish ahead of able-bodied entrants in Boston Marathon.
	National Association of Sports for Cerebral Palsy founded.
	Cerebral Palsy-International Sports and Recreation Association organized.

(continued)

Table 3.2 *(continued)*

Year	Event
1979	USOC Handicapped in Sports Committee formed, chaired by Kathryn Sallade (AAAD).
1980	Olympics for Disabled held in Arnhem, The Netherlands. Cerebral palsy athletes (ambulatory) included for the first time.
	Sit skiing introduced at Winter Skiing Championships in Winter Park, CO.
	Curt Brinkman finished Boston Marathon in under 2 hours.
1981	First National Veterans Wheelchair Games held in Richmond, VA.
	First annual World Wheelchair Marathon Championships held with Orange Bowl Marathon.
	International Blind Sports Association formed.
	United States Amputee Athletic Association founded; first annual National Games held in Nashville.
1981	First wheelchair athletes, George Murray and Phil Carpenter, crossed the United States.
	UN International Year for Disabled Persons.
	USOC and IOC issued formal statement rejecting use of term *Olympics* for competitions involving disabled athletes except for Special Olympics.
1982	First international meets held exclusively for specific wheelchair sports (e.g., WC archery in Spain, WC table tennis in England).
	Linda Downs, Class 5 CP athlete, finished New York Marathon in 11 hours, 15 minutes.
	UNESCO sponsored International Symposium on Physical Education and Sport Programs for Physically and Mentally Handicapped in College Park, MD.
	Karen Farmer, a single-leg amputee, attends college on athletic scholarship for women's track at Eastern Washington University.

(continued)

Table 3.2 *(continued)*

Year	Event
1982 (cont.)	Blind women compete for the first time in the World Goal Ball Championships at Butler University in Indianapolis.
	International Coordinating Committee (ICC) of the World Sports Organizations formed in Leysin, Switzerland.
1983	First International Women's Wheelchair Basketball Tournament held in France.
	Six wheelchair racers finish a mile in less than 4 minutes.
	Seven wheelchair racers finish Boston Marathon in less than 2 hours.
1984	Neroli Fairhall (N.Z.) first wheelchair athlete to meet eligibility and compete in Olympics in women's archery.
	First wheelchair races as demonstration events for 1984 Oympics (1500m won by Paul Van Winkle at Belgium in 3:58.50; 800m won by Sharon Rahn Hedrick in 2:15.50).
	First disabled skiing events at 1984 Olympics in Sarajevo.
	International Games for Disabled held for the first time in United States (Hofstra University in Hempstead, NY).
	George Murray (wheelchair marathoner) pictured on Wheaties Box.
1984	First full-length article in commercial magazine, *Runner's World*, about female disabled athlete: Linda Downs for the 1982 New York Marathon.
	Disabled sport featured among topics of Olympic Scientific Congress for the first time.
1985	World Games for the Deaf held in United States (Los Angeles) for the first time.
	The 1985 U.S. Olympics Sports Festival includes athletes with disabilities for the first time: 16 females and 26 males.

(continued)

Table 3.2 *(continued)*

Year	Event
1987	Candace Cable-Brooks wins the Boston Marathon for the fifth time in the Open Female Wheelchair division; Andre Viger wins for the third time in the Open Male Wheelchair division; John Brewer wins Quad division for the seventh time.
	Rick Hansen finishes his "Man-in-Motion" tour; Hansen wheeled 24,901.55 miles across 34 countries to raise money for research.
1988	Winter Olympics in Calgary include demonstration events (three-track Alpine, blind Nordic) for males and females.
	Summer Olympics (South Korea) include wheelchair races as demonstrations events (1,500m for men; 800m for females).
	Sharon Hedrick wins second gold medal in Olympic wheelchair 800m (2:11.49).
	Very successful 1988 Paralympics held in Seoul, South Korea; staged similar to Olympics.
1989	Seven females and seven males named Disabled Athletes of the Year.
1990	Shirley Platt becomes the first female (Deaf) executive secretary of AAAD.
	Dr. Donalda Ammons appointed the first Deaf female director of the World Games for the Deaf U.S. team.
	Diana Golden, three-track skier, signs sponsorship agreement with Subaru and also becomes spokesperson for ChapStick Challenge for Disabled Skiers.
1991	Jean Driscoll becomes the first disabled athlete to be named the Sudafed Female Athlete of the Year.
	Sue Moucha is the first athlete with a disability to attend the Olympic Academy.
1992	Exhibition events for athletes with disabilities continue at 1992 Summer Olympic Games; Candace Cable (U.S.) and Connie Hansen (Denmark) become the only two women to compete in all Olympic exhibition events.

(continued)

Table 3.2 *(continued)*

Year	Event
1992 (cont.)	Winter Paralympics held in Albertville/Tigne, France.
	Summer Paralympics in Barcelona; IOC President Samaranch attend and endorsed the games.
	First Paralympics for Mental Handicaps held in Madrid.
	Demonstration events (qualifying events) for wheelchair, blind, and mentally retarded athletes held in conjunction with U.S. Olympic Trials.
1993	COSD reorganized with USOC.
1994	Winter Olympics and Winter Paralympics in Lillehammer, Norway.
1996	Summer Olympics and Summer Paralympics in Atlanta.

the rehabilitation of disabled veterans. The competitive sports of the time included punch ball exercises, rope climbing, and wheelchair polo (Guttmann, 1976). Under Guttmann's tutelage, the First Stoke Mandeville Games for the Paralyzed were held in 1948. At these games, 26 British veterans (including 3 women) competed in archery.

In the late 1940s, sport as a part of medical rehabilitation spread throughout Europe and ultimately to the United States. At this same time, European competitions and sporting events for wheelchair athletes emerged.

In 1952, Guttmann organized the first international competition for wheelchair athletes. These games were held at Stoke Mandeville, and the British competed against a team from The Netherlands. In 1956, the International Olympic Committee recognized Guttmann's work and awarded him and his associates the Fearnley Cup in honor of the social and human value derived from the wheelchair sports movement.

Since the beginnings of the Stoke Mandeville Games, wheelchair sports have increased tremendously. The first sports added were lawn bowling, table tennis, shot put, javelin, and club throw. In the 1960s, wheelchair basketball, fencing, snooker, swimming, and weight lifting were introduced. Additional countries participated. South America and the United States sent teams to the competitions held in 1957 and 1960, respectively. By 1960, the ISMWSF had been formed to sanction all international competitions for individuals with spinal cord injuries. Although originally sanctioned for those with spinal cord injuries, the games were expanded in 1976 to include other physical impairments, including blindness.

During the 1960s, international sport competitions were expanded to include other disability groups not eligible for the World Games for the Deaf or the International Stoke Mandeville Games. The leadership for these additional disability sport competitions came in the form of the International Sports Organization for the Disabled (ISOD). In Paris in 1964, the ISOD was officially formed to provide international sport opportunities for the blind, amputee, and other locomotor disabilities (Lindstrom, 1984). Its founders intended that ISOD would become an entity parallel in structure and functions to the International Olympic Committee (IOC).

In part due to dissatisfaction with existing competitions, the International Cerebral Palsy Society (ICPS) was founded in 1968 to sponsor the first international games for individuals with cerebral palsy in France. ICPS continued this competition every two years until 1978 when the Cerebral Palsy–International Sports and Recreation Association (CP–ISRA) became recognized by ISOD as the official sanctioning body for cerebral palsy sports (see Figure 3.1).

Similarly, the International Blind Sports Association (IBSA) was formed in 1981 in response to increasing interest and expanding opportunities for competitions for blind athletes. These two groups (IBSA, CP–ISRA) became the last disability groups to seek and attain recognition from ISOD.

1888 – First Sport Club for the Deaf founded in Berlin, Germany

1924 – Comité International des Sports des Sourds (CISS)

1932 – British Society of One-Armed Golfers

1948 – First Stoke Mandeville Games for the Paralyzed

1952 – First international competition for wheelchair athletes

1960 – International Stoke Mandeville Wheelchair Sports Federation (ISMWSF)

1964 – International Sport Organization for Disabled (ISOD)

1978 – Cerebral Palsy–International Sport and Recreation Association (CP–ISRA)

1981 – International Blind Sports Association (IBSA)

1982 – International Coordinating Committee (ICC)

1986 – International Sport Federations for Persons With Mental Handicap (INAS-FMH)

1989 – International Paralympic Committees (IPC)

1992 – IPC assumes authority for international disability sport

---

Figure 3.1   Chronology of international disability sport organizations.

Joint interest in expanded international sport for individuals with disabilities brought the CP–ISRA, IBSA, ISMWSF, and ISOD together in 1982 to form a new umbrella organization. The International Coordinating Committee of the World Sports Organizations (ICC) was formed to coordinate disability sport worldwide and to negotiate with the IOC on behalf of athletes with disabilities. CISS (Deaf sports) and International Federation for Sports for Persons with Mental Handicap (INAS–FMH) joined the ICC in 1986.

Inasmuch as the ICC served as a fragile alliance of international sport federations and experienced an uneasy history from 1982 to 1987, representatives of 39 countries and representatives from the six international federations met to determine the future of international disability sport. This meeting, known as the Arnhem Seminar, was held March 14, 1987, in Arnhem, The Netherlands. Seminar participants decided that a new international sport organization should be created to represent disabled sportsmen and sportswomen around the world, and they appointed an ad hoc committee to draft the constitution. As specified during the Arnhem Seminar, the new organization was to have national representation from every nation with a disability sport program and was to govern itself through a council of nations. Athletes and disability sport organizations were to have a voice in the governance of disabled sport on an international level. The new structure was also charged with responsibility for developmental and recreational activities in addition to international and elite sport. The existing members of the ICC were recognized and were to become an integral part of this new organization.

In Dusseldorf, Germany, on September 21 and 22, 1989, the International Paralympic Committee (IPC) was born. At this meeting, officers were elected and the governance structure was adopted, along with a draft of the constitution. The IPC began a most significant chapter in the history of sport and disability. Initial efforts were devoted to streamlining operations, coordinating international sport, and securing communication between the IPC and IOC. Inasmuch as the 1992 Paralympics in Barcelona were to be held under the auspices of the ICC, the final exchange of power from the ICC to the IPC was set to occur at the end of the 1992 Paralympics. As of September 1992, the IPC has been recognized as the sole international coordinating entity for athletes with disabilities worldwide.

UNITED STATES DISABILITY SPORT ASSOCIATIONS

The United States sport associations are presented here in two sections. The first section includes current members of the United States Olympic

Dr. Robert Steadward

At a glance:

Professor, University of Alberta, Edmonton

Director of the Rick Hansen Center, Alberta

President of the International Paralympic Committee

Athletes are not the only ones who have contributed to the sport movement for individuals with disabilities. Dr. Robert Steadward, who describes himself as "author, teacher, coach, sport scientist, and administrator," is such an individual. His contributions are broad and have had an impact on the sport movement for individuals with disabilities. As the current president of the International Paralympic Committee, Bob is playing an instrumental role in the Olympic movement. He is also actively involved in planning for the 1996 Paralympics in Atlanta.

Dr. Steadward's participation in sport for individuals with disabilities in Canada and internationally has been a lifelong professional and personal commitment. This native Canadian began participating in the early 1970s and held positions such as national coach, team manager, and chef de mission of the Canadian Wheelchair Sports Association and Paralympic Teams. He also has founded several sports associations for individuals with disabilities throughout the 1970s and 1980s. In the 1990s, Dr. Steadward received several distinguished Canadian awards and honorary life memberships to sport associations for individuals with disabilities. He pursues a program of research, writing, and public speaking.

Bob Steadward's commitment and passion to sport for individuals with disabilities continues, to the benefit of all.

Committee (USOC). The second section describes U.S. associations that do not qualify for membership in the USOC but that actively provide sport opportunities for individuals with disabilities.

American Athletic Association of the Deaf

The oldest U.S. disability sport organization, the American Athletic Association of the Deaf (AAAD), was founded in 1945 (see Figure 3.2). Its purpose is to provide year-round sports and recreation opportunities to individuals with hearing impairments. The AAAD comprises 2,001 member clubs and affiliated organizations dispersed throughout eight geographical regions. The total number of Deaf or hearing impaired individuals represented by these associations and clubs exceeds 25,000.

Individuals with a hearing loss of 55 dB or greater in the better ear are eligible for competition under AAAD. No classification other than separate female and male divisions are found. Although initially focused upon the three team sports of volleyball, basketball, and softball, the AAAD now offers competitions in athletics, basketball, volleyball, swimming, tennis, table tennis, badminton, cycling, water polo, team handball, soccer, shooting, wrestling, softball, ice hockey, speed skating, and skiing (Alpine and Nordic).

1945 – American Athletic Association for the Deaf (AAAD)

1949 – First wheelchair basketball tournament; founding of National Wheelchair Basketball Association (NWBA)

1957 – National Wheelchair Athletic Association (NWAA)

1967 – National Handicapped Sport and Recreation Association (NHSRA)

1968 – Special Olympics International (SOI)

1976 – United States Association for Blind Athletes (USABA)

1978 – National Association of Sports for Cerebral Palsy (NASCP)*

1978 – Amateur Sports Act passed

1979 – USOC Committee on Sports for the Disabled (COSD)

1981 – U.S. Amputee Athletic Association (USAAA)

1989 – Dwarf Athletic Association of America (DAAA)

1990s – Reorganization of COSD/USOC

* Now known as U.S. Cerebral Palsy Athletic Association (USCPAA).

Figure 3.2   Chronology of disability sport organizations in the United States.

The AAAD also provides training programs for athletes and coaches, and educational programs for the public. It annually inducts Deaf individuals into its Hall of Fame and selects the Deaf Athlete of the Year.

An integral part of the AAAD organization is the U.S. Team/World Games for the Deaf (U.S. Team/WGD). The U.S. Team/WGD is a standing committee of the AAAD and has responsibility for fielding the U.S. team of Deaf athletes to compete in the Winter and Summer World Games for the Deaf. The U.S. Team/WGD sponsors competitions in the Pan American Games for the Deaf, U.S. Olympic festivals, development camps, cultural/sport exchange with foreign countries, clinics and workshops for athletes and coaches, dissemination of information through visual media, and qualifying trials prior to world games.

AAAD is a DSO member of the United States Olympic Committee, and it participates in the activities of the Committee on Sports for the Disabled

---

Jane Herrmann

At a glance:

Javelin and discus thrower

Collegiate varsity athlete

World Games participant

A hearing-impaired varsity athlete was a rarity at Bowling Green State University in the late 1970s. In fact, it was a rarity to be a collegiate athlete with a disability. Jane Herrmann was a physical education major at the university. She came from a rich school athletic experience that included varsity basketball, volleyball, and track at St. Joe's Institute for the Deaf in St. Louis and her hometown high school (Portsmouth, OH). In track she found a niche as a walk-on athlete at the collegiate level. In the javelin and discus she was invited to try out for the AAMD national team to go to Cologne, Germany to participate in the World Games for the Deaf (July 1981). Although not a medal winner, Jane was a winner in life. She successfully completed her student teaching and was contemplating graduate school when she was killed in a car-train accident 5 days before graduation.

(COSD). AAAD is also affiliated with the Comité International des Sports des Sourds (CISS).

Wheelchair Sports, USA

Recognizing that recreational and competitive sports could play an integral part in one's rehabilitative process and daily life, the first national wheelchair games were held in 1957 at Adelphi College in New York. Among the competitors were disabled men from the New York–New Jersey area who expressed interest in competing in wheelchair sports other than just wheelchair basketball. What resulted was the formation of the National Wheelchair Athletic Association (NWAA) in conjunction with these games. In 1994, the NWAA changed its name to Wheelchair Sports, USA.

Wheelchair Sports, USA has organized and sponsored competitions in seven different "Olympic" sports: athletics, archery, air pistol and rifle shooting, swimming, weight lifting, table tennis, and fencing. The competitions often have included wheelchair slalom as well. In the late 1980s, Wheelchair Sports, USA was reorganized as an umbrella organization that governs six Olympic sports (air guns, archery, athletics, swimming, table tennis, and weight lifting) with these separate sport organizations. Although these are autonomous groups, Wheelchair Sports, USA also represents wheelchair basketball and tennis at Olympic-level venues.

Wheelchair Sports, USA programs include publications, video rental, local and regional wheelchair games for adults and juniors, local wheelchair sports development, national training camps, road racing series, national workshops, and national wheelchair games and junior national wheelchair games. In addition, Wheelchair Sports, USA fields teams for participation in the world wheelchair games, events in the U.S. Olympic festivals, events in Summer Olympic Games and Pan American Wheelchair Games. Wheelchair Sports, USA also fields the U.S. Disabled Team for competition in the Paralympics and International Team trials.

Wheelchair Sports, USA is a DSO member of the United States Olympic Committee and one of the original members of the Committee on Sports for the Disabled (COSD). Internationally, Wheelchair Sports, USA is represented by the ISMWSF.

Disabled Sports USA

In 1967, a small group of Vietnam War veterans with amputations formed the National Handicapped Sports and Recreation Association (NHSRA). They did this with the belief that participation in recreation and sport activities was important for restoring self-esteem. In 1989, NHSRA changed its name to National Handicapped Sports (NHS); in 1995 it became Disabled Sports USA (DS/USA).

DIANA GOLDEN

At a glance:

Skier

Olympic gold medalist

Women's Sports Foundation Flo Hyman award

Honorary doctoral degree from Rhode Island College

U.S. Female Skier of the Year in 1988

World-class speaker, Olympic gold medalist, outstanding humanist. These are the words most often used to describe Diana Golden, a cancer survivor, a single-leg amputee, and a world-class skier.

Diana Golden grew up in Lincoln, MA, where she learned to ski when she was 5 years old. At age 12 she was diagnosed with bone cancer of her right leg after it collapsed on her. When informed that it would be necessary to amputate the leg, Diana asked if she would be able to continue to ski. And continue to ski she did.

For more than 6 years Diana Golden dominated disabled skiing. She won 19 U.S. National Disabled Championship gold medals, 10 World Disabled Championship gold medals, and a gold medal in the 1988 Disabled Giant Slalom at Calgary. But there is more to Diana Golden than medals. She has also participated in able-bodied events and proved that athletes with disabilities are indeed athletes, not "novelties."

She has succeeded off the slopes as well. Her list of awards, honors, and tributes is extensive. Many are also noteworthy because they are the first to be presented to a person with a disability. The 1991 Flo Hyman Award from the Women's Sports Foundation, the U.S. Olympic Committee Female Skier of the Year in 1988, and the 1986 U.S. Ski Writers' Association Outstanding Competitor Award are such examples.

Diana Golden has been widely respected as a first-class competitive skier. And now that she is retired from competitive skiing, what is she doing? Why, rock climbing, of course!

Initially, DS/USA was primarily involved with winter sports, especially Alpine skiing. As the organization grew, local DS/USA chapters began, and continue, to promote year-round recreational activities and various levels of competitive sports. Chapters are actively involved in snow and water skiing, swimming, scuba diving, sailing, canoeing, river rafting, tennis, hiking, biking, horseback riding, climbing, and sky diving.

In the 1980s, DS/USA established links with United States Skiing Association (USSA) to sponsor the U.S. disabled ski team. USSA employs the team's director.

DS/USA competitions and programs are open to individuals with a wide range of physical impairments including amputations, birth defects, neurological disorders, and visual impairments. Since 1972, DS/USA has sponsored the National Handicapped Ski Championships and Winterfestival, the largest winter sport events for individuals with disabilities. The adaptive equipment used and how one performs on skis determines the competition classification rather than the specific disability. The classification system for DS/USA winter sports is discussed in chapter 7. In September 1990, DS/USA was granted authority for summer amputee sports by the USOC Committee on Sports for the Disabled.

A list of DS/USA chapters is contained in Appendix E. As of 1992, DS/USA offered winter ski programs, summer programs and competitions, fitness programs (fitness videotapes are listed in Appendix G), and youth programs.

DS/USA is a DSO member of the United States Olympic Committee and has been an active participant on the COSD. Athletes who compete under the auspices of DS/USA are represented internationally by ISOD for winter sports and for summer sports, by ISOD for amputee athletes, and by IBSA for blind/visually impaired athletes.

Special Olympics International

In 1968, Eunice Kennedy Shriver founded Special Olympics and hosted the first International Special Olympic Games in Soldier Field, Chicago (see Figure 3.2). Special Olympics was created by the Joseph P. Kennedy, Jr. Foundation for the benefit of individuals with mental retardation. The mission of Special Olympics is to provide year-round "Olympic-type" sports training and competition for children and adults with mental retardation in the United States and around the world.

The goal of SOI is to help "bring all persons with mental retardation into the larger society under conditions whereby they are accepted, respected and given the chance to become useful and productive citizens" (*Special Olympics Fact Sheet*). Individuals with mental retardation who are 8 or more years of age and those persons who have impairments due to

ANDY LEONARD

At a glance:

Powerlifter

Featured in *Sports Illustrated*

State, regional, national, and international competitor

Andy Leonard came to America in 1968 in the "baby lift" from war-torn Vietnam. He was physically scarred from his ordeals. His brain damage from bombings resulted in speech and hearing problems and delayed physical development. But this 7-year-old did not let his short stature or his developmental disability stop him from learning a new life. His adoptive parents and siblings in Pennsylvania provided the kind of love and support in which children thrive. As a result, he is living and working independently in State College, PA, and powerlifting about four times his body weight. Andy Leonard is 4'11" and weighs 114 pounds.

In 1990 Andy deadlifted 380 pounds. At the Drug-Free Powerlift competition in 1994, he went for a record 430 pounds. These are records for his age and weight class for athletes with and without disabilities! As a Special Olympics athlete Andy placed first in bench press (182 pounds) and deadlift (402 pounds) in the 1991 International Special Olympics competition. He has placed first, second, or third in Pennsylvania power meets, and in regional and national competitions against able-bodied athletes.

Andy practices three times per week for about two hours under the watchful eyes of Coach Clyde Doll (who is still competing at age 60). Andy is ranked in the top five nationally in his weight class. Doll indicates that Andy has become more self-confident and self-sufficient as a result of his successes.

cognitive delays and have significant learning or vocational problems are eligible to participate in SOI programs.

Official summer sports include aquatics, athletics, basketball, bowling, equestrian events, gymnastics, roller skating, soccer, softball, and volleyball. Official winter sports include Alpine skiing, Nordic skiing, figure skating, speed skating, floor hockey, and poly hockey.

These official sports and demonstration sports are found on the program of the International Winter and International Summer Special Olympics. International competitions are held every two years, alternating between the Winter and Summer Games. A recent addition to the competitions sponsored by SOI is the European Summer Special Olympics.

Within Special Olympics, classification for competition is based upon the athletes' previous performances and/or preliminary heats. Athletes of all ability levels are accommodated through this system, and everyone has a "reasonable opportunity to win" (*Special Olympics Fact Sheet*). Athletes from each state and U.S. Territories compete with teams from countries around the world.

SOI is organized around its headquarters in Washington, DC. Policies and procedures are determined by a board of directors that includes business and government leaders, professional athletes, educators, and experts in mental retardation around the world. SOI was officially recognized by the International Olympic Committee in February 1988 and authorized to use the term *Olympics* in conjunction with *Special*. SOI is a DSO member of the United States Olympic Committee. It was also one of the original members of the COSD. Inasmuch as it was designed to be international and autonomous, SOI is not affiliated with any other international disability sport organization.

United States Cerebral Palsy Athletic Association

Prior to 1978, individuals with cerebral palsy and those with similar neurological conditions had no formal organization to meet their specific sport needs. As a result, the National Association of Sports for Cerebral Palsy (NASCP) was formed and sponsored its first national competition in Detroit in 1978.

Shortly after the 1979 National Games, NASCP became affiliated with United Cerebral Palsy Associations (UCPA). After almost 7 years as a program component of UCPA, the majority of NASCP members fought for an independent sport organization. In November 1986, NASCP became known as United States Cerebral Palsy Athletic Association (USCPAA). Its purpose is to "provide competitive sports opportunities and support mechanisms to persons with cerebral palsy, strokes, or closed-head injuries with motor dysfunction acquired congenitally or

Duncan O. Wyeth

At a glance:

16 years in competitive sport

Regional, national, and international competitions

Cycling, discus, javelin

Member, Atlanta Paralympic Organizing Committee Board of Directors

Staff member, U.S. Disabled Sport Team, Barcelona Paralympics, 1992

Duncan O. Wyeth is a man of many talents and interests. He has participated in cycling, discus, and javelin, and has won gold, silver, and bronze medals in the Michigan Regional Cerebral Palsy Games; National Cerebral Palsy Games; and 1988 Paralympics in Seoul.

Duncan started competition specific to persons with disabilities in 1979 at the age of 32. Duncan states, "As with all individuals my age born having cerebral palsy, there existed no appropriate sports programs for participation during my youth and early adulthood." Duncan played in intramural sports in junior and senior high school and after college. He continues an active lifestyle today with cycle touring, and works out three times a week in the off-season.

Duncan recounts his involvement in sports as one in which his parents encouraged him to take risks, to go beyond "the passive experience that is so much a part of life for those with disabilities." Duncan's self-motivation facilitated his success not only as an athlete but also as a member of many sports games staffs at the national and international levels. His membership on the Atlanta Paralympic Organizing Committee Board of Directors for the 1996 games, as well as his serving as a U.S. representative to the International Committee on Inclusion of Athletes with Disabilities and the United States Olympic Committee Board of Directors, indicates just how far this elite athlete has come.

Duncan O. Wyeth is an elite athlete, rehabilitation professional, family man, public servant, photographer, and cyclist. Duncan's love affair with sport is summed up in the following manner: "We live in a very competitive society. Participation in sports is a valid avenue for persons with disabilities to learn physical skills and socialization skills that will allow them to more effectively compete in all areas of their lives. Attitudes change when people observe other people breaking stereotypes and dispelling misconceptions."

at any age" (USCPAA pamphlet, n.d.). USCPAA programs and competitions are open to individuals of all ages and ability. Classification for competitions is based on a functional eight-level system. The emphasis is upon competition among individuals with similar ability.

Competitions for athletes with cerebral palsy are offered at local, regional, national, and international levels. The official sports include archery, boccie, bowling, cycling, horseback riding, powerlifting, shooting, slalom, soccer, swimming, table tennis, track and field, and wheelchair team handball.

USCPAA is a DSO member of the USOC. Cerebral palsy athletes have been represented on the COSD since its initiation under NASCP and then USCPAA. USCPAA participates with other DSOs in selecting the U.S. disabled team for the Paralympics and world championships. International representation is achieved through Cerebral Palsy–International Sport and Recreation Association (CP–ISRA).

United States Association for Blind Athletes

The United States Association for Blind Athletes (USABA) was established in 1976 as the official organization promoting athletic competition for individuals with visual impairments. The establishment of the USABA was a direct result of the success of blind athletes who competed in the 1976 Olympiad for the Physically Disabled in Toronto and the need for an organization to oversee the sport opportunities for blind and visually impaired individuals. USABA has chapters in most states and more than 1,500 members throughout the United States.

Official sports include goalball, gymnastics, judo, powerlifting, swimming, tandem cycling, athletics (track and field events), wrestling, Alpine skiing, Nordic skiing, and speed skating. Under the auspices of USABA, blind and visually impaired athletes can compete in the Winter and Summer Paralympics, Winter National Games, World Judo Championships, World Powerlifting Invitational, Summer National Games, World Cycling Invitational, Pan American Games for Physically Disabled Youth, and World Championships and Games for the Disabled. Athletes compete in one of the three vision classifications and by age and gender in selected sports.

Goalball is a unique sport played by visually impaired or blind athletes. Goalball was invented in Europe to help war veterans with visual impairments to increase their auditory tracking ability, agility, and coordination. The game is played on a court similar in size to a volleyball court. Teams of three defend goals at the opposite ends of the court. All players are blindfolded to remove advantage from any player. The players, generally on their hands and knees, try to prevent the ball (rubber ball with bells)

JAMES V. MASTRO

At a glance:

First doctorate in physical education for a person with a visual impairment

Greco-Roman wrestling Olympic alternate

USABA medals winner in wrestling, track and field, goalball, and judo

Third-degree black belt in judo

Beep baseball and audio dart enthusiast

Dr. Jim Mastro is visually impaired, but don't let that fool you. This Minnesotan is a world-class athlete in several sports. His 10-page vita is full of gold, silver, and bronze medal finishes in goalball, wrestling, judo, shotput, discus, javelin, and powerlifting. He medaled in the 1992 Paralympics in Barcelona, the 1991 Judo Championships in Japan, the 1984 International Games for the Disabled in New York, the 1978 Pan-American Games for the Blind, and the 1976 Paralympics in Toronto. Jim has also competed with able-bodied athletes. When he was a national champion (wrestling) in 1973 he was named a member of the U.S. team for the first World University Games. In 1976 Jim was the first alternate to the U.S. Greco-Roman Wrestling Team. Beep baseball, goalball, audio darts, and judo are his continuing passions.

Sport is not the only venue in which Jim has excelled. He was the first individual with a visual impairment to earn a doctoral degree in physical education, from Texas Woman's University in 1985. Along with this academic honor have been many presentations and publications at the national and international level. Jim Mastro continues to put significant energy into the promotion of sports for individuals with disabilities. He is an outstanding athlete, educator, and gentleman who can "see" the role of sport for individuals in a unique way.

from crossing the endline. Points are scored when the ball crosses the endline.

USABA is a DSO member of the United States Olympic Committee, participates in the activities of the COSD, and is represented internationally by the International Blind Sport Association.

Dwarf Athletic Association of America

In 1985, 25 dwarf athletes participated in the 1985 National Cerebral Palsy/Les Autres Games. At that time, these short-stature athletes and physically impaired athletes (other than cerebral palsy) had no formal structure for organizing disabled sport opportunities. As a result, the Dwarf Athletic Association of America was formed shortly after the games in 1985.

The purpose of the DAAA is to develop, promote, and provide quality amateur athletic opportunities for dwarf athletes in the United States. The organization is independent of Little People of America (LPA), but drew heavily from LPA for membership. DAAA maintains ties to LPA, the Short Stature Foundation, and the Billy Barty Foundation.

Approximately a quarter million Americans are classified as dwarfs (4 feet, 10 inches) due to chondrodystrophy and other related causes. It is for this population that the DAAA has organized sport opportunities. The DAAA sponsors events in athletics, basketball, boccie, powerlifting, swimming, skiing (Alpine and Nordic), table tennis, and volleyball. The DAAA sponsors the National Dwarf Games and athletes compete by age, gender, and functional ability classifications.

The DAAA also offers clinics, developmental events, and formal competitions at local and regional levels. The youth events (7 to 15 years) emphasize achieving one's personal best. Selection as a young dwarf athlete for competition at the Pan American or World Disabled Youth Games is based upon one's athletic potential and demonstrated personal performance. For children under 7 years of age, the DAAA offers a noncompetitive sports program.

Dwarf athletes can be selected to join the United States Disabled Sport Team (USDST) and participate at the Paralympics and other international competitions.

The DAAA is a DSO member of the USOC and participates in the activities of the COSD. For international representation, DAAA is affiliated with ISOD.

Additional United States Disability Sport Associations

Numerous disability sport organizations exist in the United States today. Many of these are listed in Appendix E. Only a few associations are highlighted in this section.

National Foundation of Wheelchair Tennis

The National Foundation of Wheelchair Tennis (NFWT) was formed in 1976 as the governing body for wheelchair tennis in the United States. NFWT sponsors competitions, tournaments, instructional clinics and exhibitions, and multisport camps for disabled youth. The Wheelchair Tennis Players Association (WTPA) administers the rules and regulations that govern wheelchair tennis in the United States. Everest and Jennings sponsors the annual Grand Prix Circuit, which culminates in the U.S. Open Wheelchair Tennis Championship.

National Wheelchair Basketball Association

The National Wheelchair Basketball Association (NWBA) is one of the oldest wheelchair sports organizations in the world and certainly the oldest in the United States. Formed in 1945, the NWBA serves as the national governing body for wheelchair basketball in the United States, sponsors regional and national tournaments for men and for women, and selects the team(s) to represent the United States in international wheelchair basketball competitions.

National Wheelchair Softball Association

Wheelchair softball in the United States has been officially governed since 1976 by the National Wheelchair Softball Association (NWSA), which sponsors national tournaments each September.

North American Riding for the Handicapped Association

One of the earliest organizations for therapeutic horseback riding in the world, the North American Riding for the Handicapped Association (NARHA), was established in the 1970s. Today, NARHA provides programs and training in horseback riding for individuals with disabilities throughout the United States.

Wheelchair Athletics of the USA

Wheelchair Athletics of the USA (WAUSA) is not only a member of the NWAA but is affiliated with U.S.A. Track and Field Association (formerly The Athletics Congress), the national governing body for athletics in the United States and a member of the USOC. WAUSA represents and sanctions events in several sports including track, field, slalom, and road racing. WAUSA is responsible for selecting wheelchair athletes to represent the United States in international competitions.

Brenda Gilmore

At a glance:

Wheelchair tennis player

Regional and national tennis singles and doubles champion

Special recognition awards

Brenda Gilmore is a "forty-something" retired nationally ranked wheelchair tennis player. She hails from Largo, MD, and was involved in the competitive wheelchair tennis circuit from 1985 until 1989, reaching sixth place in the United States in the Women's Open Division. Brenda trained four to five times a week along with cross-training in track and weights.

Previous recreational pursuits like jogging, cycling, and bowling turned Brenda on to serious competition. Self-motivated, Brenda did not let a spinal cord injury leave her high and dry as concerns physical activity. To Brenda, sport is "crucial to my mental and physical well-being. It allows me to exercise and have fun at the same time. It gives me something to look forward to after a hard day and has allowed me to meet a wide range of people, not just in my hometown but from around the world."

Brenda won two sportsmanship awards from the Midwest and Southwest National Wheelchair Tennis Championships in 1986 and 1987, respectively. She also received a community service award from the Women's Competitive Tennis Club in 1989. Four years later, the Maryland Tennis Association recognized Brenda for outstanding contributions to the game of tennis in Maryland.

Brenda describes herself and others who are active in sport as "a group who tends to challenge life instead of waiting around for things to come to us. We are the high-profile 'hot shots' that help change the image of the physically challenged by our social appeal and appearance."

United States Les Autres Sport Association

The United States Les Autres Sport Association (USLASA) was formed after the 1985 National Cerebral Palsy/Les Autres Games as a separate sport governing body. USLASA organizes and sanctions competitions for les autres. Les Autres athletes include those with physical impairments not associated with any other disabled sport organization. USLASA works closely with USCPAA and DAAA in providing programs and competitions for physically impaired athletes at the local, national, and international levels.

United States Organization for Disabled Athletes

The United States Organization for Disabled Athletes (USODA) was formed as a nonprofit organization in 1985. The purpose of USODA is to bring together the various U.S. organizations serving athletes with disabilities and to provide a coordinated approach to scheduling, promotion, management, and funding for national and international sport events. Current members include USABA, USCPAA, DAAA, NWAA, and USLASA. Since 1985, USODA has sponsored numerous sport competitions including Pan Am Youth Games for the Physically Disabled, Winter Sports Festival, and Victory Games.

SIGNIFICANT EVENTS IN DISABILITY SPORT CHRONOLOGY: UNITED STATES PERSPECTIVES

The earliest known athletic event for individuals with disabilities in the United States was a wheelchair basketball game played by war veterans at California's Corona Naval Station in 1945. While still in its infancy, the Flying Wheels from Van Nuys, California, toured the United States in 1946. As result of this tour, the public became increasingly aware not only of wheelchair basketball as a sport but also that the players were capable individuals despite their impairment.

In 1947 and 1948, wheelchair basketball teams emerged: the Pioneers from Kansas City, MO; the Whirlaways from Brooklyn; the Gophers from Minneapolis; the Bulova Watchmakers of Woodside, NY; the Chairoteers of Queens; and the New York Spokesmen from Manhattan.

Since 1946, wheelchair basketball in the United States has increased so much in popularity that a wheelchair basketball tournament was desired. Tim Nugent, director of student rehabilitation at the University of Illinois, organized the first wheelchair basketball tournament in 1949 in Galesburg, Illinois. During the preparations for the tournament, it became necessary for Nugent to form a planning committee to oversee administrative aspects.

This evolved into the National Wheelchair Basketball Association (NWBA), the governing body for wheelchair basketball in the United States.

In the early 1950s, while Guttmann was organizing the first international competition for wheelchair athletes, Ben Lipton (from the United States) was contemplating the development of organized wheelchair sports, in addition to wheelchair basketball, on both the national and international levels. In 1957, with the cooperation of the Paralyzed Veterans Association of America and Adelphi College in New York, Lipton organized the first national wheelchair games. These games, patterned after Stoke Mandeville, introduced several events at the inaugural event: 60-, 100-, and 220-yard dashes and the 220- and 400-yard shuttle relays.

As a result of the successful national wheelchair games, Ben Lipton and his committee founded the National Wheelchair Athletic Association (NWAA). The prime function of this organization was to establish rules and regulations governing wheelchair sports other than basketball. Ultimately, the NWAA would expand its purpose to sponsoring various competitive sports on a state, regional, and national level.

With Lipton as director, the U.S. team entered its first international competition in 1960. (In that year, the wheelchair games were held shortly after the Olympics in Rome. This gave rise to the term *Paralympics*.)

Although many wheelchair sports were available, they were summer sports. Up to 1967, no organization attempted to serve the winter sport interests of individuals with disabilities. As a result, the National Handicapped Sports and Recreation Association (NHSRA) was formed by a small group of Vietnam veterans with amputations. This group is now Disabled Sports USA (DS/USA).

The United States was represented at the 1976 Olympiad for the Disabled in Toronto by 27 blind men and women. As a result of their successes in these games, a group was convened to discuss the formation of an organization to promote sport for blind athletes. In late 1976, national leaders, educators, and coaches of blind athletes formed the United States Association for Blind Athletes (USABA).

The National Association of Sports for Cerebral Palsy was founded in 1978 as the United States' governing sport organizing body for individuals with cerebral palsy and similar neurological conditions. In 1986, the NASCP was reorganized as the United States Cerebral Palsy Athletic Association (USCPAA) and continues to sponsor competitions in a variety of events including archery, horseback riding, powerlifting, table tennis, soccer, bowling, swimming, and track and field events.

A significant event in the history of the U.S. disability sport movement was the passage of PL 95-606, the Amateur Sports Act of 1978. This law charged the United States Olympic Committee with encouraging and promoting amateur athletic activity for individuals with disabilities. In meeting this mandate, the USOC established the Committee on Sports for the Disabled (COSD) and a separate category of membership for disabled sport organizations (DSOs). Since 1979, disability sport has been a part of the U.S. Olympic Movement. (The details are discussed in chapter 4.)

A small group of amputee athletes founded the United States Amputee Athletic Association (USAAA) in 1981. Although two other organizations (NHS, NWAA) served athletes with amputations, the USAAA was formed to offer these athletes another outlet. As the governing body for amputee sport, USAAA sponsored competitions for amputee athletes in events not offered by NHS and NWAA such as archery, stand-up basketball, sit-down and stand-up volleyball, swimming, weight lifting, and track and field events. (In 1989, USAAA filed for bankruptcy and ceased to exist as an organization.)

Under the auspices of the 1985 National Cerebral Palsy/Les Autres Games, dwarf athletes and physically disabled athletes with conditions other than cerebral palsy (les autres) were allowed to compete for virtually the first time. Inasmuch as there was no organization devoted to serving either dwarf athletes or les autres athletes, two new organizations were formed.

With the demise of USAAA, two organizations vied for the right to coordinate and sponsor athletic events for individuals with amputations. The two groups were Disabled Sports USA (formerly NHS) and National Amputee Summer Sports Association (NASSA). In September 1990, the COSD gave DS/USA provisional authority to conduct summer sports for amputee athletes. After months of negotiations, DS/USA and NASSA agreed to a transition plan that specified the manner in which DS/USA would assume responsibility for summer sports programs for amputees, allowed for significant involvement by the leaders from NASSA, and ensured appropriate athlete representation within DS/USA.

Numerous sport and recreational organizations were formed in the 1970s and 1980s. These were in response to growing interest in sport by individuals with disabilities. Examples of these include Handicapped Scuba Association (1974), National Foundation for Wheelchair Tennis (1976), and North American Riding for the Handicapped Association (NARHA). As the disability sport movement continues to gather momentum, new sport organizations serving individuals with disabilities will continue to emerge. For a comprehensive listing of these, see Appendixes D, E, and F.

Since the 1970s, numerous significant events and happenings have occurred in disability sport. A brief review of these includes the following:

- Recognition was given to athletes with disabilities by the United States Olympic Committee (USOC) and International Olympic Committee (IOC),

- Athletes with disabilities entered races and competitions primarily for able-bodied athletes, such as the Boston Marathon and exhibition events at both Summer and Winter Olympic Games,

- Sporting events for female athletes with disabilities were established, such as the first women's national wheelchair basketball tournament in 1974,
- Additional competitions were established to provide additional outlets for athletic competitions, such as the Pan American Games for the Disabled (1967), Victory Games for the Physically Disabled (1989), and the National Veterans Wheelchair Games (1981), and
- The athletic performances of athletes with disabilities have improved tremendously, such as George Murray breaking the sub 4-minute mile in 1985 and repeated victories by Candace Cable-Brooks in the Boston Marathon (see Figure 3.3 as an example of significant changes in athletic performance of athletes with disabilities).

THEMES OF CHANGES

As indicated previously, many of the significant changes are highlighted in Table 3.2. In addition to the identification of significant events, it is important to give meaning to the collective history. Thus, the following themes were identified:

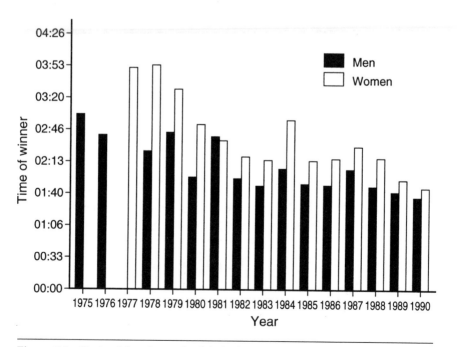

Figure 3.3   Boston Marathon wheelchair division winners.

1. Wheelchair sport has been prominent throughout the history of sport and disability.

2. Men have had early involvement in and primary access to sport.

3. There has been an increase in the number of sport associations serving individuals with disabilities.

4. There has also been an increase in the number of competitions available to athletes with disabilities.

5. Increasing emphasis has been placed on sport-specific competition and specialization in sport.

6. As expected, there has been a dramatic increase in the athletic performance of athletes with disabilities.

7. More girls and women are entering sport.

8. There are increasing opportunities for athletes with disabilities to compete alongside able-bodied athletes and more emphasis on integration.

9. Athletes with disabilities have experienced increased visibility through media coverage (television, advertisements, endorsements, public relations), corporate sponsorships, recognition and award ceremonies, etc.

10. There is increasing acknowledgment and acceptance of individuals with disabilities as athletes by the IOC in particular and the able-bodied sporting world in general (e.g., exhibition events at Olympic Games, development of IPC) as well as by society in general (e.g., television coverage, articles in sport pages of newspapers).

CONCLUDING COMMENTS

Numerous sport organizations serve individuals with disabilities. Much of the progress made in the disability sport movement has been a result of individual efforts as well as the efforts of the sport organizations highlighted in this chapter.

In terms of competitive sport worldwide, the major international sport organizations serving individuals with disabilities were presented in this chapter. Also highlighted were a selected few of the disability sport organizations found in the United States, many of which are members of the United States Olympic Committee and are therefore considered as playing a leading role in disability sport in the United States.

Paralímpics
Barcelona'92

CHAPTER 4

Structure of Sport and Disability

To understand the structure of disability sport, it is necessary first to briefly describe the social framework for sport. Understanding the structure of Olympic and Pan American sport at the international level is important as well as understanding the structure of sport in the United States. Although the international organization of sport remains consistent, the national structure varies in relation to the given cultural or societal context (see chapter 6).

INTERNATIONAL OLYMPIC SPORT

The major players in the international sport arena are the International Olympic Committee (IOC), international federations (IFs), Olympic organizing committees (OOCs), and national Olympic committees (NOCs).

The IOC serves as the final authority in regard to the Olympic movement throughout the world and the Olympic and Pan American Games. By official action of the Congress of Paris, the IOC was created on June 23, 1894, and thereby given the control and development of the modern Olympic Games. The specific purposes of the IOC are as follows (adapted from the *1993 USOC Fact Book*):

1. Encourage the organization and development of sport and sport competitions,

2. Inspire and lead sport within the Olympic ideal, thereby promoting and strengthening friendship between the sportsmen (and women) of all countries,

3. Ensure the regular celebration of the Olympic Games, and

4. Make the Olympic Games even more worthy of their glorious history and of the high ideals which inspired their revival by Baron Pierre de Courbertin and his associates.

Perhaps the most important international organizations for specific sports are the international federations (IFs), autonomous single-sport organizations that are each solely responsible for the governance of their sports on the international level; an example would be the International Amateur Athletic Foundation (IAAF). The IFs have the authority over eligibility, rules, and the events offered in their sports at the Olympic Games and other international competitions. In this capacity, the IFs work closely with the IOC, OOCs, and NOCs. Because of the IFs' role as final authority over a given sport, national sport associations (e.g., national governing bodies, NGBs) must be recognized by their respective IFs.

An additional entity concerned with international sport is the Olympic organizing committee. In those cities around the world which desire to host the Olympic Games, an OOC is formed. Initially, the OOC is responsible for preparing the official bid to the NOC and perhaps the IOC. If its city is selected to host, the OOC is responsible for preparations, management, and conduct of the Olympic Games.

National Olympic committees are recognized by the IOC and are found in more than 166 countries. Each NOC has sole responsibility for its country's representation at the Olympic Games and other events under the patronage of the IOC (including the Pan American Games). Although these organizations' responsibilities and authority may vary by country, these NOCs are responsible for fielding an Olympic team. In preparing a team for international competition, the NOCs must work closely with the NGBs in each sport, which in turn must be recognized by and must work closely with the IFs.

INTERNATIONAL DISABILITY SPORT

The structure of international sport for individuals with disabilities is similar to that of Olympic sport. For international disability sport, there exist umbrella organization(s), international sport federation(s), and "Olympic (International Games)" organizing committees. In addition, national sport organizations serve as the responsible agencies for disability sport in a given country.

The International Paralympic Committee (IPC) was designed to serve as the "IOC" of sport for and including individuals with disabilities. The IPC has been recognized by the IOC and serves as its liaison on behalf of athletes with disabilities. (A detailed discussion of the IPC is presented in chapter 3.)

HUGO STORER

At a glance:

A-K amputee

Seoul and Barcelona
Paralympic competitor

Pan-Am Games medal
winner

Born in San Juan, Puerto Rico, Hugo Storer is a shotputter. He has been involved in competitive sport for the past 7 years. Training 11 months of the year, Hugo is serious about his sport. In 1986 Hugo won a gold medal in the shotput and a bronze in the discus at the Pan-Am Games. In 1988 in Seoul, he finished 8th, while the 1992 Barcelona Paralympics were a bit of a disappointment.

A professor from the University of Puerto Rico was the first to encourage Hugo to become involved in disability sport competition. The importance of sport in Hugo's life enables him to work hard and focus on winning a medal in the Paralympics. Eventually, Hugo would like to coach others. He would like to encourage young people with disabilities to become involved in sport so they can travel, meet people, and perhaps win medals. "Even if they do not make a team, they can be a super role model for others," he says.

As shown in Figure 4.1, six international governing bodies for disability sport organized the IPC. These include the International Committee of Sports for the Deaf (CISS), International Blind Sport Association (IBSA), International Sports Organization for the Disabled (ISOD), International Stoke Mandeville Wheelchair Sports Federation (ISMWSF), Cerebral Palsy–International Sport and Recreation Association (CP–ISRA), and International Sports Federation for Persons with Mental Handicap (INAS–FMH). In contrast to their Olympic counterparts, which are organized around sport, these "international federations" are multisport and mostly organized around disability; that is, IBSA for blind, CP–ISRA for cerebral palsy, ISMWSF for spinal cord injured and wheelchair users, ISOD for amputee and les autres, CISS for Deaf, and INAS–FMH for mentally handicapped persons. Although these groups are active in the business of the IPC, only four (IBSA, CP–ISRA, ISMWSF, ISOD) participate in the Paralympics.

Although a member of IPC, INAS–FMH held separate world championships until 1992. With the cooperation of the International Coordinating Committee and the Barcelona Paralympics Organizing Committee, INAS–FMH scheduled the first Paralympics Games for Persons with Mental

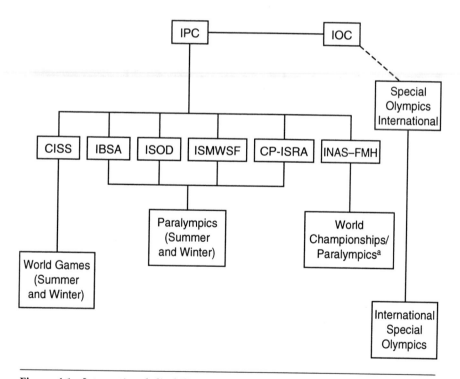

Figure 4.1 International disability sport structure. [a]Competitions for the mentally handicapped currently considered within the Paralympics.

Handicaps for September 1992 in Madrid. These games were identified as the "mentally handicapped sector" of the Paralympics that were held in Barcelona in September 1992. Yet unresolved is the status of separate or integrated international competitions for athletes who compete under the auspices of INAS–FMH; lengthy and heated discussions have been held about the inclusion of the mentally handicapped among the competitors in the Paralympics. The organizers of the Winter Paralympics in Lillehammer, Norway, in February 1994 included two demonstration events for athletes with mental retardation.

Despite the controversy, the IPC decided that full medal events for athletes with mental retardation were to be held during the First World Championships in Athletics in Berlin in July 1994. Four events were offered for men (shot put, long jump, 200m, 800m) and two events for women (long jump, 200m). The World Championships in Swimming held in Malta in October 1994 also included athletes with mental retardation. The decision to include these athletes in future Paralympic Games and World Championships rests with the IPC.

Deaf athletes have not yet participated in the Paralympics, but the CISS does remain a member of the IPC. For most of the 20th century, the CISS has hosted the World Games for the Deaf and has gained recognition by the IOC as the only federation responsible for the administration of all sporting events involving Deaf athletes. In keeping with this autonomy, CISS secured a similar agreement with the IPC on July 16, 1990. Although the CISS has maintained autonomy over sporting events including Deaf athletes, the inclusion of Deaf athletes in the Paralympics has been considered and the debate will continue well into the 21st century.

Special Olympics International (SOI) is not a member of IPC, nor does it participate in any of the Paralympics activities or events. On the other hand, SOI has established a link to the IOC. In 1988, Special Olympics International was formally recognized by IOC and given permission to use the word *Olympics* in their title. This permission was granted under the condition that the word *Olympics* only be used in conjunction with *Special*.

UNITED STATES OLYMPIC SPORT

The United States Olympic Committee (USOC) serves as the IOC-recognized national Olympic committee (NOC) and as such has the responsibility for Olympic sport in the United States. The roots of the USOC can be traced back to a small group that entered the first U.S. athletes into the Olympics in 1896. Since these early beginnings, the USOC has undergone many structural changes as well as name changes. The most significant change occurred in 1978 with the enactment of the Amateur Sports Act, which specified that the USOC would serve as the organization for amateur athletic activity in the United States and would coordinate U.S. athletic activity related to the international Olympic movement (see Figure 4.2). USOC has the following goals (adapted from *1993 USOC Fact Book*):

1. To provide the most comprehensive financial and facilities support possible for American athletes,

2. To coordinate and develop athletic activity in the U.S. directly related to international athletic competitions and to foster productive working relationships among sports-related organizations with the Olympic family,

3. To exercise exclusive jurisdiction over all matters pertaining to the participation of the U.S. in the Olympic Games,

4. To obtain the most representation possible in each competition and event of the Olympic and Pan American Games,

5. To provide for the resolution of conflicts and disputes among athletes, NGBs, or sport organizations,

6. To foster the development of athletic facilities and assist in making existing facilities available,

7. To encourage and support research, development, and dissemination of information in the areas of sports medicine and science and sport safety, and

8. To encourage and provide assistance for athletic activities for women, individuals with disabilities, and athletes of racial or ethnic minorities.

In meeting its mission, the United States Olympic Committee

1. Provides athlete support services (Olympic Job Opportunities Program, special grants programs, health insurance, tuition assistance)

2. Supports information resources (library, archives, publications, conferences)

3. Encourages development activities (licensing, fundraising, marketing, television revenue, corporate sponsorship)

4. Offers sports medicine programs (clinical, dental, vision, nutrition) and sport science programs (engineering and technology, sport psychology, biomechanics, sport physiology)

5. Provides drug education and testing programs

6. Endorses the Olympic festivals

Inasmuch as the USOC is an organization of organizations, different member categories exist. There are 42 Olympic/Pan American Games

Figure 4.2 Structure of U.S. Olympic sport. A dotted line indicates the organization is affiliated with, but not officially part of, the USOC.

sport organizations (NGBs), 9 affiliated sports organizations, 11 community-based multisport organizations, 4 education-based multisport organizations, 1 armed forces sport organization, and 7 disabled in sport organizations (DSOs). Table 4.1 lists these organizations. In addition, state Olympic organizations sponsor fundraising and other Olympic events on a state level.

DISABILITY SPORT IN THE UNITED STATES

Although individuals with disabilities have long participated in sport and recreation activities, disability sport has rapidly become a more formalized entity in itself and a legitimate part of the U.S. sport world.

Table 4.1 USOC Member Organizations

Olympic/Pan American Games Sport Organizations

National Archery Association

U.S. Track and Field

U.S. Badminton Association

U.S. Baseball Federation

USA Basketball

U.S. Biathlon Association

U.S. Bobsled and Skeleton Federation

U.S. Tenpin Bowling Federation

USA Boxing

U.S. Canoe and Kayak

U.S. Cycling Federation

U.S. Diving, Inc.

American Horse Shows Association

U.S. Fencing Association

Field Hockey Association of America (Men)

U.S. Field Hockey Association (Women)

U.S. Figure Skating Association

U.S.A. Gymnastics

USA Hockey

United States Judo, Inc.

U.S. Luge Association

U.S. Modern Pentathlon Association

American Amateur Racquetball Association

U.S. Amateur Conference of Roller Skating

U.S. Rowing Association

U.S. Sailing Association

U.S. Shooting Team

U.S. Skiing

U.S. Soccer Federation

Amateur Softball Association

U.S. International Speedskating Association

U.S. Swimming, Inc.

U.S. Synchronized Swimming, Inc.

U.S. Table Tennis Association

U.S. Taekwondo Union

U.S. Team Handball Federation

U.S. Tennis Association

U.S. Volleyball Association

U.S. Water Polo

U.S. Weightlifting Federation

USA Wrestling

U.S. Yacht Racing Union

Affiliated Sports Organizations

U.S. Cycling Association

USA Karate Federation

U.S. Orienteering Federation

U.S. Sports Acrobatics Federation

U.S. Squash Racquets Association

American Trampoline and Tumbling Association

Triathlon Federation USA

Underwater Society of America

American Water Ski Association

Community-Based Multisport Organizations

Amateur Athletic Union

American Alliance for Health, Physical Education, Recreation and Dance

Boys and Girls Clubs of America

Catholic Youth Organization

(continued)

Table 4.1 *(continued)*

Community-Based Multisport Organizations (cont.)	
Jewish Community Centers Association	National Federation of State High School Associations
National Exploring Div., Boy Scouts of America	National Junior College Athletic Association
National Association of Police Athletic Leagues	**Armed Forces**
National Congress of State Games	U.S. Armed Forces Sports
U.S. National Senior Sport Organization	**Disabled in Sports Organizations**
YMCA of the USA	American Athletic Association of the Deaf
YWCA of the USA	Disabled Sports USA
Education-Based Multisport Organizations	Dwarf Athletic Association of America
	Special Olympics International
National Association of Intercollegiate Athletics	U.S. Association for Blind Athletes
	U.S. Cerebral Palsy Athletic Association
National Collegiate Athletic Association	Wheelchair Sports USA

U.S. Legislative History

The 20th century provided most, if not all, of the legislative impetus for the development and growth of sport for and including athletes with disabilities. Although several other western countries have utilized legislation, charters, and/or federally endorsed strategic planning efforts to effect change on behalf of individuals with disabilities, legislation mandates have been largely American phenomena. Legislation has assisted in the development of sport opportunities for individuals with disabilities in the United States. (Information about legislation in other countries is discussed in chapter 3.)

Legislation affecting the rights of individuals with disabilities started in 1958, and the rights of disabled persons to access programs, facilities, education including physical education, and sport have all been secured. Of specific import here are PL 90-170, the Elimination of Architectural Barriers Act (1968); PL 93-112, the Rehabilitation Act (1973), which made discrimination on the basis of disability illegal; PL 94-142, the Education of All Handicapped Children Act (1975), which mandated education including physical education for disabled children; and PL 95-606, the Amateur Sports Act (1978), which recognized athletes with disabilities as part of the United States Olympic Committee. Although they did not mention disability specifically, the civil rights legislation of 1964 and Title IX legislation of 1972 influenced the disability rights movement (see Table 4.2).

In 1975, President Gerald Ford formed the President's Commission on Olympic Sports to examine the structure and status of Olympic sport in the United States. The Commission's 1977 report actually formed the basis for the Amateur Sports Act of 1978. The civil rights movement of the 1960s resulted in the passage of the Civil Rights Act of 1964, Title IX in 1972, and the Rehabilitation Act of 1973, setting the stage for the inclusion

Table 4.2 Significant U.S. Legislation Affecting Physical Education and Sport for Individuals With Disabilities

Year	Public law	Title	Effect of law
1964	PL 88-352	Civil Rights Act	Nondiscrimination on basis of race
1967	PL 90-170	Elementary and Secondary Education Act (ESEA) amended.	Training programs in physical education and recreation for persons with disabilities
1968	PL 90-480	Architectural Barriers Act	
1972	PL 92-318	Title IX	Nondiscrimination on basis of gender
1973	PL 93-112	Rehabilitation Act	Nondiscrimination on basis of disability
1975	PL 94-142	Education of All Handicapped Children Act	Instruction in physical education required as part of special education
1978	PL 95-606	Amateur Sports Act	Recognized athletes with disabilities as part of the Olympic movement and the USOC
1990	PL 101-336	Americans With Disabilities Act	Civil rights reaffirmed for individuals with disabilities

of ethnic minority individuals, women, and individuals with disabilities into future legislation. Inasmuch as the essence of the Amateur Sports Act was formulated during the mid-1970s, lawmakers couldn't help but be influenced by earlier civil rights legislation. As a result, the Amateur Sports Act included specific reference to opportunities in sport for ethnic minority individuals, women, and individuals with disabilities (De-Pauw & Clarke, 1986).

The enactment of the Amateur Sports Act led to the inclusion of the following purposes listed in the constitution of the United States Olympic Committee (*USOC constitution*, 1989, p. 2): "To encourage and provide assistance to amateur athletic programs and competition for handicapped individuals, including, where feasible, the expansion of opportunities for meaningful participation by handicapped individuals in programs of athletic competition for able-bodied individuals." To achieve this objective, a separate USOC category known as Group E membership and a Committee on Sports for the Disabled (formerly known as the Handicapped in Sports Committee) were established. Group E membership (now known as disabled sport organizations, DSO) was open to national amateur sports organizations serving individuals with disabilities that sponsored national athletic competitions in two or more sports included on the program of the Olympic or Pan American Games.

Although not directly related to sport, legislation passed in the late 1980s reaffirmed the civil rights of individuals with disabilities. The Americans With Disabilities Act of 1990 (ADA) extends the broad protections offered by the Civil Rights Act of 1964 to individuals with disabilities. It provides protection against discrimination on the basis of disability in employment, public services, and public accommodations. Although not specifically mentioned, sport and recreational programs are interpreted to be included among the public services.

Committee on Sports for the Disabled

The Committee on Sports for the Disabled (COSD) was established as a standing committee of the USOC. It was originally composed of two representatives from each of the then Group E members (AAAD, USAAA, USABA, USCPAA, NHSRA, NWAA, Special Olympics) and members-at-large appointed by the USOC president. The COSD coordinates amateur athletic activity for individuals with disabilities in the United States. By law, at least 20% of the membership has to be active athletes with disabilities. Members are appointed for the Olympic quadrennium and can be reappointed. Although modified in the late 1980s, the COSD has remained a critical component in the disability sport movement. (For a comprehensive history of the COSD through 1984, see DePauw & Clarke, 1986. The activities of the COSD since 1984 are chronicled in the COSD

Forum section of *Palaestra*.) Inasmuch as the COSD and USOC member-ship were a direct result of federal legislation, the Amateur Sports Act remains the most influential piece of legislation in regard to individuals with disabilities and their right to participate in sport.

Over the years the COSD has assumed some of the responsibility for representing American athletes with disabilities on the international level. The majority if not all of this representation has been related to the Paralympic movement as opposed to efforts on behalf of Deaf athletes or mentally retarded athletes. Representation for Deaf athletes has been conducted by the American Athletic Association of the Deaf; representa-tion for mentally retarded persons has been handled by Special Olympics.

Since 1979, as a standing committee the COSD has advised the USOC on matters affecting the rights of individuals with disabilities. In per-forming its duties as outlined in the USOC constitution, the COSD has met regularly, established criteria and evaluated requests by disabled sport organizations for membership in the USOC, reviewed and approved budgets for committee activities, provided financial support for develop-mental programs as well as elite sport programs sponsored by the disabled sport organizations, designed workshops and media productions for the dissemination of information about disability sport, resolved conflicts among groups, coordinated efforts for combined (multidisability and cross-organizational) U.S. teams for Winter and Summer Paralympics, assisted in the review of grant proposals, established criteria for evaluating membership services funds allocations, coordinated disabled athlete par-ticipation in Olympic festivals, and recommended changes to the USOC constitution.

Disability Sport Organizations

Prior to 1992, the COSD was composed of representatives from each of the USOC-recognized disability sport organizations (DSOs). Membership in the USOC requires the DSOs to sponsor national competitions in two or more sports found on the Olympic or Pan American program. As such, DSOs are required to be multisport and organized around disability to the extent that at least two sports are represented. DSOs must also be affiliated with international sport federations serving individuals with dis-abilities.

At one time eight DSOs were recognized by the USOC:

- American Athletic Association of the Deaf (AAAD)
- Dwarf Athletic Association of America (DAAA)
- United States Cerebral Palsy Athletic Association (USCPAA)
- Disabled Sports USA (DS/USA)

ROD HERNLEY

At a glance:

Skier

18-year competitor

Member of the U.S. Disabled Ski Team

USOC Committee on Sports for the Disabled

Inventor

Rod Hernley was born in Goshen, IN, with arthrogryposis of the lower extremities. Rod's parents were instrumental in his attempts to be actively engaged in the sporting community. Rod recalls his father spending hours coaching him to place hit in softball. When his family moved to Denver, Rod was able to join a city softball league and had the highest batting average (.900+) in the league, even though some people could walk faster than he could run! Later, Hal O'Leary, Jack Benedict, and others assisted him.

Rod has been actively involved in community, national, and international organizations related to sports for individuals with disabilities. As a competitive skier from 1976 to 1986, Rod garnered 20 gold and silver medals in national competition. In 1984, Rod won a bronze medal at the 3rd World Winter Games in Innsbruck. However, his reputation for service is also noteworthy. Rod has been recognized as an outstanding federal employee in an eight-state region. He has received the Jim Winthers Memorial Award (1990) for service to disabled winter sports, and has served on various national and international boards and commissions related to disability sport, including several on the United States Olympic Committee.

Rod's thoughts on the role of sport in his life reflect his positive philosophy. "The fact that I can't run like others does not always put me at a disadvantage. It just means that I may have to train better and play more intelligently to compete on a level playing field. Maybe that's what conquering a disability is all about—figuring out how to level the playing field." Now retired, Rod encourages young people with disabilities to "never give up" and to remember that a physical disability is not a handicap! Words well spoken from a competitor, family man, creative/adaptive sport equipment developer, and spokesperson for people with disabilities.

- National Wheelchair Athletic Association (NWAA)
- Special Olympics International (SOI)
- United States Association for Blind Athletes (USABA)
- United States Amputee Athletic Association (USAAA).

The USAAA filed for bankruptcy in 1989, and the athletes are currently being served by National Handicapped Sports. The remaining disability sport organizations are current members of the USOC (see Figure 4.3).

Each of these DSOs has a network of regional, state, or local affiliates. The responsibilities of these DSOs run the gamut from grassroots developmental sport programs to elite athletic competitions and representation by athletes at international competitions (details about each of these groups can be found in chapter 3). See Table 4.3 to compare the relationships between the NGBs and DSOs.

Recently each DSO has established contacts with the NGBs in the USOC. Through these ties, programs for athletes with disabilities have been incorporated within selected NGBs, training and educational programs have been offered for DSOs and their athletes, information has been shared regarding technological advances, and events for athletes with disabilities have been included among the normally sanctioned competitions. With improved relations between DSOs and NGBs, the NGBs will be able to assume greater responsibility for elite disabled athletes and the DSOs will focus on quality developmental sport programs.

USOC Task Force on Sport and Disability

From the beginning, sport for individuals with disabilities in the United States has been organized both around disability (e.g., Special Olympics

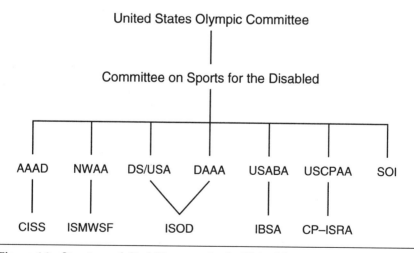

Figure 4.3 Structure of disability sport in the United States.

Table 4.3   USOC National Governing Bodies and Affiliated Disability Sport Organizations

NGBs	AAAD	DAAA	USCPAA	USABA	DS/USA	WS-USA	SOI	NWBA	USLASA
Athletics	+	+	+	+	+	+	+		+
Basketball	+	+			+		+	+	
Cycling	+		+	+	+				
Equestrian events			+						
Racquetball						+			
Shooting	+	+	+	+	+	+			+
Skiing			+	+	+		+		
Soccer	+		+				+		
Softball		+					+		
Swimming	+	+	+	+	+	+	+		+
Table tennis	+	+	+	+	+	+			
Team handball	+		+			+	+		
Tennis	+				+				
Volleyball	+	+		+	+				
Weight lifting	+	+	+	+	+	+			

for mentally retarded individuals) and around sport (e.g., National Wheelchair Basketball Association). Those associations organized around disability (and multisport) were given access to the USOC through the COSD; those organized around sport (single sport, single or multiple disability) were denied membership to the USOC as well as participation on the COSD. These associations could attempt to gain access to the NGBs of the USOC, and some have been successful. As the USOC is organized around sport, specifically the vertical structure sport, difficulties have ensued in attempting to integrate disability sport into the USOC.

Since 1979, the COSD has functioned in a role for disability sport similar to the role of USOC for Olympic sport. Much of the early efforts were devoted to coordination among the disability sport organizations and seeking access into the components of the USOC, especially the NGBs.

Although a part of the USOC, the COSD tended to function outside its mainstream of activity. Whereas the USOC was organized around sport, the COSD effort was organized by disability. This type of organization created difficulties in the actual acceptance of athletes with disabilities within the Olympic movement, let alone the USOC.

One of the most significant changes for disability sport arose from the impasse created by the different structural organization of the USOC and disability sport within it. In January 1989, a USOC task force was appointed to examine all aspects of the USOC commitment to athletes with disabilities and to recommend appropriate policy and direction. Over the next year and a half, the task force met with representatives of the USOC NGBs, USOC staff and officers, individuals involved with writing the Amateur Sports Act, disabled sport organizations, COSD members, and athletes with disabilities. At its May 3-4, 1991 meeting, the COSD approved the following (adapted from *COSD Minutes*, May 1991):

1. Sport for individuals with disabilities is an integral part of the Olympic movement. The USOC and NGBs have a legally mandated responsibility to provide, encourage, and support amateur athletic programs for athletes with disabilities.

2. The goals of disabled sport programs within the U.S. Olympic movement are (a) integration, where feasible, into open competition programs, and (b) development of elite athletes with disabilities.

3. Amateur athletic programs for persons with disabilities should be organized around sport rather than around disability.

4. Development of athletic opportunities for all persons, including those with disabilities, should be a shared responsibility of NGBs and DSOs.

5. DSOs and athletes with disabilities should be represented through NGBs to provide for a more vertical governance structure of sport in the United States.

JAN WILSON

At a glance:

First United States Olympic Committee disabled sport coordinator

Amputee Hall of Fame inductee

U.S. disabled sports team member 1980, 1984, and 1988

Gold, silver, and bronze medal winner

Jan Wilson, a Lexington, NC, native, spent 10 years as an elite competitor in swimming. A member of three U.S. disabled sports teams, she competed in Arnhem, New York, and Seoul, and brought home a total of 12 medals, including a gold. As a member of the U.S. Amputee Team in 1983, 1986, and 1988, Jan won more medals. She trained 3 to 5 hours 6 days a week. That's commitment!

Jan has also gained notoriety out of the pool. She was female captain of the U.S. Amputee Team at the 1988 Paralympics, and she has been recognized as an athlete-of-the-year by the U.S. Amputee Athletic Association, the United States Olympic Committee, and the Colorado Amateur Sports Corporation. More recently, Jan served as the first coordinator for disabled sport for the USOC.

The value of sport in Jan's life means having the opportunity for the "same rewards as for the nonhandicapped—a healthier body." Sport to Jan means "improved mental outlook and a chance to test and challenge myself in all areas of life."

Jan Wilson's record of medal-winning performances is testament to her beliefs and her advice for young persons with disabilities. "Find what it is you love and do it as often and as passionately as you desire."

6. The COSD should become a regular standing committee of the USOC composed of DSO representatives, NGB representatives, and other individuals representing the interests of persons with disabilities and should coordinate and oversee the fulfillment of the responsibilities outlined herein and contained in the Amateur Sports Act of 1978.

7. USOC financial support for sports for persons with disabilities should be focused on programs for athletes and coaches.

8. USOC financial support for athletes with disabilities should continue to be made available through specific grant programs and member services funds.

9. USOC should provide as a priority budgeted funding for Olympic-equivalent multisport, multidisability games.

10. Participation by elite athletes with disabilities should be ensured in USOC programs, training centers, and services.

CONCLUDING COMMENTS

From its beginnings, international disability sport has essentially functioned as a parallel model for able-bodied sport, in particular, Olympic sport. On the other hand, the structure of disability sport in the United States has been complicated by the emphasis on disability rather than sport. This discrepancy between the vertical structure of sport and the manner in which disability sport in the United States was organized was finally addressed in the early 1990s. Sport for and including athletes with disabilities has finally become an integral part of the U.S. Olympic movement.

CHAPTER 5

Sport Opportunities for Athletes With Disabilities

Throughout the 1900s, sport opportunities for athletes with disabilities have increased tremendously. Now there are major international competitions for elite athletes with disabilities in addition to numerous national and regional competitions and a multitude of sport and recreation opportunities found in local communities.

INTERNATIONAL COMPETITIONS FOR ATHLETES WITH DISABILITIES

The international organizations serving sport for individuals with disabilities have tended to pattern themselves after the "able-bodied" sporting world and the international Olympics. In doing so, a parallel system of sport has been created. As naturally follows, parallel international competitions exist and most likely will continue to emerge.

Multisport multidisability world championships as well as single-sport single-disability international competitions are held on a regular basis. Today, in virtually all disability sports, world or regional competitions can be found. These can be specific to the disability type as well as the sport such as international wheelchair archery tournaments, world goalball championships, international wheelchair marathons, and so on. In addition, multisport and multidisability competitions are found, including the Pan American wheelchair games, World Cup Alpine disabled skiing championships, and European championships for athletics and swimming, as well as multisport single-disability events such as the European Special Olympics and competitions offered under the auspices of the North American Deaf Sports Association (NADSA). For more specific information, the reader is referred to disability sport organizations in the United States, Canada, and around the world (see Appendixes D, E, and F). Listings of international competitions can be found in the *IPC Newsletter* and *Palaestra* as well as in publications of disability sport associations.

In addition to multisport and multidisability international competitions, there are Olympic-equivalent international competitions for individuals with disabilities. These are:

- the Paralympics (summer and winter),
- World Games for the Deaf (summer and winter),
- International Special Olympics (summer and winter), and
- Paralympics/World Championships for the Mentally Handicapped.

Paralympics

The Paralympics can be considered the equivalent of the Olympics for elite physically and visually impaired athletes. Both summer and winter games are held every four years, in the same host country as the Olympics whenever possible. The Paralympics include many of the sports found on the program of the Olympics and are open to athletes who are paraplegic and quadriplegic, blind, amputee, cerebral palsied, and les autres. Although the first games were held in 1952 at Stoke Mandeville, England, and in 1960 in Rome, the term *Paralympic* has only been used to describe the games since 1964. Paralympics refers to games that are "next to" the Olympics. See Table 5.1 for a chronology of the Paralympics.

A significant milestone in Paralympic history occurred during the Summer Paralympics, held October 15-24, 1988, in Seoul. Some 3,200 athletes from 62 countries competed in 732 different events. These games utilized

Table 5.1 Brief History of the Paralympics

The Summer Paralympics have been held every four (4) years since 1960.

1960 Rome
- Coincided with Olympics
- 400 athletes, 23 countries
- Wheelchair events only

1964 Tokyo
- Olympics in Tokyo
- 390 competitors and escorts, 22 countries
- Wheelchair events only

1968 Tel Aviv
- Olympics in Mexico City
- 1,100 competitors and escorts, 29 countries
- Wheelchair events only

1972 Heidelberg
- Olympics in Munich
- 1,400 competitors and escorts, 44 countries
- Demonstration events—blind and amputee events

1976 Toronto
- Olympics in Montreal
- 2,700 competitors and escorts, 41 countries
- First full competition—blind, wheelchair, and amputee events

1980 Arnhem, Holland
- Olympics in Moscow
- 2,560 competitors and escorts, 42 countries

1984 New York
- Olympics in Los Angeles
- 2,500 competitors and escorts, 45 countries
- First competition to include athletes with cerebral palsy

1988 Seoul
- After Olympics
- 4,200 competitors and escorts, 62 countries

1992 Barcelona
- After Olympics
- 4,500 competitors and escorts, 90 countries

The Winter Paralympics have been held every four years since 1976.

1976 Oshevik, Sweden
- Olympics in Innsbruck

1980 Geilo, Norway
- 322 competitors, 18 countries
- Olympics in Lake Placid, NY

1984 Innsbruck, Austria
- 458 competitors, 21 countries
- Olympics in Sarajevo, Yugoslavia (Bosnia)

1988 Innsbruck, Austria
- 400 competitors, 22 countries
- Olympics in Calgary, Canada

1992 Tignes, France
- First time Paralympics held at same site as Olympics
- 603 competitors and escorts, 24 countries

the same facilities, housing, competition sites, etc., as the 1988 Olympics, and the opening and closing ceremonies were identical. Competition was held in 17 different sports: archery, athletics, basketball, boccie, cycling, equestrian events, fencing, goalball, judo, shooting, volleyball, soccer, swimming, table tennis, weight lifting/powerlifting, lawn bowling, and snooker.

The momentum of Seoul continued into the 1992 Paralympic Games held September 3-14 in Barcelona. Over 3,000 athletes representing 90 countries marched into the Olympic Stadium before a crowd of 60,000 spectators (Sherrill, 1993). They competed in archery, athletics, boccie, cycling, fencing, goalball, judo, seven-a-side soccer, shooting, swimming, table tennis, volleyball, weight lifting/powerlifting, wheelchair basketball, and wheelchair tennis. The Barcelona Paralympics have been heralded for their unparalleled success: 1,386,000 spectators attended 46 events, including spectacular opening and closing ceremonies. For a full discussion of the 1992 Paralympics, see Sherrill (1993).

The sports programs for the 1996 Paralympics in Atlanta will include 16 sports: archery, athletics, basketball, boccie, cycling, equestrian events, fencing, goalball, judo, powerlifting, shooting, soccer, table tennis, tennis, and volleyball. In addition, wheelchair racquetball, wheelchair rugby, and sailing will be demonstrated. It is anticipated that 4,000 athletes (amputees, blind, cerebral palsy, dwarf, and spinal cord injured/wheelchair users) from 102 nations will compete in the Paralympics August 16-27, 1996 (two weeks after the close of the Olympics). The 10 days of competition will allow for some 500 different events held in 12-14 different venues (also used for competitions during 1996 Olympic Games). For the first time, a Paralympic Congress and Expo will be held in conjunction with the games.

The Winter Paralympics are held every four years similar to the Summer Paralympics. In 1988, they were held in February in Innsbruck, Austria, and utilized the same facilities and venues as the 1968 Olympics. In the Winter Paralympics, competition includes a variety of Alpine and Nordic events, skating, ice picking, and more. Physically impaired (amputee, cerebral palsy, les autres) athletes and visually impaired/blind athletes compete. As is the case with the Summer Paralympics, these games are to be held in the Olympic host city near the time of the Olympics. The 1992 Winter Paralympics were held in Albertville/Tigne, France. Lillehammer, Norway hosted both the 1994 Winter Olympics and 1994 Paralympics (see Table 5.1).

World Games for the Deaf

World Games for the Deaf (WGD) have been held regularly since the first in 1924 in Paris. The first Winter World Games for the Deaf were held in

GUNTHER BELITZ

At a glance:

Track and field athlete

World champion

Olympic medalist

Gunther Belitz, from Germany, has been competing for 12 years at the elite level. His high jumping and long jumping ability has earned him gold and bronze medals at three Paralympics and two world championships. In 1992 Gunther set a world record in the long jump as an above-the-knee amputee with a leap of 4.82m and he also placed 3rd in the 100m race.

To Gunther, sport is "a good way to communicate with other people and to get to know your body. Competitive sport is, to my mind, the challenge to move the body toward its limits." Gunther further notes that competitive sport has a social function in reducing the stigmatizing image of disability in society. When thinking about younger people who might enter the realm of sport, Gunther notes that "sport can help you to accept a disability within a functional context, . . . to overcome prejudices toward disability, and to form a self-confident identity." Gunther Belitz knows what he is talking about and has the sports records to prove it.

Seefeld, Austria, in 1949. Since then, the WGD have been held every four years, the year following the Olympic year and whenever possible in the same host country or city. For example, the 1985 WGD were held in Los Angeles and utilized many of the same venues as the Olympics the year before. Deaf athletes have also been able to compete in Pan American Games for the Deaf.

Events on the Summer WGD program include men's and women's basketball, cycling, soccer, swimming, tennis, water polo, badminton, shooting, table tennis, team handball, men's and women's athletics, men's and women's volleyball, and wrestling. For the Winter WGD, athletes compete in Alpine events (men's and women's downhill skiing, giant slalom, slalom, and parallel slalom), Nordic skiing events (men's 15K,

TANNI GREY

At a glance:

Track competitor

Road racer

British and international medal
  winner

Competing for the past 11 years, Tanni Grey is serious about her racing. Tanni was born with spina bifida, but has not let the condition stop her from competing in a wide range of wheelchair racing events. From the 100m and 400m sprint to 1,500m, 5,000m, and the marathon, Tanni has made her mark. She won four gold medals at the 1992 Barcelona Paralympics in competition from 100 to 800m and holds the world record. Additionally, Tanni holds British records in the 1,500m, 5,000m, and half and full marathon.

Sport plays a significant role in Tanni's life. She says she "can't imagine wanting to be involved in anything else." For those youngsters thinking about sport, Tanni offers the following: "It's a great way to learn discipline and achieve personal aims. I would advise anyone to participate in sport at whatever level possible."

Tanni recognizes the gains in sport for individuals with disabilities, and she is looking to the future. She would like to see better organizational structure, positive changes in attitudes, and recognition of performances at the elite level.

30K, and 3 × 10K relay, women's 5K, 10K, 3 × 5K relay), speed skating (500m, 1,000m, 1,500m, 3,000m), and ice hockey.

Perhaps somewhat unique to the WGD is the concerted effort to provide an international forum for exchange of culturally relevant information (Stewart, 1990, p. 32). The WGD offer participants the experience to be identified with the unique cultural identity of the Deaf. They are much more than athletic competition; they represent a celebration of community.

Special Olympics International

Special Olympics International (SOI) sponsors both summer and winter games for individuals with mental retardation. The first Special Olympics were held at Soldier Field in Chicago; 1,000 athletes from 26 states and Canada participated. SOI competitions are held every two years, alternating winter and summer games. The most recent summer games were held at the University of Notre Dame in South Bend, Indiana, and in Minneapolis. For these games, over 5,000 athletes from 70 countries participated. Official sports include aquatics, athletics, basketball, bowling, equestrian events, soccer, gymnastics, roller skating, softball, and volleyball; demonstration events include cycling, powerlifting, table tennis, team handball, and tennis. In addition to competitions held regularly in the United States, European Summer Special Olympics have been held in Belgium (1981) and Dublin (1985). Unlike the WGD and the Paralympics, media coverage is extensive for SOI events.

In March 1993, the Fifth SOI World Winter Games were held in Schladming, Austria. These were the first International Special Olympics ever held outside of the United States. Approximately 1,600 athletes from 63 countries competed in Alpine and cross-country skiing, figure skating, speed skating, and floor hockey (Cowan, 1993).

Paralympics for the Mentally Handicapped

In addition to those held under the auspices of Special Olympics International, rival competitions for mentally handicapped individuals have been held since 1985. These games have been sponsored by the International Sports Federation for Persons With Mental Handicaps (INAS–FMH). In September 1992 in Madrid, the first Paralympics for Persons with Mental Handicaps were held in a close proximity and timing to the Paralympics.

These Paralympic Games included 1,400 competitors from 74 countries (DePauw & Rich, 1993). To attend, the athletes had to be mentally retarded (mentally handicapped), at least 15 years of age, and able to meet qualifying athletics standards. The competitive events included five sports: athletics, swimming, table tennis, indoor soccer, and basketball. The competitions were open to both men and women. For more information, see DePauw and Rich (1993).

Inasmuch as the IPC serves as the international governing body for disability sport, the establishment of Paralympic Games for all athletes regardless of the type of disability remains under consideration. It is not likely that Deaf athletes will compete in the Paralympics in the foreseeable future, but it is possible that athletes with mental handicaps will be included.

Although these major international events have sport competition in common, the emphases are quite different. Special Olympics appears to focus less on athletic competitions and more on participating; athletes who compete at international games are not selected based upon standards of athletic performance. In contrast, the World Championships for the

Mentally Handicapped (and as of 1992, Paralympics for Persons with Mental Handicaps) focus upon athletic performance and competition. The WGD encourages elite athletic performance; standards are used to select the U.S. team members, but a sense of community and unique cultural identity permeates the atmosphere. The Paralympics is probably most like the Olympics: elite athletic performance is important and the primary reason for attending. Across all international competitions, these athletes share a sense of pride and accomplishment.

Future International Competitions

Through alignment with the international Olympic movement through the IOC and national Olympic committees (NOCs), athletes with disabilities are receiving recognition and acceptance into the Olympic family. Athletes with disabilities have participated in exhibition events at the Winter Olympics in Sarajevo (1984) and Calgary (1988) and at the Summer Olympics in Los Angeles (1984) and Seoul (1988). Unless the IOC places a restriction upon the number of events included on the Olympic program, such events could be included in future Olympic Games. Although not yet considered as equals in elite athleticism, some athletes with disabilities were allowed to wear the official uniform of their country in Olympic competition and to march with their country in the opening and closing ceremonies. Efforts are under way to secure the right of selected athletes with disabilities to compete in full medal events in the Olympics (see discussion in chapter 12).

NATIONAL DISABILITY SPORT OPPORTUNITIES

Throughout the world, sport opportunities and competitions exist for individuals with disabilities. Although many of these occur within the general context of sport in a given society (e.g., sport clubs, sport-specific events), there are competitions specifically designed for individuals with disabilities. In the United States and Canada, sporting events are held regularly in a number of sports. A listing of the sports offered by selected U.S. disability sport organizations is shown in Table 5.2.

Sport events and competitions for individuals with disabilities are found at the local, state, and regional levels. These take many forms such as local parks and recreation programs (e.g., wheelchair basketball league, Deaf softball, local Special Olympics bowling program) and even interscholastic, intramural, and intercollegiate sport programs for individuals with disabilities. Increasingly so, locally organized fun runs include a

CONNIE HANSEN

At a glance:

Holds six world records and one European record in racing

Has competed for 12 years

Serves on Danish and international sports governing boards

When viewing Connie Hansen's sports vita, one immediately is drawn to the *WR* (world record) appearing six times since 1992 in distance races around the world. In September 1992 at the Barcelona Paralympics, Connie established two world records in the 400m and 10,000m runs. Also in 1992 Connie established world records in the 1,500m, 800m, 15K, and a marathon. Placing second in the 1993 Boston Marathon, Connie established a European record. What kind of a person races from 100m to marathons and performs at this consistently high level?

Connie was born in May 1964 in Denmark. As a child she was active with her family in sports and outdoor activities. At 3 she started gymnastics. A fall from a tree at 13 left Connie a paraplegic. Two weeks in intensive care followed by 9 months of rehabilitation gave Connie time to think. She writes, "I didn't feel lost or left by friends or family. Actually, they were very good in their support by letters, visits, and straight talk."

Connie was focused. As a result, her rehabilitation went well. When she got home she was "basically independent." She was successful because she "had done lots of sports and physical activities and was used to challenging myself." Three months after leaving the hospital, Connie started swimming.

Because Connie did not have a car, she wheeled 4-8K daily. Often she took long tours in the forest. She did not want to give up her active lifestyle and, in fact, used it to her advantage. She did not "feel disabled." Going away to college in 1982 increased her access to sporting opportunities, including wheelchair racing.

Connie Hansen finds sport appealing because she is able to "bring myself where I want to go, in the place I want to be." Connie finds that sport lets her feel her body work and get tired and to "better listen to myself and to be able to hear others."

That sound you hear is Connie practicing because there is another challenge to conquer and because of her love of physical activity.

Table 5.2 Competitive Sports and Recreational Activities Offered by Disability Sport Organizations

Sport	AAAD	DAAA	DS/USA	NWAA	SOI	USABA	USCPAA
Alpine skiing	X	X	X		X	X	
Archery			X				X
Basketball	X	X	X	X	X		
Boccie		X					X
Bowling	X				X		X
Canoeing			X		X		X
Cross country	X				X		X
Cycling	X		X			X	X
Diving	X						
Equestrian events		X			X		X
Figure skating					X		
Floor hockey					X		
Goalball						X	
Gymnastics					X	X	
Handball	X						
Ice hockey	X						
Judo						X	

Sport	1	2	3	4	5	6
Nordic skating	X			X	X	
Poly hockey				X		
Powerlifting	X	X	X	X	X	X
Racquetball			X			
Road racing	X	X	X	X		
Roller skating				X		
Shooting	X	X	X	X		X
Slalom		X		X		X
Soccer	X			X		X
Softball	X			X		
Speed skating	X			X	X	
Swimming	X	X	X	X	X	X
Table tennis	X	X	X	X		X
Team handball	X			X		X
Tennis	X		X	X		
Track and field	X	X	X	X	X	X
Volleyball	X		X	X		
Weight lifting		X	X			
Wrestling	X			X		

wheelchair division, track meets include heats for Special Olympians, and wheelchair basketball tournaments are scheduled on a regular basis. State games (e.g., Sunshine State Games, Empire State Games) now often include events for athletes with disabilities.

In this section, the reader is provided with a brief overview of selected examples of the numerous sport opportunities and competitions available in the United States and Canada. An attempt was made to provide examples across various disability groups and the wide variety of sports available. These are offered as examples only and are not intended to be an exhaustive or even extensive review. Many of the examples presented are similar to offerings by a number of disability sport organizations.

New York State Games for the Physically Challenged

The New York State Games for the Physically Challenged were the first in the nation to offer fitness and training workshops for individuals with disabilities as well as open competition in a variety of sports. These games are primarily designed for disabled youngsters from 8 to 21 years of age with cerebral palsy, amputations, hearing or visual impairments, or spinal cord injuries. Since 1987, the New York State Games have been held annually. The events are open, requiring no qualifying competitions, and include events such as track and field, swimming, wheelchair slalom, equestrian sports, and table tennis. The athletes compete with others of similar disability, and awards are given for the top three scores. The emphasis of these games, however, is placed upon sport participation and the educational and training workshops.

Winter Park Disabled Skiing Program

Located in Winter Park, Colorado, the Winter Park Disabled Skiing Program offers the largest and best-known skiing program for disabled individuals in the world. Although originally intended for fun and games, the program grew into a serious educational and sports training enterprise. The program is designed to teach skiing to visually and hearing-impaired persons as well as those with physical impairments including postpolio, amputations, spinal cord injuries, cerebral palsy, muscular dystrophy, and spina bifida. Local programs run essentially once a week for 8 weeks but are structured on a weekly basis for out-of-state programs.

The program includes not only actual ski lessons but sessions for training volunteer ski instructors and professional certified ski instructors. Specific lessons are designed to teach two-, three-, and four-track skiing as well as mono and sit-skiing, and specific techniques for teaching skiing

MITCHELL SEIDENFELD

At a glance:

Table tennis—able-bodied and disability sport

Pseudoachondrophasia dwarfism

Paralympic medalist

World champion

Mitch Seidenfeld has competed in both able-bodied and disability sport. Between 1979 and 1989, Mitch was the Minnesota State Doubles Champion in able-bodied table tennis. His entrance into disability sport occurred after his successful competition in the able-bodied arena. In his 6 years of competition, Mitch has won gold medals at national and international Paralympic competitions for individuals with disabilities. Mitch's current training regime consists of physical and mental workouts, which attests to his commitment to remain competitive.

The importance of sport in Mitch's life was established early. His father, also a dwarf, encouraged Mitch to be active. Mitch says, "Sport is a big part of my health and fitness maintenance. It has also strengthened my self-esteem, confidence, and friendships. It has meant extensive travel and exposure to many different people and cultures. In many ways, sport is a way of life for me."

Mitch's late involvement in disability sport is not unique, but involvement after a highly successful career in able-bodied sport is. Mitch states, "I did not become involved in disabled sports until after I was almost finished competing in able-bodied sports. I was not aware of the tremendous opportunities. I was not open to them, and I did not accept myself and my disability as completely as I thought I did. Competing in disabled sports does not have to be how you define yourself, but the opportunities and challenges are worthy of anyone's time and effort." These are the words of a true champion.

to Deaf, blind, physically impaired, and developmentally delayed persons. Lessons are provided on adaptive equipment and safety as well. Much of the instruction is conducted in conjunction with the Winter Park Ski School. In addition, races and competitions are regularly scheduled throughout the ski season. For more information, see O'Leary (1987).

Variety Village Sport Training and Fitness Center

The Variety Village Sport Training and Fitness Center, located in Scarborough, a suburb of Toronto, is hailed as North America's model of accessibility. Variety Village is a multipurpose sport training facility with no physical or psychological barriers in an integrated setting of able-bodied and disabled sport enthusiasts. Once a Variety Club community service activity in the form of a residential training school for physically disabled boys, it has become a hub of integrated sport activity. Throughout its history, Variety Village has maintained its priority on serving persons with disabilities, but it has done so with the specific purpose of integration as well.

Every attempt has been made for complete accessibility. For example, flooring throughout the facility is tiled with raised squares in the main hallways, carpeting in the offices, and ceramic raised-square surfaces in the baths and showers for easy discrimination for visually impaired persons. The alarm system includes both a visual alarm and auditory alarm system to accommodate persons with visual and hearing impairments. Baseboards are actually bumper guards for the wheelchairs.

All sport areas were specifically designed to include individuals with all types of impairments. Among the adaptations of the track lanes are a synthetic surface with more give for those with amputations, corners without a bank ideal for wheelchair users, inside lanes near special railings for blind runners, and typical lanes for able-bodied runners. The lighting was designed to eliminate all shadows on the playing surfaces, and appropriate adapted equipment is available. In addition to offering a year-round training center, Variety Village sponsors competitive events, which are designed for competition by able-bodied and disabled persons alike.

Tampa General Rehabilitation Center

Among the ongoing activities of the Tampa General Rehabilitation Center is the annual Wellness Classic, advertised as a fun-filled event for the entire family. The Wellness Classic tends to include cycling events (12.5, 25, or 50 miles), 5K wheelchair invitational, invigorating wellness walk, 5K road race, rollerblading, and a children's fitness circuit. The Tampa

General Rehabilitation Center also regularly sponsors sports clinics, DS/USA fitness workshops, ski tours, wheelchair tennis tournaments, health workshops, a triathlon for the disabled, and the annual Catch the Leisure Wave. The Leisure Wave events include exhibitions of adapted golf, adaptive racquetball, walleyball, scuba diving, and quad rugby. The program at Tampa General Rehabilitation Center is but one example of many around the country.

Training and Sport Camps

Numerous training and sport camps have been developed for children and adults with disabilities. Among these are

NWBA/PVA Wheelchair Basketball Camp

Randy Snow Wheelchair Tennis Camp

Wheelchair Racing Camp

Junior wheelchair sport camps

Paralyzed Veterans of America (PVA) National Trapshoot Clinic

U.S. Aquatic Association of the Deaf Water Polo Camp

Canoe White Water Wilderness Experience

Kayak the Everglades

Float the Rio Grande

Movement Unlimited Sports Camp at California State University at Chico

Specific coaches' training programs have also been developed. These clinics are offered by all the disability sport organizations, often in conjunction with the USOC and the NGBs. Coaching materials, as well as videos and other media products, are available through the disability sport organizations (see Appendixes F and G).

Additional Competitive Events

Competitive events for individuals with disabilities are held in the United States on a weekly basis. These vary by season, geographic location, sponsoring agency, sport, and disability. Examples of these can include

DS/USA Ski Spectacular

Ski for Light International Week (annual)

USCPAA Bowling Tournament (Tucson)

U.S. Deaf Flag Football Super Bowl (Buffalo)

SSAD Basketball Tournament (Virginia)

AAAD National Men's and Women's Slow Pitch Softball Tournament (Canoga Park, CA)

Blister Bowl Wheelchair Football Tournament (Santa Barbara)

(continued)

SportsFest (Atlanta)

AFL-CIO International Invitational Junior Wheelchair Basketball Tournament

Honolulu Wheelchair Marathon

Annual Open Powerlifting Meet (Oregon)

Can-Am World Games

Chicagoland Regional Beep Baseball Tournament

Pre-Paralympic Powerlifting Competitions

Midwest Deaf Annual Golf Tournament (Minnetonka, MN)

National Disabled Waterskiing Championships

USABA Judo Paralympic Trials (Colorado Springs)

Mitsubishi Open Wheelchair Tennis

National PVA Trapshoot

Midnite Sun Wheelchair Marathon

Florida State Cerebral Palsy Games

Deaf Women's Bowling Tournament (Palm Beach)

Intercollegiate/Interscholastic Athletic Programs

Recent legislation (Section 504 of Rehabilitation Act, PL 94-142, ADA) in the United States has increased access to education by individuals with disabilities. Even before the passage of these laws, individuals with disabilities have participated in intercollegiate and interscholastic athletic programs on a very selective basis. A few individuals with disabilities were able to overcome the obstacles to sport competition and participate alongside able-bodied athletes (Appenzeller, 1983; D'Alonzo, 1976).

Although increasing numbers of persons with disabilities are attending colleges and universities, their access to intramurals and other extracurricular activities including intercollegiate athletics has been minimal (Hedrick & Hedrick, 1993). In 1993, only 6 of the 803 NCAA member institutions offered complementary sport opportunities for individuals with disabilities.

The earliest of these was the University of Illinois at Urbana-Champaign. In 1948, Tim Nugent created a disability sports program out of which grew the National Wheelchair Basketball Association. This program provides athletic competitions in men's and women's basketball, wheelchair track and field, and quad rugby.

Wright State University in Dayton, Ohio, offers a variety of sports including wheelchair basketball, wheelchair tennis, wheelchair softball, quad rugby, tandem cycling, and downhill skiing. Wright State also provides aquatics, fitness, and intramural programs for students with disabilities. For a listing of colleges and universities offering sport scholarships, see Appendix H.

Sport opportunities for individuals with disabilities in public schools are very limited. For example, in 1986 Dade County public schools offered a Disabled Sports Program that allowed students with disabilities to compete in athletics, swimming, and weight lifting "sport days" and gave them access to selected competitions outside the public school system (i.e., Special Olympics).

Minnesota is the only state to formally establish an interscholastic athletic program for individuals with disabilities (Hedrick & Hedrick, 1993). This competitive program is housed within the Minnesota High School League (Hanson, 1993).

CONCLUDING COMMENTS

Numerous sport opportunities exist for individuals with disabilities. International and national events occur on a regular basis. Among these are Paralympics, Special Olympics International, World Games for the Deaf, World Championships for the Mentally Handicapped, and numerous world championships in specific sports (e.g., wheelchair basketball). Additionally, athletes with disabilities regularly participate in events such as the Boston Marathon, Bay to Breakers Race, Bloomsday, and wheelchair marathons held around the world.

Since the 1970s, sport opportunities and competitions for individuals with disabilities have greatly increased. Although numerous opportunities exist, they are often not widely promoted. Concerted efforts must be made to share information about the existence of disability sport organizations and the opportunities for sport participation and competitions with disabled youth through our school systems as well as our recreation departments. College and university personnel can also play a major role in sharing information about sport for and including individuals with disabilities in coursework provided to physical educators, athletic trainers, physical therapists, therapeutic recreation specialists, sport management majors, and others.

CHAPTER 6

Sport and Disability: A World View

Sport for and including individuals with disabilities is found throughout the world. Its organization varies in relation to the societal context of a given country; disability sport varies not only in relation to the societal structure of sport but also to the societal context of disability.

In this chapter, a variety of structures of sport and athletes with disabilities from regions around the world are presented. The discussion is limited to selected countries, reflecting the availability of literature and an intent to present diversity. The structure of international disability sport and the United States perspective are discussed in chapter 4.

TERMINOLOGY

One of the greatest challenges to understanding and communicating about disability sport worldwide is the terminology and the different meanings attached to the same terms. A discussion of this phenomenon has been adapted from Doll-Tepper & DePauw (1989). Within the context of the United States, the terms *physical education, sport,* and *recreation/leisure* are used to describe separate, although related, entities; the term *sport* is used in Europe to represent that which is encompassed by all of the above. Specifically, *physical education* translates into German as *Sportunterrich an Schulen* (sport instruction in the schools), *leisure* or *recreation* as *Freizeit Sport* (free time sport), and *competitive sport* as *Wettkampf*. Additionally, the term *Sport for All* is commonly used to describe sport and physical activity for all persons regardless of ability or disability. Sport and physical activity programs for individuals with disabilities are conducted under such titles as *sport and physical activity for disabled individuals* (Finland), *disabled sport* (Denmark), *education physique adaptee* (Belgium), *Sport* (the Netherlands, Norway, Austria), and *Sportunterricht* (sport instruction)/ *Bewegungserziehung* (movement education) (Germany). Those professionals involved with disability sport are known as physical educators, sport teachers, trainers, coaches, and even therapists.

Although the World Health Organization's definitions of impairment, disability, and handicap are accepted throughout the world, the actual use of these terms and others to describe individuals with disabilities can differ by country. For example, learning disabled persons in Germany are those who have learning difficulties and an IQ between 70 and 90; only those with an IQ below 70 are classified as mentally retarded. In the United States anyone with an IQ below 90 would be classified as mentally retarded. *Special populations* in the United States usually implies disabled persons, but in Finland, *special groups* include "the disabled, the aged, and persons suffering from long-term illnesses" (Koivumaki, 1987, p. 57).

In this book, every attempt has been made to use words that are consistent in meaning and to describe any differences as they occur. Throughout, the frame of reference is sport, not physical education or leisure. In most instances, sport refers primarily to the formal organization of competitive sport and includes developmental sport opportunities. Any deviations are noted.

SELECTED LEGISLATIVE MANDATES

Each country is unique in its approach to accessibility, opportunity, education, physical activity, and sport for individuals with disabilities. Laws, regulations, and rules vary accordingly and are not universal. On the other hand, two organizations (United Nations and UNESCO) have proclaimed the universal rights of individuals with disabilities.

On December 9, 1975, the General Assembly of the United Nations adopted the following passage, Resolution 3447, as part of the Declaration on the Rights of Disabled Persons:

> Disabled persons, whatever the origin, nature and seriousness of their handicaps and disabilities, have the same fundamental rights as their fellow citizens of the same age, which implies first and foremost the right to enjoy a decent life, as normal and full as possible.

As a direct result of this and other United Nations declarations, education of individuals with disabilities was ensured as an integral part of cultural development, equal access to leisure activities became inseparable from social integration, and the general quality of life of disabled individuals was vastly improved (Sherrill, 1986).

In April 1976, the first International Conference of Ministers and Senior Officials Responsible for Physical Education and Sport was held under the auspices of UNESCO. At this conference, the right of persons with disabilities to participate in physical education and sport was established (Stein, 1986).

The United Nations not only enacted a "bill of rights" for persons with disabilities but declared 1981 the International Year for Disabled Persons. Many nations followed this lead and declared a National Year for Disabled Persons in 1982.

EUROPEAN PERSPECTIVES

Throughout Western Europe, sport programs for persons with disabilities are found in the schools and throughout a sport club system. Because clubs are locally organized and developed in response to community interests and initiatives, there are sport clubs whose members include individuals with disabilities as well as able-bodied persons. There are also clubs for persons with a variety of disabilities and clubs for able-bodied persons or persons with one specific disability (e.g., Deaf). These sport clubs are associated with a rehabilitation center (e.g., Belgium, Austria), school, or community/town/city (DePauw & Doll-Tepper, 1989).

In anticipation of the "unification" of Europe in 1992, the Conference of European Ministers Responsible for Sport passed a series of resolutions, entitled the *European Charter for Sport for All: Disabled Persons*. Although passed in 1987, the history of the *European Charter* can be traced back to 1980, when the Committee for the Development of Disabled Sport (CDDS)

MANUEL ROBLES AGUILA

At a glance:

Partial paraplegia

Wheelchair table tennis player for 14 years

Manuel Robles Aguila of Granada, Spain, has won the Spanish table tennis championships 12 times and has been second twice. He has placed second or third in the French table tennis championships and in the European championships. It is obvious that Manuel has been a consistent world-class athlete.

His participation in disabled sport "means everything to me. My life would not make much sense without it, I work with it and even met my wife through it." Further Manuel says that youngsters with disabilities should "not doubt it at all. Go for it. It is the best way for integration. Depending on the sport, one can even compete against nondisabled people." Manuel Robles Aguila is an athlete with focus and a love of sport.

commissioned a study as a contribution to the 1981 International Year for the Disabled. During that same year, the European Ministers Responsible for Sport adopted a resolution outlining the main priorities for European and national policies for sport for disabled individuals. Six years later, the *European Charter* was finalized. It is divided into two parts: one devoted to discussion of disability sport and the other to the accessibility of sport and recreation facilities. The major points of the *European Charter* are summarized below (for more discussion see DePauw & Doll-Tepper, 1989):

1. Disabled persons are defined as those who are not able to participate in most sports or physical recreation without some adjustment in the form of special equipment or training. These individuals include those who are mentally retarded, physically or multiply disabled, chronically ill (diabetic, asthmatic, cardiac), blind, Deaf, or mute.

2. Sport for All is comprehensive and includes four main types of sport: top level (elite) sport, organized sport (club sport), recreational sport, and health sport for medical reasons or for fitness

purposes. In addition, sport is purported to be beneficial as therapy and/or rehabilitation for disabled persons.

3. Sport for All for disabled persons must be promoted because (a) disabled persons have the same right to sport as able-bodied individuals, (b) sport adds to the quality of life of participants, (c) disabled persons can achieve to the highest level of competition, and (d) disabled persons receive both the physiological and social benefits of participation.

4. Governments have the responsibility to ensure that every person, disabled or not, has the opportunity to participate in sport and physical recreation at the level one desires. Sport and recreation facilities must be accessible to disabled persons.

5. National sport organizations, public or semipublic agencies, and clubs must consider the needs of disabled persons in decisions concerning sport or policies.

6. In sport, as well as in other areas of society, integration of disabled individuals and able-bodied persons is essential. An adequate and sufficient range of appropriate sport opportunities should be provided for individuals with disabilities. Able-bodied sport federations must assume increasingly more responsibility for the sport needs and interests of disabled individuals including (a) educating trainers and coaches, (b) officiating and refereeing sport events, (c) organizing competitions for disabled individuals, (d) developing youth programs, (e) including events for disabled athletes at competitions for able-bodied athletes, and (f) organizing regular integrated activities and events.

7. Sport for disabled persons requires the coordination and cooperation of physicians, physical therapists, occupational therapists, physical education teachers, elementary school teachers, special education teachers, and sport administrators. A coordinated effort should include the provision of sport programs, accessibility to sport facilities, transportation assistance, and technical aids for sport participation.

8. Physical education for disabled students should be provided in regular schools.

9. Research on sport for individuals with disabilities should include (a) "state of the art review," (b) benefits of participation, (c) classification and integration, (d) coaching and training, and (e) professional preparation.

10. Training and education must be provided for sport personnel including (a) knowledge of impairment or disability, (b) understanding of specific disabilities and the implications for daily activities,

(c) knowledge of physical activity appropriate for specific disabilities, (d) knowledge of technical and scientific research in adapted physical activity, and (e) ability to communicate with individuals with disabilities.

11. Sport for disabled persons should receive media coverage to (a) positively impact the public's attitudes toward disabled individuals, (b) recruit disabled persons into sport, and (c) create an appreciation of disabled athletes similar to able-bodied athletes.

12. Governments should ensure that disabled persons receive a fair share of money available to sport in general.

13. Individuals with permanent illness, chronic impairment, or mental illness must also have access to sport programs organized on their behalf.

Although the *European Charter* stands as the basis of Sport for All including individuals with disabilities throughout Europe, each country is unique in its application of the principles espoused. Sport in selected European countries is discussed in the following narrative.

Denmark

Sport is reported to be the primary cultural activity in which Danish citizens participate; approximately 45% participate in numerous clubs. These sport clubs are self-organized and self-governed, and many include individuals with disabilities. In addition, there are a few separate sport clubs formed only by visually impaired, mentally retarded, or Deaf members.

The Danish Sport Organization for the Disabled (DSOD), formed in 1971, serves as the national governing body for disability sport. Its purpose is to promote and organize recreational as well as competitive sports for all individuals with disabilities and to promote the use of sport for rehabilitation. Inasmuch as the DSOD serves all disability groups, it is recognized as representing the national disability organizations and sport federations alike. Many of its activities are conducted conjointly with the Danish sport federations.

The organizational structure of the DSOD is depicted in Figure 6.1. Four organizational levels exist: club, country, region, and national. Clubs have the primary responsibility for daily sport activities in a given community. At the county level, the primary tasks include disseminating information, recruiting new members and coaches (trainers), and assisting in forming new clubs. The primary regional responsibility is sponsoring regional sport tournaments including the qualifying events for national tournaments. The responsibilities of the national level include sponsoring

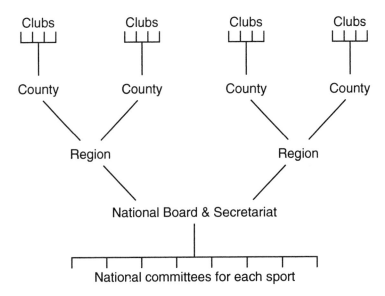

Figure 6.1 Structure of the Danish Sports Organization for the Disabled.

national sport events, establishing sport rules and regulations, educating and training coaches and officials, public relations, and fielding a disabled team to represent Denmark at international competitions.

The organizational structure of DSOD is similar only to that found in Sweden, Norway, and Iceland. Other European countries, and most of the rest of the world, have more than one national disability sport organization. Although Special Olympics International reports an SOI chapter in Denmark and Deaf sport is very active there (the executive secretary of CISS works in Copenhagen), DSOD remains the only officially recognized national sport group serving individuals with disabilities.

Scandinavia (Norway, Sweden, Finland)

Norway and Sweden have structures of disability sport similar to that of Denmark. Only one national disability sport organization exists in each country: Norwegian Sport Organization for the Disabled (NSOD) and Swedish Federation for Sports for the Disabled (SHIF). In addition, the Nordsk Handicapped Sport Organization fosters communication and co-operation among Iceland, Denmark, Sweden, Finland, Faroe Islands, and Norway.

Deaf athletic associations are active in both Norway and Sweden. Autonomous associations exist for Deaf sports, but these are affiliated officially with NSOD and SHIF. Special Olympics International reports an SOI chapter in Norway but not in Sweden (the offices of INAS–FMH are located in Sweden).

Disability sport in Finland is structured slightly differently and includes a broader segment of the population. In Finland, "special groups" include individuals with disabilities, the aged, and persons suffering from long-term illnesses. Although Finnish sport clubs are prevalent, only just recently have a few begun to provide opportunities for individuals with disabilities. For the most part, the sport and physical activity needs of these individuals have been met by municipal sport offices and specific organizations serving segments of the population referred to as "special groups."

Four national sport organizations serve the disabled population in Finland: the Finnish Association of Sports for the Disabled (FASD), the Sports Committee of the Finnish Central Association of the Visually Handicapped, the Finnish Athletic Association of the Deaf, and the Disabled War Veterans Sports Association. In addition, a welfare organization meets the needs of individuals with mental retardation; this group has joined both Special Olympics International and INAS–FMH.

These organizations are responsible for providing the main sport forms including rehabilitation, physical education in the schools, sport for all, and competitive sports for the disabled. The FASD local sport offices are the most important entity for offering sport opportunities, whereas its national office has the primary responsibility for sponsoring competitive sport experiences, including championships.

Selected Western European Countries

Sport in Germany is organized around the German Federation of Sport (Deutsches Sportbund, DSB); disability sport is a part of this structure (DePauw & Doll-Tepper, 1989). The German Sport Federation for the Disabled (Deutsches Behinderten Sportverband, DBS) is the officially recognized representative of sport for individuals with disabilities throughout Germany.

Germany also utilizes a sport club system. Opportunities are organized by sport clubs at the city or community levels, by state sport associations (Landessportbunde), and by the DSB. This pattern is the same for disability sport. At the national level, the DBS is responsible for all types of sport including rehabilitation, recreation, and competitive sport. Under its auspices, sport is offered for the disabled (physically, sensory, and mentally retarded) and for health-impaired persons as well. The DBS organizes national competitions and selects the team members to represent Germany

ANDREAS SIEGL

At a glance:

High jump and long jump competitor

Paralympic medalist

Asian World Champion

Andreas Siegl of Austria has been involved in the world of competitive sport for 9 years. In that short time this athlete, who is a left-sided arm and leg amputee, has earned silver and bronze medals at the 1988 Paralympics in Seoul, the 1990 Asian Games, and the 1992 Barcelona Paralympics in the high jump, long jump, and 100m race. This talented athlete practices three times a week for 3 hours and spends additional time stretching for flexibility.

Why high jumping? Andreas writes, "Since my childhood I was fascinated by high jumping. My role models were able-bodied high jumpers." To accentuate the significance of sport in her life Andreas states quite simply, "Sport is my life." Andreas also urges "every person with a disability to give it a try and experience physical activity and sport." Andreas particularly encourages younger people to participate in sport so that they can meet new people, experience success, improve physically, and show others, "Here I am!"

in European and world competitions. The German Sport Federation for the Deaf (Deutsches Gehörlosen Sportverband) appears to have status equal to that of the DBS, and the German Wheelchair Sport Association exists under the DBS umbrella.

Since the early 1980s, a nonprofit organization (Lebenshilfe) focusing on the needs and interests of mentally retarded individuals has coordinated Special Olympics activities. The Lebenshilfe exists outside the officially recognized disability sport structure in Germany (Doll-Tepper & DePauw, 1989).

Disability sport in the other European countries is not unlike that found in Germany. Sport clubs form the dominant system; individuals with disabilities can be found within the clubs. Every European country has a national sport organization for individuals with disabilities officially recognized by and affiliated with the government. Slight variations exist. For example, the Austrian Sport Organization for the Disabled serves the competitive sport needs and interests of blind, amputee, cerebral palsy,

Corina Robitjcho

At a glance:

Involved in sport for 13 years

Wheelchair basketball player

Corina Robitjcho of Germany was motivated to become a champion wheelchair basketball player following a traumatic amputation. She trains four or five times a week. She has been a member of the national team five times, most recently in the 1993 Paralympics in Barcelona. Corina writes "Sport is my life. I can't imagine a life without sport." To young children she says "If you find yourself in sport, it will be a great enrichment. Go looking for yourself and see the wonderful things that sport can give you."

and spinal cord injured persons. It also serves individuals with mental retardation, but only for recreational sport. The Federation of Sport for the Disabled in The Netherlands provides sport opportunities for individuals with physical disabilities, mental retardation, visual impairments or blind, and hearing impairments or Deaf.

United Kingdom

The British Sports Association for the Disabled (BSAD) was founded in 1961 as an outgrowth of the efforts of Sir Ludwig Guttmann. It was then, and is now, an association composed of national disability sports organizations. In addition, the BSAD has a network of 10 regional associations including Wales, Scotland, and Northern Ireland and more than 450 sport clubs. The BSAD organizes educational conferences and seminars, coaches training programs, and sport events at the county, regional, and national levels. The BSAD is also responsible for representation by British disabled athletes at international sport competitions.

Other national associations exist in Britain; some are affiliated with the BSAD and some are separate and enjoy official recognition by the Sports

Council. The disability-specific associations affiliated with BSAD include British Amputee Sports Association, British Association for Sporting and Recreational Activities of the Blind, British Deaf Sports Council, British Paraplegic Sports Society, United Kingdom Sports Association for People with Mental Handicap, CP-Sports Within the Spastics Society, and British Les Autres Sports Association. Other associations include Riding for the Disabled Association, BSAD Water Sports Division, PHAB (Physically Handicapped and Able-Bodied) youth sport clubs, and Special Olympics UK. Addresses of these organizations and others are found in Appendixes D and F.

CANADA

The organization of sport in Canada revolves around the Minister of State for Fitness and Amateur Sport. This office oversees national sport organizations, including disability sport. Specifically, the Canadian Federation of Sport Organizations for the Disabled (CFSOD) serves as the national governing body. Informally organized in 1979, CFSOD was formally incorporated in 1981. Its purpose is to facilitate, coordinate, and promote sport for athletes with disabilities through cooperative action among its member organizations.

CFSOD members include the Canadian Wheelchair Sports Association, the Canadian Association for Disabled Skiing, the Canadian Blind Sports Association, the Canadian Amputee Sports Association, the Canadian Deaf Sports Association, and the Canadian Cerebral Palsy Sports Association. The Sports Funds for the Physically Disabled is a nonprofit, federally incorporated organization whose sole purpose is to raise money to support sports competitions among disabled Canadian athletes. In 1988, it was successful in supporting the Canadian team at the 1988 Winter and Summer Games for the Disabled.

In 1986, Canada undertook a collaborative effort to address the physical activity needs of its disabled citizens. This effort, known as the Jasper Talks Symposium, was sponsored by the Adapted Programs Special Interest Group of Canadian Association for Health, Physical Education and Recreation (CAHPER), Fitness Canada, and the University of Alberta. Inasmuch as Section 15 of the Canadian Charter of Rights and Freedoms (1982) forbids discrimination on the basis of disability and calls for suitable opportunities for all to be physically active (Wall, 1990), the Jasper Talks resulted in a strategic plan for adapted physical activity in Canada.

AUSTRALIA AND NEW ZEALAND

In 1962, a lone participant from New Zealand entered the first British Commonwealth Paraplegic Games held in Perth, Western Australia. Since then, a team of New Zealanders has been sent to the major international sport events for athletes with disabilities.

In cooperation with local "associations," sport competitions for disabled athletes were initiated in New Zealand: specifically, the First Inter Provincial Games in Christchurch (1966) and the First National Games for the Disabled in Auckland (1968). The New Zealand Paraplegic Physically Disabled Federation was formed in 1968 to enable athletes to officially enter the Paralympics in Tel Aviv.

The National Games continue today, but the Commonwealth Games were replaced eventually by the 1975 Far East and South Pacific International Games (FESPIC) in Japan. New Zealand has continued to send athletes to regional games, world championships, and the summer and winter Paralympics. In addition, New Zealand attempted to send Neroli Fairhall to the Olympics in Moscow and was successful in sending her to compete in archery from a wheelchair at the Los Angeles Olympics in 1984.

The New Zealand Paraplegic and Physically Disabled Federation is the national governing body and works closely with 17 local associations and with individual members. In addition, it represents New Zealand with ISOD, IBSA, CP–ISRA, and ISMWSF. The Federation is closely affiliated with other disability sport organizations in New Zealand, including the Royal N.Z. Foundation for the Blind, N.Z. Skiing for the Disabled, N.Z. Road Wheelers Association, N.Z. Wheelchair Basketball Association, and N.Z. Amputee Sports Association.

The first sport opportunities for individuals with disabilities in Australia were available to Deaf individuals in 1954, under the auspices of the Australian Deaf Sports Federation.

Wheelchair sports in Australia began in 1972. Shortly thereafter, a group of disabled sport representatives convened to develop one organization that would speak on behalf of all handicapped sport groups to the Australian government (Grant & Pryke, 1987). By 1979, a constitution was adopted for the national body, the Australian Sports Council for the Handicapped. Its name was changed in 1984 to Australian Confederation of Sports for the Disabled.

The Australian Confederation provides a means whereby associations serving disabled sport can discuss matters of importance to disabled athletes. Members include the Australian Paraplegic and Quadriplegic Sports Federation, Australian Deaf Sports Federation, Ltd., Australian Cerebral Palsy Association, Riding for the Disabled Association of Australia, Amputees Sporting Association of Australia, Australian Blind Sports Federation, and Australian Disabled Skiers Federation.

Under the auspices of the Australian Paraplegic and Quadriplegic Sports Federation (APQSF), the national governing body of wheelchair sports, there are seven state sport organizations (e.g., New South Wales Wheelchair Sports Association, Western Australia Disabled Sports Association). Collectively and individually, these associations provide sport opportunities for wheelchair users throughout Australia. Deaf sport, cerebral palsy sport, and amputee sport are also organized by a national governing body with state associations.

Sport for intellectually handicapped, or mentally retarded, persons in Australia follows a different model: sport is considered at all levels and depends upon access, awareness, attitudes, acceptance, ability and advocacy (Little, 1987). These led to the establishment of both integrated and segregated sport programs for intellectually handicapped persons at the local and state levels. The Sport and Recreation Association of Intellectually Disabled Persons (SRAIDP) acts as an advocate for the participation of intellectually disabled persons in sport. Much of its efforts are coordinated with the sport associations. The programs are established to integrate intellectually disabled persons into the regular club sport programs and competitions as well. The programs are unique to the club, the sport, and the persons involved. Sport for intellectually disabled persons varies across the states of Australia. State associations affiliated with SRAIDP are found in Western Australia, New South Wales, Queensland, and Victoria. Special Olympics programs are found in Tasmania, New South Wales, Australian Capital Territory, and Victoria.

ASIA

Sport opportunities for individuals with disabilities exist in Asian countries. Disability sport is a more recent development in Asia than in Europe or North America. To date, programs are continuing to emerge. The following discussion presents but a sketch of disability sport in Asia. (It remains somewhat difficult to obtain current information from these countries.)

China

Disability sport in China is a very recent phenomenon. Minimal sport opportunities existed for individuals with disabilities prior to the 1980s. The first evidence of international competition by disabled Chinese athletes was recorded at the Third Far East and South Pacific Games (FESPIC) in 1982. The Chinese Sports Association for the Disabled was then founded on October 21, 1983, in Tianjin with the assistance of the Chinese government. The vice director of the Physical Culture and Sports Commission of the People's Republic of China not only attended the inaugural meeting but participated in the activities.

The First China National Games for the Disabled were held in Hefei, Anhui, in 1984. Over 500 athletes representing 29 provinces, municipalities, and regions including Hong Kong participated in 168 separate events.

The Third National Games were held March 18-23, 1992, in Guangzhou. Over 1,200 athletes from all over the country and Hong Kong and the Macao regions competed in six events: athletics, swimming, table tennis, shooting, weight lifting, and wheelchair basketball. Interestingly, these were the first national games after the passage of the Protection Law for the Disabled People.

The Chinese Sports Association for the Disabled has represented disabled athletes internationally in such organizations as CP–ISRA, IBSA, and ISOD. Since the 1980s, Chinese disabled athletes have been regular participants at international competitions and world championships. China sent its first official delegation to the 1984 International Games for the Disabled (Paralympics) held at Hofstra University in New York City.

In 1985, the Chinese Sports Association for the Mentally Retarded was formed and was accepted as a member of Special Olympics International one month later. China sent its first delegation to the 1987 International Special Olympics held at Notre Dame University in South Bend, Indiana.

Hong Kong

Disability sport in Hong Kong is organized around three groups: Deaf, mentally retarded, and physically impaired. Three organizations attempt to provide sport opportunities: Hong Kong Sports Association of the Deaf (1987), Special Hong Kong Olympics, and the Hong Kong Sports Association for the Physically Disabled.

The oldest of these, the Hong Kong Sports Association for the Physically Disabled, was established in 1972. Its purposes are to (a) promote and encourage sports activities among physically disabled persons, (b) organize a variety of sports and training programs, (c) promote public awareness of disability sport, (d) select and organize the Hong Kong teams for all international competitions, and (e) increase athletic performances.

HKSAP sports include archery, athletics, wheelchair basketball, fencing, lawn bowls, judo, rifle shooting, swimming, table tennis, and wheelchair tennis. Training sessions are regularly scheduled. In addition, the HKSAP offers special school programs, community sport programs, national team training, and participation in international competitions including Paralympics, FESPIC, world championships and games, international youth championships and games, and invitational championships and games.

In its capacity as the national governing body, the HKSAP holds affiliate membership with ISMWSF, ISOD, IBSA, and CP–ISRA. HKSAP is also recognized by the Amateur Sports Federation and Olympic Committee of Hong Kong.

Korea

In response to the International Year of Disabled Persons, the annual Korean National Games for the Disabled began in 1981. In 1988, the very successful 8th Paralympics were held in Seoul, South Korea, under the auspices of the Seoul Paralympic Organizing Committee. In 1989, this committee became the Korea Sports Association for the Disabled (KO-SAD). On April 28th, the Ministry of Health and Social Affairs officially approved KOSAD as the national governing body for disabled sport in Korea. KOSAD serves in the fields of sport, culture, and art in the greatest harmony for disabled persons in Korea. Specifically its functions include promoting disability sport throughout Korea, sponsoring cultural and art events performed by disabled persons, organizing national games and other sport events, conducting research on sport and rehabilitation, operating sport facilities for disabled athletes, and providing health and recreational sport programs.

In addition to KOSAD, Deaf athletes are served through the Korea Deaf Sports Federation. The KDSF was officially recognized as a CISS member in 1987. It is organized around a club system and offers programs in athletics, swimming, soccer, table tennis, and shooting.

Japan

Japanese athletes with disabilities have participated in sport longer than any of their Asian neighbors. The Japanese Athletic Association of the Deaf became a CISS member in 1936. Under the auspices of the JAAD, Deaf athletes are provided with competitions and training in Alpine skiing, soccer, tennis, athletics, judo, volleyball, baseball, and table tennis. The JAAD regularly fields a national team to represent Japan in the Summer and Winter World Games for the Deaf.

Japan hosted the first Far East and South Pacific Games for the Disabled (FESPIC) in Oita in 1975 to promote the general interest and welfare of disabled persons through participation in sport events. These first games included 690 athletes with amputations, visual impairments, and other physical disabilities from 18 countries in the Far East and South Pacific region.

Wheelchair sports are quite popular in Japan, especially tennis, basketball, skiing, and marathon racing. There are eight major sport centers for disabled athletes and 50 smaller ones. These centers are government financed and open year-round to all disabled persons and their families and friends.

Japan has also played a significant role in wheelchair roadracing. In 1981, as part of the celebrations for the International Year for Disabled Persons (IYDP), the annual Oita International Wheelchair Marathon began.

AFRICA

Sport for individuals with disabilities in Africa tends to be structured differently in each country. These structures include a sport society for the disabled, an "Olympic type" sports federation for the disabled, and a government ministry office for organizing disability sport. In addition, opportunities can be found in conjunction with rehabilitation institutions. Although included in these instances, medical rehabilitation is often given priority over sport.

In selected African nations, such as Algeria and Senegal, a specialized federation for disability sport is organized at the local, regional, and national levels. Often the federation includes technical and sport-specific committees. In general, it is an umbrella organization serving various types of disabilities.

One example is the South African Sports Association for Physically Disabled. Established in 1962, it was originally called the South African Paraplegic Games Association (Barrish & Ndungane, 1988). It has since expanded to include other physically disabled individuals. The South African Sports Association for Physically Disabled is the only national governing body that serves without regard to race, creed, or color. It is an "autonomous amateur sport organization which conducts its affairs on a nonracial and nonpolitical basis" (Barrish & Ndungane, 1988, p. 13). Currently, the South African Sports Association holds membership in ISMWSF, ISOD, IBSA, CP–ISRA, and the IPC.

CONCLUDING COMMENTS

Selected countries have been highlighted to illustrate the similarities and differences in disability sport around the world. Some countries have very well established programs and organizations; others are still developing. Regardless, sport for and including individuals with disabilities exists throughout the world.

PART II

Sport and Sport Modifications

CHAPTER 7

Classification

Classification in sport has existed since the beginning of organized sport. Essentially, classification was, and continues to be, used to account for differences in muscle mass. Initially, this classification was by sex: the exclusion of women and the development of separate events for men and for women. Classification is also used as delineation by weight for "fairness" in competition: weight classifications in boxing, rowing, judo, and the like. Classification has now been extended as a variation in the ability to move and is applied to individuals with disabilities (Lindstrom, 1986).

MEDICAL CLASSIFICATION

The first type of sport classification for athletes with disabilities was the medical classification system developed in the 1940s in conjunction with the beginning of disability sport in England. The development of this medical classification system was based upon the level of spinal cord lesion. This system was designed to enable individuals with similar severity of impairment to compete "more fairly" against one another.

Medical classification was later extended to athletes using wheelchairs, including those with amputations. The medical classification system is shown in Figure 7.1, along with examples of functional classification systems.

From the 1940s until the early 1990s, the medical classification system was the dominant system worldwide. As a result, additional medical-based classification systems evolved for athletes with disabilities other than spinal cord injuries: classification systems for cerebral palsy athletes, amputees, les autres, and the blind, and classifications for winter sports and wheelchair basketball (see Tables 7.1 through 7.6). These classification systems were developed, or officially adopted, by the national and international sport federations for athletes with disabilities. By the 1980s, the multiple classification systems, based upon type and extent of impairment, were as follows:

- Spinal cord injured wheelchair users (7 classes): NWAA, ISMWSF

- Amputee wheelchair users (3 of the 7 classes above): NWAA, ISMWSF

- Cerebral palsy athletes (8 classes): USCPAA, CP–ISRA

- Blind and visually impaired athletes (3 classes): USABA, IBSA

- Physical impairments for winter sports (7 classes, 3 sit-ski classes): DS/USA, ISOD

- Ambulatory amputee athletes (9 classes): DS/USA, ISOD

- Les Autres athletes (6 classes): USLASA, DS/USA, ISOD

- Wheelchair basketball players (3 classes, required team balance): NWBA

FUNCTIONAL CLASSIFICATION SYSTEM

These disability-specific medical-based classifications allow for relatively little consideration of the nature and demands of the specific sport performance or of cross-disability competition. In addition, the large number of classes often resulted in cancellations of events because of the small number of athletes in selected events. Although the medical classification system was constituted as a "leveling factor between physical capacity and competitivity" (p. 3), its use ultimately diminished the competitive

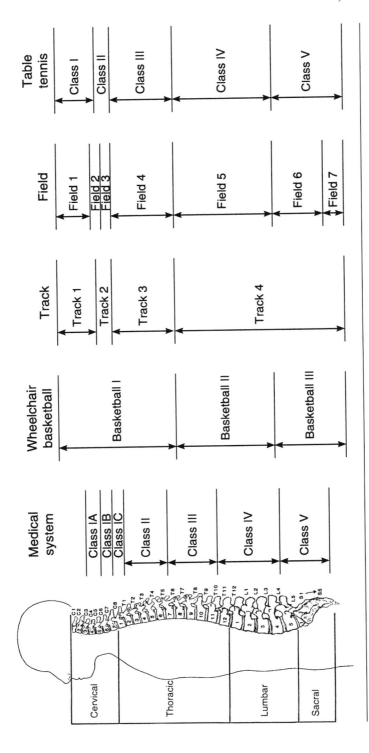

Figure 7.1 Examples of functional classification systems.

Table 7.1   Cerebral Palsy Athletes (USCPAA and CPN-ISRA) Functional
Profiles

Class	Functional profiles
Class 1	Moderate to severe spasticity—severe involvement of all four limbs. Poor trunk control. Poor functional strength in upper extremities.
Class 2	Moderate to severe spasticity—severe to moderate involvement of upper extremities and trunk. Poor functional strength and control of upper extremities. Propels wheelchair with legs.
Class 3	Fair functional strength and moderate control in upper extremities. Almost full functional strength in dominant upper extremity. Propels wheelchair with one or both arms slowly.
Class 4	Moderate to severe involvement of lower limbs. Functional strength and minimal control problems in upper extremities. Uses wheelchair for daily activities and sports.
Class 5	Good functional strength; minimal control problems in upper extremities. Ambulates on two legs for competition.
Class 6	Moderate to severe involvement of all four extremities and trunk; walks without aids. May use assistive devices for track events.
Class 7	Moderate to minimal hemiplegia. Good functional ability is nonaffected side. Walks without aids.
Class 8	Minimally affected hemiplegic or monoplegic. Minimal coordination problems. Good balance and is able to run and jump freely.

Note. 1–4 wheelchair for competition, 5–8 ambulatory for competition.

aspect of Paralympic sport (*General and Functional Classification Guide for the 1992 Paralympics,* 1992).

In the late 1980s and early 1990s, attempts were made to develop an "integrated" classification system that placed greater emphasis on sport performance by disability groupings rather than by specific disability. This represented the logical evolution of disability sport from sport as an element of rehabilitation to elite competitive sport.

"Wheelchair basketball was the first Paralympic sport to experiment with a functional classification system" (Paciorek, 1993, p. 37). Horst Strohkendl (1986) first proposed an integrated classification system for use at the 1984 World Games for the Disabled held in England. This system was refined for use at the 1992 Paralympic Games in Barcelona.

As a result of the efforts of wheelchair basketball and the general trend toward integrated (or functional) classification, a sport-specific functional classification system was developed (Curtis, 1991) to be used for the first

Table 7.2 Winter Sports (DS/USA) Classification System for Physical Impairment/Amputee/Les Autres Athletes

Class	Description of skiing technique or classification
LW1	Four track, impairment in both legs, skiing with outriggers and two skis or skiing with one ski and using a prosthesis
LW2	Three track, impairment in one leg, skiing on one ski and outriggers and poles
LW3	Two skis with poles, impairment in both legs
LW4	Two skis with poles, impairment in one leg
LW5/7	Two skis, no poles, impairment in both hands or arms
LW6/8	Two skis, one pole, impairment in one hand or arm
LW9	Combination of arm and leg impairment using equipment of choice

Sit-Ski Classifications:

Group 1 Impairment in lower limbs (T1 to T10, inclusive)

Group 2 Impairment below T10 to L3, inclusive

Group 3 All others

time at the 1992 Paralympic Games in Barcelona. The proposed use of a functional classification system was met with much controversy, and the debate continues over medical versus functional classification (Curtis, 1991; Higgs, Babstock, Buck, Parsons, & Brewer, 1990; Labanowich, 1988; Lindstrom, 1986; McCann, 1987; Richter, Adams-Mushett, Ferrara, & McCann, 1992; Sherrill, 1993; Sherrill, Adams-Mushett, & Jones, 1986; Squires, 1987; Strohkendl, 1986; Thiboutot & Curtis, 1990; Weiss & Curtis, 1986).

In accordance with the perspective that the Paralympic Games do represent the most important top-class competition for athletes with disabilities (physical and visual impairments), the cognizant international federations (CP–ISRA, IBSA, ISMWSF, ISOD) and the Paralympic Division of the Barcelona '92 Olympic Organizing Committee devised a classification system with the following features (*General and Functional Classification Guide for the 1992 Paralympics*, 1992, p. 3):

1. The introduction of "functional" classifications.
2. The grouping together of different classes of athletes with similar disabilities and performance in competition.
3. The cancellation of events that have attracted few competitors over the years.

Table 7.3 Classification for Summer Sports (DS/USA, ISOD): Amputee/Les Autres Athletes

Class	Description of classification

Amputee

A1   Amputation of both legs above or through the knee joint. Uses wheelchair for competition.

A2   Amputation of one leg above or through the knee. Uses wheelchair for competition.

A3   Amputation of both legs below the knee. Uses wheelchair for competition.

A4   Amputation of one leg below the knee. Ambulatory with prosthesis for competition.

A5   Amputation of both arms above or through the elbow.

A6   Amputation of one arm above the elbow.

A7   Amputation of both arms below the elbow but through or above the wrist.

A8   Amputation of one arm below the elbow but through or above the wrist.

A9   Combined lower plus upper limb amputation.

Les Autres

L1   Uses a wheelchair. Reduced function of muscle strength and/or spasticity in throwing arm. Poor sitting balance.

L2   Uses a wheelchair. Good function in throwing arm and poor to moderate sitting balance or reduced function in throwing arm with good sitting balance.

L3   Uses a wheelchair. Good arm function and sitting balance.

L4   Ambulatory with or without crutches and braces or problems with balance together with reduced function in throwing arm.

L5   Ambulatory with good arm function. Reduced function in lower extremities or difficulty in balancing.

L6   Ambulatory with good upper extremity function in throwing arm and minimal trunk or lower extremity impairment.

Table 7.4 Classification for Blind Athletes (USABA/IBSA) for Summer and Winter Sport

Class	Description
Class B1	Totally blind; may possess light perception but unable to recognize hand shapes at any distance.
Class B2	Recognizes hand shapes; up to and including 20/600 or field limited to less than 5 degrees.
Class B3	Visual acuity greater than 20/600 up to 20/200. Field limitation from 5 to 20 degrees.

Table 7.5 Classification for Wheelchair Basketball (NWBA)

Class	Description
Class 1	Complete motor loss at T7 or above or comparable disability. Poor to absent sitting balance and trunk control.
Class 2	Complete motor loss T8 through and including L2 where there may be some motor strength in the hips and thighs. Fair to good sitting balance and trunk control. Includes bilateral hip disarticulations.
Class 3	All others with paralysis originating at or below L3. All lower extremity amputees except above class 2. Good to normal sitting balance and trunk control.

Team balance: At no time can there be greater than 12 value points in the game or more than three class 3 players on the floor. Points assigned as follows: Class 1—1 point, Class 2—2 points, and Class 3—3 points.

The new functional system of classifications requires that athletes be evaluated on what they can and cannot do in a particular sport (Sherrill, 1993). In short, athletes are assigned to a class based on a functional profile. An example of the difference between the medical classification and the functional classification systems is graphically represented in Figure 7. 1 for selected sports for athletes using wheelchairs.

The system for wheelchair track reduced the number of classes from seven (Table 7.7) to four as follows:

1. Class T1—severe reduction of power in the arms affecting grip and elbow extension; severe shoulder problems and reduced triceps power.

Table 7.6 Classification for Wheelchair Users (NWAA, ISMWSF)

Class	Description
Class 1A	All cervical lesions with complete or incomplete quadriplegia who have involvement of both hands, weakness of triceps, with severe weakness of the trunk and lower extremities interfering significantly with trunk balance and the ability to walk.
Class 1B	All cervical lesions with complete or incomplete quadriplegia who have involvement of upper extremities but with preservation of normal or good triceps, generalized weakness of the trunk and lower extremities interfering significantly with trunk balance and the ability to walk.
Class 1C	All cervical lesions with complete or incomplete quadriplegia with impairment of upper extremities with preservation of normal or good triceps, good finger flexion and extension (grasp and release), without intrinsic hand function, with a generalized weakness of the trunk and lower extremities interfering significantly with trunk balance and the ability to walk.
Class II	Complete or incomplete paraplegia below T1 down to and including T5 or comparable impairment with total abdominal paralysis or poor abdominal muscle strength, no useful trunk sitting balance.
Class III	Complete or incomplete paraplegia or comparable impairment below T5 down to and including T10 with upper abdominal and spinal extensor musculature significant to provide some element of trunk sitting balance.
Class IV	Complete or incomplete paraplegia or comparable impairment below T10 down to and including L2 without quadriceps or very weak quadriceps, gluteal paralysis.
Class V	Complete or incomplete paraplegia or comparable impairment below L2.

Amputee wheelchair users

Class	Description
Class VI	Unilateral amputee
Class IV	Bilateral above knee—Amputations above level of lesser trochanter
Class V	Bilateral above knee—Amputations below level of lesser trochanter
Class V	Above knee/below knee
Class VI	Bilateral below knee

2. Class T2—little or no use of one or both hands; propulsion of wheelchair is performed by using the back of one's hands.

3. Class T3—normal arm and hand function; gripping and pushing action unaffected; limited sitting balance, trunk rotation, and no trunk fixation.

4. Class T4—normal upper-body function; optimal sitting balance and effective trunk rotation.

As indicated previously, the 9th Paralympic Games in Barcelona used the functional system. Table 7.8 summarizes the functional classification system related to the sports on the Paralympic program, the disability groupings eligible for competition, and the new classes. As indicated, athletes across multiple disability groups competed alongside each other for the first time. Not all those who competed did so under the functional classification system; athletes who competed under the auspices of IBSA were exempted for 1992. On the other hand, athletes from CP–ISRA, ISOD, and ISMWSF not only competed under the new system but had to meet qualifying standards based on previous best performances of these three groups (Paciorek, 1993). This caused much controversy and frustrated cerebral palsy athletes during the games.

CLASSIFICATION OF ATHLETES WITH MENTAL RETARDATION

The classification system used with athletes with mental retardation varies according to the sport governing body. Both similarities and differences exist between Special Olympics International (SOI) and the International Sports Federation for Persons With Mental Handicap (INAS–FMH).

Both groups require that athletes be classified as mentally retarded (SOI terminology) or mentally handicapped (INAS–FMH terminology).

Table 7.7 Example of Functional Classification System for Wheelchair Track

New classification	Neurological impairment level	Medical classification
T1	<C6	1A
T2	CYB	1B, 1C
T3	C7–T7	1C, 2, 3
T4	T8–S2	3, 4, 5, 6

Table 7.8 Summary of Classification Systems Used in the Paralympic Games

Sport	Participating athletes	Sport association affiliation	Classification
		Summer	
Athletics	All	All	Disability
Archery	Amputee, WC	IPC	Standing, sitting, open
Basketball	WC, amputee, CP	Independent	Functional—high ability
Boccie	CP	CP-ISRA	Disability—severe
Bowls	Amputee, blind, WC	IPC	WC and blind
Cycling	CP, amputee, blind	Multifederation/IPC	Disability
Equestrian	All	IPC	Functional (minimal disability)
Fencing	WC	ISMWSF	Functional (spinal level)
Goalball	Blind	IBSA	All with goggles
Judo	Blind	IBSA	Weight
Racquetball	WC	ISMWSF	None
Rugby	WC	ISMWSF	Functional
Sailing	All	Independent	None
Shooting	Amputee, WC	IPC	Functional
Soccer	CP	CP-ISRA	None
Swimming	All	IPC	Functional
Table tennis	Amputee, WC	IPC	Functional
Tennis	WC	Independent	None
Volleyball	Amputee	ISOD	Standing, sitting
Powerlifting	All	IBSA, IPC	Blind, weight

(continued)

Table 7.8 *(continued)*

Sport	Participating athletes	Sport association affiliation	Classification
		Winter	
Alpine	All	IPC	Blind, amputee, sitting (points)
Nordic	All	IPC	Blind, amputee, sitting (points)
Sledge hockey	WC	IPC	None
Sledge racing	WC	IPC	Two levels

Adapted from a presentation by M. Riding at Sport Science Seminar in Berlin, April 1994.

Verification of mental impairment is required to participate in international competitions (e.g., Paralympics for the Mentally Handicapped, Special Olympics International). Other than the requirement of mental impairment, INAS–FMH does not utilize a classification system. To compete in international events, athletes must meet qualifying standards and be at least 15 years of age (DePauw & Rich, 1993). The athletes who compete for INAS–FMH tend to be those with mild to moderate retardation because the more severely mentally retarded individuals usually cannot meet the qualifying standards.

Special Olympics does not use either a medical or functional classification system but has adopted an approach called divisioning, whereby the athletes are classified by age and sex as well as by ability. Competitors must be at least 8 years old.

Each division must have at least three, but no more than eight, competitors or teams. Prior to placement in heats or divisions, athletes are required to submit their best times or distances. Divisions are then determined based upon the 10% rule. No division can have more than a 10% difference between the top and bottom scores for individual sports. For team sports, team scores on sport-specific skills are used to create divisions.

DEAF ATHLETES AND CLASSIFICATION

Athletes who compete in national and international competitions for the Deaf must have at least a 55 decibel (dB) hearing loss in the better ear according to the rules of the International Committee of Sports for the Deaf (Stewart, 1990). Athletes must show proof of hearing loss. Other than the requirement of severe hearing loss, there is no classification among Deaf athletes by level of hearing impairment. Deaf athletes compete together regardless of the extent of hearing loss.

ISSUES RELATED TO CLASSIFICATION

Classification of athletes with disabilities for competition has been a long-standing controversy. On one hand, the goal of classification seems to be to enable each competitor, regardless of severity of impairment, to compete in a fair manner with others of similar ability/disability (a more medical-based classification system). On the other hand, the goal of classification based upon functional ability applied to sport is to provide for meaningful athletic competition based upon ability, not disability. Given this increased emphasis on ability and less on adaptation/modification of the sport, the more severely impaired tend to be eliminated from elite athletic competition. This latter goal of classification has emerged partly because of the administrative problem and logistics of numerous classes for competitions (e.g., 50+ 100m races by gender and disability type—3 for blind, 8 for cerebral palsy, 9 for amputee, 6 for les autres, 7 for wheelchair users).

According to Sherrill (1993) sport classification theory has been consistently ranked as the sport topic where research is greatly needed. She suggested that the current issues of classification include the following:

> Should sport classifications be medical or functional?
>
> Should sport classifications be specific to each disability (e.g., cerebral palsy, spinal cord injury) or should there be one system broad enough to include all?
>
> Should there be a classification system for each sport or a general system encompassing several sports? (p. 176)

The results of research conducted on classification have been mixed, and these are often undertaken and reported based upon the differing goals identified above. Differences found in athletic performances in track and field by gender, distance, and class of athletes (Coutts & Schutz, 1988; Ridgeway, Pope, & Wilkerson, 1988; Wicks, Oldridge, Cameron, & Jones, 1983) have been used to support the need for classification for fairness.

On the other hand, the findings reported by Higgs, Babstock, Buck, Parsons, and Brewer (1990), as well as Gorton and Gavron (1987), seem to support a reduction in the number of classifications.

Throughout the 1990s and perhaps into the 21st century, integrated or functional classification systems will continue to be examined and refined for use in international competitions. These same systems will also permeate the national competitions, especially those for qualifying for international competitions.

CLASSIFICATION: INTEGRATION AND SEGREGATION

Classification is primarily a concern for the fairness of competitions among athletes with disabilities. But central to sport and disability in the broader context is the issue of competition with able-bodied athletes. This issue manifests itself in two distinct ways: the inclusion of disability sport events within competitions for able-bodied athletes and competition between athletes with disabilities and able-bodied athletes.

A growing number of athletes with disabilities advocate the inclusion of events for athletes with disabilities within major international competitions such as the Olympic Games, Pan American Games, World University Games, Commonwealth Games, World Championships, and the like (Clarke, 1986; Daignault, 1990; Labanowich, 1988). Although advocated, the classification issues for this type of competition have yet to be identified fully. For further discussion of the IPC and its Committee on Integration, see chapter 14.

Also virtually ignored in the sport and disability literature is discussion of athletes with disabilities competing alongside able-bodied athletes. Except for notable exceptions during the Olympic Games (e.g., Liz Hartel, who despite polio won a silver medal in dressage in 1952; Nerol Fairhall, who represented New Zealand in 1984 and competed in archery from a wheelchair), this type of competition exists at the regional or local level. As the future of sport and disability unfolds, it is important to consider all facets of integration/inclusion and related classification issues.

CONCLUDING COMMENTS

Classification has always been a major component of disability sport, particularly for international competitions. In the 1990s, the medical classification system gave way to the functional classification system as utilized in the Paralympic movement. Although classification issues are themselves controversial, they are related to the underlying philosophies of disability sport.

CHAPTER 8

Sports Medicine and Athletes With Disabilities

Ronald W. Davis and Michael S. Ferrara, ATC
Ball State University, Muncie, Indiana

In the 1990s, sports for individuals with disabilities are becoming more visible in the able-bodied sporting world. More of these athletes are participating in such major able-bodied sporting events as the Boston Marathon, U.S. Olympic Sports Festivals, and the Olympics, and their performances are more clearly recognized as true athletic endeavors. The general public is starting to see the performance and not the disability. The question is why? Why are the athletes with disabilities improving their individual performances? Why are they setting new records and becoming increasingly visible to the general public? Beyond the factors related to media coverage and promotional events, perhaps the answer lies in better athletic preparation. Athletes with disabilities are focusing more attention on an area frequently ignored in the past: sports medicine and training.

This chapter will attempt to provide a general approach to the factors related to sports medicine. This will *not* be a chapter on "how to" or "what is the best method." It will, however, provide the reader with general information concerning sports medicine (i.e., training, injuries, coaching preparation).

SPORTS MEDICINE

What is sports medicine and what is its background? Historically, the use of therapeutic exercises (medical gymnastics) was documented between 1000 and 800 B.C. (American Academy of Orthopedic Surgeons, 1991). As the popularity of sports grew, those professionals interested in the well-being of the participants organized to help provide a more effective service delivery system. Physicians were the first to become involved with sports care. With the emergence and development of interscholastic and intercollegiate programs, athletic trainers also gained prominence.

Today the term *sports medicine* includes the services of, but is not limited to, athletic trainers, physicians, physical therapists, coaches, athletic administrators/directors, exercise physiologists, and nutritionists. The sports medicine professional will be involved with preventing injuries and developing training schedules. Regardless of their role, sports medicine professionals have their roots in able-bodied sports.

INVOLVEMENT WITH DISABILITY SPORTS

The earliest documentation of sports medicine involvement with disability sports centered around athletic injuries. Kathleen Curtis (1981a, 1981b, 1982), a physical therapist, wrote a series of articles concerning the wheelchair athlete and basic exercise physiology, training, stretching routines, and athletic injuries. Curtis's work provided the foundation for other professionals in the area of sports medicine for the disabled to expand upon. While Curtis's efforts were descriptive in nature, Mangus (1987) reported on injuries to disabled athletes from a prevention and treatment perspective. An athletic trainer, Mangus divided his work between athletes with sensory and physical impairments.

Perhaps the most comprehensive involvement related to sports medicine and injury surveillance is a project supported by the United States Olympic Foundation under the direction of Dr. Michael Ferrara, entitled Athletes With Disabilities Injury Registry (ADIR). This was the first epidemiological study to use a cross-disability design. Ferrara's work was initiated in 1989 and continued through 1992. ADIR is a comprehensive injury surveillance system in which injury and exposure information is collected and analyzed. Location of injury (head, neck, wrist, etc.), type of injury, surface on which the injury occurred, time of injury (e.g., during training or competition), time lost to the injury, and medical caregiver (physician, athletic trainer, therapists) are all analyzed. Three major disability sport organizations are involved with ADIR: the National Wheelchair Athletic Association (NWAA), representing individuals with spinal cord injuries, the United States Association of Blind Athletes (USABA), and the United States Cerebral Palsy Athletic Association (USCPAA). While research on injury is continuing, field experience by the sports medicine professionals at disability sport competitions is increasing.

Medical practitioners on site at the various competition venues have verified the increased involvement of sports medicine professionals with disability sports. Kowalski and McCann (1991) reported on a unique approach utilized at the 1991 Victory Games in New York. A mobile sports medicine center, sponsored by the Henry Ford Hospital in Detroit, was set up on the grounds of the games. Housed in a tractor trailer, it was billed as the largest expandable athletic sports medicine facility on wheels in the world. The mobile unit had a staff of 9 physicians, 17 trainers, 12 physical therapists, 8 chiropractors, 14 nurses, and 5 emergency medical technicians. All were ready to provide medical assistance to more than 1,200 athletes with disabilities.

The 1991 International Special Olympics implemented one of the most comprehensive medical coverage systems utilizing the latest in communication technology. More than 750 medical and health care personnel volunteered to serve on sports medicine teams. Each team comprised athletic training, nursing, first aid, and emergency medical technicians. They treated more than 6,200 athletes at 16 different sporting venues. Seventeen mobile medical units, housed in large recreational vehicles, were equipped with cellular phones and facsimile machines to transmit medical information. "Never in the history of Special Olympics or Olympics has such a facsimile system been used" (Special Olympics medical director, personal communication, July 26, 1991).

SPORTS INJURIES

While it is apparent that sports medicine pertains mostly to care and prevention, injuries still occur. This section will look at the incidence, type, and treatment considerations for the athletic trainer or other medical caregiver.

Incidence, Care, Prevention

Treatment, care, and prevention of athletic injuries must be documented and called to the attention of the physician, trainer, and/or coach. Historically, physicians, athletic trainers, and physical therapists have not been alerted when athletes with disabilities are injured. Hopefully, with the increased on-site involvement of the physician and/or trainer at competitions, treatment will be greatly improved.

Curtis (1982) documented the 10 most common wheelchair sports injuries. She indicated that 33% of all injuries were classified as soft tissue (sprains, strains, muscle pulls, tendinitis, bursitis). The second and third most common injuries were blisters and lacerations. Track, basketball, and road racing were the top three sports associated with injury risk for the wheelchair athlete. According to Curtis, soft tissue injuries were most common in road racing, basketball, and tennis. Ferrara and Davis (1990) concurred with Curtis's investigation of a high number of muscular injuries, particularly to the shoulder.

Ferrara (1990) indicated that upper extremities suffer greater chronic injuries than lower extremities. Twenty-two percent of all injuries reported across disabilities were reported at the shoulder for the athlete with a spinal cord injury, cerebral palsy, or visual impairment, followed by injuries to the hand and fingers (10%). The USCPAA athletes indicated a higher percentage of hand and finger injuries than those of the NWAA and USABA. Ferrara's breakdown of these injuries is presented in Figure 8.1.

Treatment Considerations

With a few exceptions, treatment for specific types of injuries should remain the same regardless of ability or disability. The treatment of strains, sprains, lacerations, contusions, and other injuries should not change when one is treating an athlete with a sensory or physical impairment. However, communication and follow-up management should be important considerations.

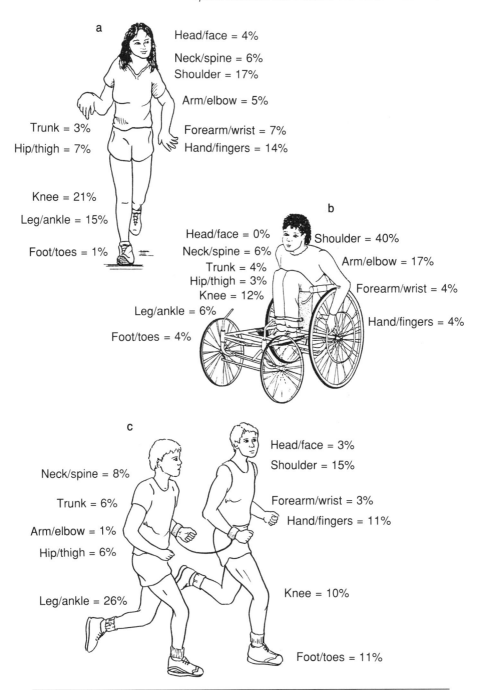

a

Head/face = 4%

Neck/spine = 6%
Shoulder = 17%

Arm/elbow = 5%

Trunk = 3%

Forearm/wrist = 7%

Hip/thigh = 7%

Hand/fingers = 14%

Knee = 21%

Leg/ankle = 15%

Foot/toes = 1%

b

Head/face = 0%

Shoulder = 40%

Neck/spine = 6%

Arm/elbow = 17%

Trunk = 4%

Hip/thigh = 3%

Forearm/wrist = 4%

Knee = 12%

Leg/ankle = 6%

Hand/fingers = 4%

Foot/toes = 4%

c

Head/face = 3%

Shoulder = 15%

Neck/spine = 8%

Trunk = 6%

Forearm/wrist = 3%

Arm/elbow = 1%

Hand/fingers = 11%

Hip/thigh = 6%

Leg/ankle = 26%

Knee = 10%

Foot/toes = 11%

Figure 8.1 Injuries to athletes compiled from the (a) USCPAA, (b) NWAA, and (c) USABA.
Note. Data from Ferrara (1990).

The following are suggested ways of caring for and preventing injuries:

Injury	Care and Prevention
Soft tissue	• stretching—warm-up/cool down
	• protective covering for old injuries
Blisters	• taping fingers
	• protective covering (gloves, socks on upper arms for wheelchair users)
	• frequent inspection of footwear
Abrasions/lacerations	• protective covering for old injuries
Pressure sores (wheelchair users)	• frequent weight shifting
	• clothing that absorbs moisture

Communication Considerations

Communication to the athlete concerning injury management and follow-up treatment does require specific considerations related to individual disabilities. The athletes with sensory impairment usually have normal cognitive abilities. Comprehending treatment procedures and follow-up responsibilities is not a problem, but compliance may be. The individual attention lies in the athletic trainer's ability to effectively communicate the information. In other words, choosing the appropriate mechanism for learning is a key factor (e.g., visual, auditory, sign language).

Hearing Impaired.   Mangus (1987) suggests the following when communicating with hearing impaired athletes:

- Try not to yell. Speak with a normal tone and directly to athlete.
- Try not to speak too fast. Watch your pace.
- Be aware the athlete might be reading your lips, and mustaches might interfere. Shaving the mustache might be necessary.
- Allow enough time when communicating, as the athlete might speak slower and need additional time. Be patient.
- Use visuals, if necessary.

Visually Impaired.   Mangus (1987) suggests the following when communicating with visually impaired athletes:

- Realize you must work through the modalities of sense and touch.
- Use the tactile sense. Allow the athlete to feel the uninjured part and compare it to the injured part.

- Allow the athlete to follow your hands through the injury evaluation procedure.
- Physically assist the athlete through any rehabilitative exercises while under your supervision to help clarify proper procedures.

Cerebral Palsy. The etiology of cerebral palsy (CP) is often explained as a neurological impairment affecting voluntary motor control. According to Sherrill (1986), less than 20% of the athletes reported by the USCPAA have an associated condition related to mental retardation. Therefore, the majority of athletes with CP have normal cognitive abilities. However, greater associated dysfunctions are reported in the sensory modalities of speech, vision, hearing, and perceptual deficits. Thus, communicating the injury treatment and follow-up management does not hinge on the athletes' ability to understand but rather on the athletic trainers' ability to communicate.

Some considerations for explaining injury treatment to an athlete with CP:

- Use word boards or other visuals related to the injury and follow-up treatment.
- Allow enough time to communicate. The athlete's speech might be very slow and difficult to understand. Be patient.
- Straps, slings, and wraps might be needed to appropriately position and secure ice bags/cold packs. The nature of the CP (spasticity, athetoid) might not allow the athlete the muscle control to hold treatments on the injured body part.
- Position the athlete carefully during examination, treatment, and follow-up. Incorrect positioning on a treatment table might elicit abnormal reflexive tones, which will interfere with movement.
- Avoid ballistic movements during examination. Move body parts slowly to avoid increased muscle tone or abnormal reflexive responses.

Athletes Using Wheelchairs

Some suggestions for treatment and injury management for the athlete using a wheelchair:

- Document all injuries. Use a log or any means of recording regardless of degree. Keep the trainer, coach, and athlete informed.
- To regulate temperature, replace fluids often. Use of spray bottles and cool towels is recommended for the quadriplegic athlete.
- Don't allow the athlete to be exposed to the sun for extended periods of time.

- Evaluate conditions for pressure sores:
  a. Check skin frequently.
  b. Remove pressure from the site.
  c. Treat local infection with disinfectant.
  d. Keep the area clean. Use a dressing to promote healing.
  e. Maintain proper nutrition and hygiene.

Decubitus ulcers are perhaps the most debilitating injury for the wheelchair athlete. Decubitus ulcers (pressure sores) are not necessarily directly related to the athletic endeavor. Athletes who use a wheelchair need to guard against this condition on a daily basis. Pressure sores can negatively affect an athlete's preparation and training for weeks or months. Constant inspection is imperative. Early signs of skin breakdown must be treated immediately, and close supervision by sports medicine professionals is vital.

PROFESSIONAL PREPARATION

While it is clearly documented that sports medicine professionals are becoming increasingly involved with disability sports, attention must now be shifted to their professional preparation. Athletic trainers and coaches should have formal training related to the etiologies of the various disabilities. A review of their current curricula reveals a void in preparation concerning characteristics and etiologies of individuals with disabilities. Course work related to athletic care and prevention for the disabled is virtually nonexistent. A survey completed at the 1991 Victory Games in New York by coaches and team leaders of disabled athletes indicated a modest professional preparation (see Table 8.1). For a profile of those

Table 8.1 Preparation for Coaching Athletes With Disabilities

Subjects (N = 84)	Yes	No
Had an educational course in disabled sport?	33%	67%
Completed a workshop/clinic on disabled sports?	63%	33%
Attended a coaching conference related to disabled sport within the last 3 years?	50%	50%

Note. From *Training Profiles of Elite Wheelchair Athletes* by R. Davis and M. Ferrara, November 1991. Paper presented at the 8th International Symposium of Adapted Physical Activity, Miami, FL.

coaching athletes with disabilities, see DePauw and Gavron (1991) and Gavron and DePauw (1989).

If sports medicine professionals are to continue their involvement in sports for the disabled, it would seem logical for them to have formal training in sport and disability. Suggestions for addressing this situation might be the inclusion of course work within the higher education curriculum, especially for degrees in physical education (kinesiology, exercise science), adapted physical education, athletic training, and coaching. Revision of coaching curricula to include a course related to sports for individuals with disabilities is another approach. Extended workshops through university continuing education programs might also be successful.

Several universities have utilized a very effective venue for professional preparation by hosting elite training camps. Ball State University in Muncie, Indiana, the University of Illinois at Urbana-Champaign, and the University of California at Sacramento have each sponsored training camps for athletes with disabilities. Ball State University has hosted training camps for three disability sports organizations (NWAA, USCPAA, USABA) in preparation for the 1988 and 1992 Paralympics. The University of Illinois, a long-time leader in preparing athletes using wheelchairs, has hosted developmental camps and clinics for coaches and athletes. Under the direction of Marty Morse and Brad Hedrick, the University of Illinois has produced several world-class athletes. Rory Cooper, a wheelchair athlete and engineer, has conducted several training camps at the University of California at Sacramento. Kevin Hansen has developed and offered a racing camp (Myers, 1991) specifically for wheelchair racers. These camps/clinics follow similar formats and provide the participants the opportunity to gain additional knowledge related to sports medicine and athletic preparation. The camps usually include the components of education, training, and research. Educational topics include the areas of exercise physiology, biomechanics, nutrition, sports psychology, and athletic preparation. Research investigations follow similar topic areas and are designed to minimize the time between data collection and feedback to the athlete and/or coach. Utilizing any of these camp/clinic options will help in the professional preparation of sports medicine personnel involved with disability sports.

TRAINING

This section will deal with athletic preparation. It is not meant to be a "cookbook" approach to competitive training (also see chapter 10 on coaching athletes with disabilities). The information presented will address the composition of a sound training program, review several training principles, document training profiles of athletes with disabilities, and show specific exercise considerations.

Components of Training

Before any considerations can be made to the physiological aspects of training, something must occur unrelated to the physical domain of a training paradigm. This component is goal setting. Without question, goal setting can be the most influential component of the training program. Without goal setting athletes will lose focus, become increasingly difficult to motivate, and subject themselves to lower retention rates. In other words, the athlete stands a greater chance of failing and dropping out.

Goal setting needs to be dynamic. Both the coach and the athlete need to be actively involved with this dimension of training. A dynamic plan for goal setting requires close supervision of training. If necessary, goals need to be modified, either extended or shortened to make them attainable. Unrealistic goals will contribute to poor training habits and motivation. "Goal setting helps athletes to stay focused on relevant, attainable performance objectives that are within their control, while concurrently helping to prevent them from attending to or worrying about events or factors that are beyond their control" (Hedrick & Morse, 1991, p. 64).

Comprehensive goal setting should include behavioral and athletic performance goals. Several factors should influence goal setting: level of commitment, time available to train, and level of athletic ability. Goal setting should be multidimensional to include immediate, intermediate, and long-range goals. Last, coaches, trainers, and athletes must work together to reach the goals. Success breeds success. Setting and reaching goals will contribute to a very successful training program; however, physical training is equally important.

If performance in an athletic event is dependent upon the physiological factors of strength, power, flexibility, endurance, and coordination (technique), then a comprehensive training program should include these same factors. While training principles will direct the training program, the athlete must assemble these basic ingredients for optimal performance.

For the sake of clarity, let us operationally define what is meant by these basic components of training:

Strength—The athlete's ability to exert a force against some form of resistance.

Power—The rate at which muscular force is exerted. Anaerobic power might be measured in seconds, while aerobic power would last 5 minutes or more.

Flexibility—The athlete's full range of motion around a joint. Flexibility might be specific to a functional limb or an entire body position.

Endurance—Performance at a desired rate for extended periods of time. Endurance can be muscular or cardiovascular, and it can be considered anaerobic (short time period) or aerobic (longer time period).

Coordination—Timing, precision, accuracy, balance, and more. Coordination brings into play the perceptual factors of training. It is the performance-related component of training (e.g., shooting free throws, drafting in turn in racing, starting techniques).

All of the components of training must be guided by principles. It is difficult to talk about the components of training without discussing the myriad training principles.

Training Principles

This section will not discuss specific training principles utilized for athletic preparation but will take a more general approach. Training principles remain the same. It is the individual athlete who must make the adjustments to training based on his/her commitment, available time, outside responsibilities, and access to equipment. Training centers around three ingredients: frequency, intensity, and duration. Sometimes a fourth ingredient, mode of training, needs to be considered. Mode of training is specific to the athlete's use of special equipment (e.g., racing wheelchair, tethered runner, beeper devices).

Frequency refers to how often the athlete applies a training overload. Several factors influence this ingredient: work or school schedules, availability of facilities, and transportation to and from the training site. Intensity is training at a set percentage of work effort (energy) over a period of time. For example, athletes who are weight training might train at 85% of their maximum for three days per week, then drop to 70% for two days, and then increase to 90% for one day, depending on their event. This type of training would allow the athlete's body to recover during a typical training week. Runners might train at 80-85% of maximum heart rate four days per week. Duration refers to the length of time set aside for training. This might be set daily, weekly, or monthly depending on the specific event. Endurance athletes will have different training durations than sprinters.

Training must address two key principles: overload and specificity of training. Utilizing the principle of overload, the athlete must stress the various systems of the body (musculoskeletal, cardiovascular, and respiratory). All of these systems must be placed in a state of stress above the normal level. By utilizing various combinations of the ingredients of frequency, intensity, and duration, overload will occur.

While applying the overload principle is important, making the training sessions specific to the athletic performance emphasizes specificity of training. This is critical to optimal training. The elements related to race pace, positioning, speed, cornering and starting techniques, and early race versus late race strategy must be included within this dimension of training. Perhaps no other element of training requires the utilization of a coach more than this one. A coach will be able to teach and evaluate performances during training sessions, thus allowing the athlete time to implement necessary changes. Despite all we know about training and how to apply it, there is minimal documentation of training programs for elite athletes with disabilities.

Documentation of Training

Few efforts have been made to document the training profiles of athletes with disabilities. Hedrick, Morse, and Figoni (1988) reported the training practices of elite wheelchair roadracers competing in a national 10K roadrace. Their findings reflected the need for coaching and more appropriate sources of training information. Their findings can be summarized as follows: nearly all of the male paraplegic athletes (90%) reported receiving training information from other sources before getting input from a coach, 45% of the quadriplegic athletes reported not having a coach, and cycling magazines were the leading source of training information followed by other athletes and coaches.

Davis and Ferrara (1991) reported significant differences in frequency, duration, and intensity of training between elite wheelchair athletes training with a coach versus those training without a coach. The average frequency for training was 3.5 days per week. Ferrara (1990) reported similar training frequencies across disabilities for strength, flexibility, anaerobics, and aerobics (see Figure 8.2).

The American College of Sports Medicine (1990) recommends that an individual should exercise at least three days per week for a minimum of 15 continuous minutes to receive cardiovascular and health benefits. One would expect elite athletes to be training at greater frequencies than is shown in Figure 8.2. Sparling, Wilson, and Pate (1987) indicated elite women runners practiced seven times a week and experienced runners (nonelite) practiced five or six times per week. When comparing training frequencies of athletes with disabilities to able-bodied athletes, Blair, Kohl, and Goodyear (1987) and Marti, Abelin, and Minder (1988) indicated that elite athletes with disabilities appear to have the same training frequencies as recreational able-bodied runners.

Elite level training must improve and sports medicine professionals must get involved at the professional preparation level. Available resources should include college and/or university professionals. Today's

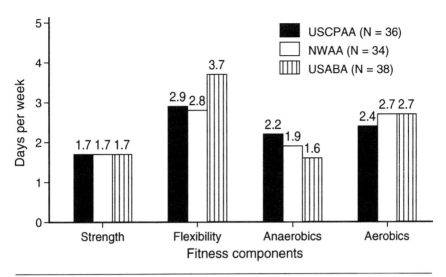

Figure 8.2 Training frequencies for track athletes with disabilities compiled from the USCPAA, NWAA, and USABA.
Note. Data from Davis & Ferrara (1991).

college and university physical education curricula have heavy concentrations of exercise science courses. Professionals directing these programs must make a more conscious effort to include training regimes for athletes with disabilities in their curricula. Elite athletes with disabilities need to expand their resources and seek assistance from local able-bodied coaches for development of training programs.

The following suggestions for developing a seasonal approach to designing a training program are from Marty Morse at the University of Illinois. Four periods of preparation should be targeted for the specific competitive event:

Foundation Period—Includes general conditioning, laying a solid base for future intensive training.

Preparation Period—Sport-specific training; training is focused on specific sport activity.

Competition Period—The peak of the training year.

Transition Period—End of the season, active rest and relaxation, good time for recreational basketball, tennis, swimming.

Training programs must be individually designed and engineered. Athletes should strive to know as much as they can about themselves and their responses to training. Learn to recognize these responses, and you will program for more successful training. Successful training is not without special considerations for specific populations.

Exercise Considerations for Athletes With Disabilities

Everyone regardless of disability should be provided the opportunity to be involved in some type of exercise program. Suggestions for exercise modifications from the National Handicapped Sports (NHS) are shown in Table 8.2; contraindications are listed in Table 8.3. Sample training regimens are shown in Tables 8.4a and b.

Table 8.2   Exercise Modifications for Selected Athletes With Disabilities

Disability	Component	Modification
Spinal cord injury (quadriplegic)	Aerobic	Internal approach (e.g., 2-3 exercise bouts, rest, repeat).
Muscular dystrophy	Aerobic	Be aware of time of day (e.g., late afternoon for muscular dystrophy and multiple sclerosis).
Multiple sclerosis	Aerobic	
Cerebral palsy	Aerobic	Slow gradual warm-up. Alternate easy/hard workload.
Across disabilities	Strength	Alternative devices (e.g., rubber tubing, wall pulleys, small hand weights). Caution: free weights not recommended for persons with motor coordination problems or reduced muscle control.
Spinal cord injury	Flexibility	Be aware of reduced sensations of muscle groups.
Cerebral palsy	Flexibility	Avoid ballistic movements. Stretch slowly.
Wheelchair users	Flexibility	Provide opportunities to get out of wheelchairs. Stretch hip flexors whenever possible (e.g., prone or supine on a mat).

Table 8.3 Contraindications to Exercise

Disability	Condition	Contraindications
Down's syndrome	Atlanto-axial	Forward rolls, tucking the head, diving headfirst.
Spinal cord (Quadriplegia)	Thermal regulation	Overheating, need to provide spray bottles and moist towels. Guard against overexposure to sun; stay in shade.
	Blood pooling	Make sure to do passive range of motion for lower extremities upon completion of exercise.
	Finger contractures	Avoid hyperextension of fingers during passive ROM.
(Paraplegia)	Harrington rods	Avoid rotation and twisting types of activities.
Amputee	Skin breakdown	Avoid skin breakdown with frequent checks of the stump.
	Leg length	Make sure to use the type of shoe designed for the prostheses to avoid differing leg lengths.

CONCLUDING COMMENTS

The message from this chapter is simple: stay involved. Sports medicine professionals have come a long way in terms of their involvement with sports for individuals with disabilities. However, more work is needed. Sports medicine professionals must begin to infuse new knowledge and applications related to individuals with disabilities into their professional development. Their roles must continue to be more active and dynamic.

Knowledge of the disability, the sport, and the athlete will help the professional in sports medicine better address the needs of the athlete with respect to training and injuries.

Table 8.4a   Training Vignette: Spinal Cord Injury

Name	Kenny Carnes
Disability	Spinal cord injury
Competition	Wheelchair road and track
Background	Injured April 14, 1974 in motorcycle accident. Entered his first wheelchair race October 3, 1987. Won seven gold medals in June 1990 and was voted the NWAA Athlete of the Year for Track and Field.
Training program	Kenny divides his program into three phases:
Phase I	Focus on building an aerobic base. Emphasis on use of stationary rollers. Phase I continues through February and occurs 6 days per week.
Phase II	Focus on strength training and hill work. This phase lasts until the middle of March.
	Sunday—1.5 to 2.5 hr of steady pushing Monday—Recovery 60-70 min of pushing Tuesday & Thursday—Hill work Wednesday—Easy 30-40 min of pushing Friday—Rest Saturday—Track work (e.g., 6 × 1,000 at race pace)
Phase III	Divided into three subphases
	Sub 1—Continues through May with emphasis on intervals Sub 2—Continues through June with race pace intervals Sub 3—A sharpening phase.
	Sunday—Distance at 1.5 hr Monday—Track work Tuesday—Steady push 60-75 min Wednesday—Recovery 1 hr easy Thursday—Sprints all out, 3 min rest between Friday—Rest Sunday—Time trials

Note. Adapted from "Focus on Training" by J. Jones, 1991, *Palaestra,* **7**(4), pp. 56-57.

Table 8.4b   Training Vignette: Congenital Birth Defect

Name	Tony Volpentest
Disability	Congenital birth defect
Competition	Track
Background	Tony was born without forearms or feet. Began to walk without prostheses at 14 months. Gold medal winner in 1989 Pan/Am Games in Florida for 100m, 200m races. Fitted with Flex-Foot prostheses in 1990. Named Most Outstanding Athlete at the 1989 Pan Am Games and USAAA Junior Male Athlete of the Year in 1990.
Training program	Tony trains year-round, 6 days a week, in the weight room and on the track. Uses mental imagery of his best performances and watches videotapes of his past performances.
Monday	Weights—emphasis on upper body Track—endurance workout (800m warm-up; 4 × 400m, 2 × 200m intervals; 800m cool-down)
Tuesday	Weights—emphasis lower body Track—form running (800m warm-up, 10 × 100m Q 50%; practice starts; 800m cool-down)
Wednesday	Weights—emphasis on upper body Track—speed work (800m warm-up, 5 × 100m @ 85%; 4 × 200m Q 85%; 800m cool-down)
Thursday	Weights—emphasis lower body Track—endurance work (800m warm-up; progression/regression drill/1 each 100m to 500m to 100m at 100m intervals all out; 800m cool-down)
Friday	Weights—emphasis on upper body Track—speed work (800m warm-up; 5 × 100m @ 85%; 4 × 200m @ 85%; 800m cool-down)
Saturday	Weights—emphasis on lower body Track—endurance and form work (800m warm-up; 4 × 400m; 2 × 200m; 5 × 100m @ 50%; practice starts; 800-m cooldown)

Note. Adapted from "Focus on Training" by J. Jones, 1991, *Palaestra,* 8(1), pp. 60-61.

CHAPTER 9

Access to Sport
and Adapted Equipment

Accessibility is a key issue facing individuals with disabilities in their quest to participate in sport and recreation activities. Access to sport and adapted equipment is a necessity for full participation.

ACCESSIBILITY ISSUES

Addressing accessibility issues involves identifying and eliminating common barriers. It is important to understand the legislative mandates regarding sport for individuals with disabilities.

Common Barriers

Individuals with disabilities have sometimes had difficulty in accessing opportunities in sport. Expense, fear, distance, and the lack of information, skill, physician encouragement, and appropriate equipment appear to be major contributors to this problem (Frederick, 1991; Murphy-Howe & Charboneau, 1987). Access to information about sport programs is increasing but is not yet widespread. For information about such sport programs, individuals with disabilities and their families could be referred to their local parks and recreation association, chamber of commerce, schools, and sport programs. Physical educators and recreation specialists are becoming increasingly aware of sport opportunities for individuals with disabilities and can provide valuable information. For a listing of sport organizations, see Appendixes C, D, and E.

Lack of skill is another variable that may impact on whether an individual with a disability participates in sport. Playing standing basketball is different from sitting in a wheelchair, even though the skills and the objective of the game are the same. Individuals with disabilities are encouraged to seek training through physical education in the public schools or through community recreation and youth sport programs.

The fear of failure and of making a fool of oneself is a significant factor in whether an individual with a disability chooses to become physically active. In many ways this is no different from what an able-bodied individual feels when engaging in something new. However, a person with a newly acquired disability and low self-esteem will have a greater fear of trying challenging physical activity. Related to this concept is learned helplessness, the situation in which individuals with disabilities become used to having someone else do tasks for them (Murphy-Howe & Charboneau, 1987).

Sport as rehabilitation began after World War II. The history of the development of sport elsewhere in this text provides the foundation of its existence and its development. However, even today there are many physicians, with whom individuals with disabilities have a significant amount of contact, who do not recommend sport opportunities as an adjunct for their clients' rehabilitation or lifestyle.

Similar to able-bodied individuals, those with disabilities also have problems with transportation, lack of appropriate equipment, and cost. It matters little if one is able-bodied or disabled: if the cost is prohibitive or the distance too far, participation will suffer. Frederick (1991) confirmed that these factors are magnified when in a rural setting.

Mandated Accessibility

Accessibility to sport programs is secured for individuals with disabilities by legal mandates in the United States. Several pieces of significant legislative mandates (e.g., Amateur Sports Act) have been previously covered in this text. However, the Americans With Disabilities Act (ADA), the newest federal law, mandates increased accessibility, removal of barriers, and promotion of economic, social, and personal independence (West, 1991).

The ADA encompasses five areas, or "titles." The first title is that of employment. The essence of this section is that "no entity shall discriminate against a qualified individual because of the disability in regard to job application procedures, the hiring, placement or discharge of employees, employee compensation, job training and other terms, conditions and privileges of employment" (West, 1991, p. 34). Individuals with disabilities who wish to work in a sport or recreation environment cannot be generally excluded just because they have a disability, unless they are not otherwise qualified to do the job. This is just like anyone else. This aspect of the law did not affect employers of 15-24 persons until July 1994.

Title II is related to the areas of public services and has direct impact on sport for individuals with disabilities. This title provides that "no individual with a disability shall be excluded from participation in or be denied the benefits of services, programs or activities of a public entity or subjected to discrimination by any such entity" (West, 1991, p. 37). Public transportation systems need to be responsive to the needs of individuals with disabilities to travel from homes or jobs to training centers and have the adapted equipment available.

Title III is perhaps one of the most far-reaching segments of the law. It provides that "no individual shall be discriminated against on the basis of disability in the full and equal enjoyment of the goods, services, facilities, privileges, advantages and accommodations of any place of public accommodation by any person who owns, leases or operates a place of public accommodation" (West , 1991, p. 38). This section covers places where athletes can practice, such as school or university gymnasiums, local parks, stadiums, and recreation facilities. The U.S. Olympic Training Center in Colorado Springs is now physically accessible to individuals with wheelchairs. Other training sites and competition sites across the country will need to follow suit. Administrators for the National Sports Festival, for example, a partially integrated sport competition, will need to make sure that housing, restaurants, spectator seating, and event venues are accessible. For buildings that are newly constructed, the law is very direct on this mandate (Munson & Comodeca, 1993).

Accessibility to programs (e.g., intramurals and teams) by individuals with disabilities is also included in the ADA. The focus in this area is one of not only the removal of physical barriers but the inclusion of an individual based upon ability. Exclusion from participation in activity is based upon proving that an individual with a disability is more likely to be injured than in the "normal course of participating in a program" (Munson & Comodeca, 1993).

Title IV directs that telecommunications relay systems should be available to a reasonable extent. Title V relates to insurance, exclusions of certain disabilities from the law, acceptance of accommodations by an individual with a disability, and other worksite provisions.

ADA concerns freedom of movement and access to training sites and the venues where athletic events are staged. Individuals with disabilities have the right to attend and participate in such events. This law ensures access on a much broader scale than ever before.

SPORT AND ADAPTED EQUIPMENT

Equipment for sport usage is an important aspect for future athletes. Whether it be a prosthetic leg, racing wheelchair, or adapted archery equipment, the equipment must fit the individual athlete. Equipment can be adapted at home or in a sophisticated laboratory. The most important thing is that the athlete have a good fit and be safe utilizing the equipment. Resources for equipment adaptations appear in

- Paciorek and Jones (1989) *Sports and Recreation for the Disabled: A Resource Book,*

- Adams and McCubbin (1991) *Games, Sports, & Exercises for the Physically Disabled* (4th ed.), and

- Nesbitt (1986) *The International Directory of Recreation-Oriented Assistive Devices Sources.*

Innovator of Disability Equipment and Adaptations (IDEA) publishes a yearly catalog as does J.L. Pachner, Ltd. Two excellent resources are available from the Veterans Administration:

- Kegel (1985), Sports and Recreation for Those With Lower Limb Impairment, *Journal of Rehabilitation Research and Development* (Suppl. 1), and

- Burgess and Rappoport (n.d.), *Physical Fitness: A Guide for Individuals with Lower Limb Loss.*

Palaestra and *Sports 'n Spokes* (especially its annual review of wheelchairs) are also excellent resources for viewing state-of-the-art sport equipment.

Space-age technology has made its way to the athletic arena. Prosthetic devices are lighter, stronger, and more flexible. Sport wheelchairs are lighter while also designed for maximum wind effect and wheel performance. Foamlike, egg carton seat cushions prevent pressure sores. While space-age metals have made equipment lighter, access to modified equipment is still a problem for some individuals who aspire to become elite athletes. Usually this is due to finances.

The cost of customized equipment for elite athletes can run into the thousands of dollars. Often elite athletes with disabilities have sponsors who subsidize them in return for product endorsements. This is not unlike able-bodied athletes, but there are few large corporations or businesses who support athletes with disabilities on an ongoing basis.

Equipment adaptations vary from the very subtle (a change in strap width, length, or material) to the more complex and time-consuming (design of a prosthetic leg or racing wheelchair).

Prosthetic Devices

Prosthetic devices are often made of titanium, the same material used in airplanes, or a combination of fiberglass and metal. Athletes are now demanding devices that fit well and will perform as closely to the able-bodied foot or leg as possible. Cracks in fiberglass prosthetic legs continue to be a problem with runners, while poorly fitting prosthetic devices may injure soft tissue. In one case a prosthetic leg became undone during a final race in a national meet within sight of the finish line. Examples of prostheses are shown in Figure 9.1.

Acquiring a well-fitting prosthetic device may take a protracted effort. First is where to go. Children have access to Shriners' hospitals, and Easter Seals also assists in prosthetic procurement. Adolescents and adults can utilize the U.S. Bureau of Vocational Rehabilitation, while in other countries government support is available. Second is the skill of the prosthesist. This person should have had formal training and should work in a reputable setting (private practice or clinical). A third factor is the type or style of prosthetic device. Some individuals want both cosmetic and functional ability. The materials it is made of will affect weight, and all these factors together will affect cost. The more sophisticated, lightweight, and durable the prosthetic device, the more expensive it becomes. Usually it must be fitted several times.

Sport Chairs

The size, weight, and height of the racing wheelchair may be contoured to match its owner. The sitting configurations may be molded to a particular body. The camber of the wheels is often adjusted according to the athlete's ability and track conditions. Metals such as Chromoly, titanium, or aluminum are used, and basic costs are around $1700-2000. Custom seat cushions, specialized brakes and tires, and other enhancements can

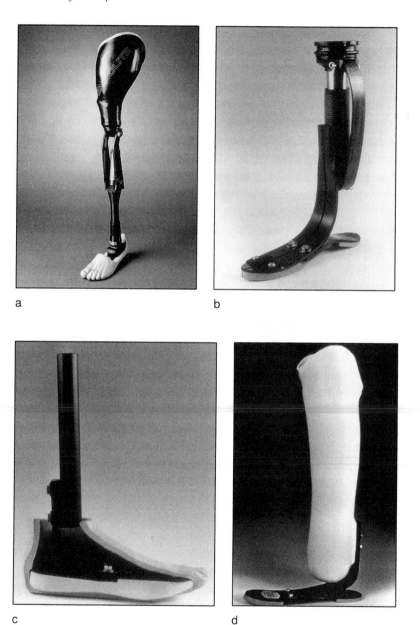

a

b

c

d

(continued)

Figure 9.1 Prostheses for sport and recreation. (a) High Activity prosthesis, courtesy of BioSculptor. (b) Vari-Flex prosthesis, (c) Sure-Flex prosthesis, (d) Flex-Foot Symes prosthesis, (e) Vari-Flex user, (f) Modular III Flex-Foot wearer, (g) Split-Toe Option prosthesis. Courtesy of Flex-Foot, Inc. (h) Weight lifting prosthesis. Courtesy of Stuart Spencer.

e

f

Figure 9.1 *(continued)*

g

h

Figure 9.1 *(continued)*

result in additional costs of $1000-3000 (*IDEA*, 1993). Thus, a fully functional and state-of-the-art wheelchair can cost up to $5000 when adjustments are completed.

Today's athletes compete in specialized wheelchairs; some are motorized, some are designed for roadracing, and some are customized for particular activities, such as wheelchair basketball, quad rugby, or tennis. Examples are shown in Figure 9.2.

There are important differences between the chairs used for daily activities and those designed for sports. Typically, sport chairs have larger wheels and smaller handrims, lowered seat position, increased camber, and a longer wheelbase. Additionally, virtually all of these aspects are adjustable by the demands of a given sport. Not only is the hardware fully adjustable for sport competition, but so are the propulsion techniques utilized and positions assumed by athletes (Axelson & Castellano, 1990; Cooper, 1988; Hedrick, Wang, Moeinzadeh, & Adrian, 1990). Athletes typically assume one of three positions: high knee, flexed trunk, or alternating forward-back (Sherrill, 1993).

Athletes who race in the high knee position do so to lower the center of gravity and opt for the maximum forward lean possible. This position aids in lowering wind resistance and provides for a better driving position for the arms.

The flexed trunk position is one in which the trunk is flexed and as close to the legs as possible to minimize aerodynamic drag. Advances in technology have allowed an increasing number of wheelchair athletes, including those with high lesions, to adopt this position for racing.

Some athletes do not utilize either of the above positions, and they allow their upper bodies to move back and forth in conjunction with arm propulsion. Athletes who compete in most wheelchair sports (basketball, tennis, rugby) other than road racing utilize this position and use short, quick, explosive strokes. In contrast, long-duration circular motions are used successfully for long-distance racing. Although most of the arm propulsion techniques utilize a grab of the handrim with the palms, some athletes with high lesions have found initial contact with the rim with the back of the hand a successful technique for wheelchair sport.

Adapted Equipment

Technique and equipment vary according to the sport, the type and extent of the disability, one's skill and training, and individual preference. Equipment is available for every conceivable sport in which individuals with disabilities wish to compete. Examples of adapted equipment appear in Figure 9.3. A listing of adapted sport equipment would include the following (for a comprehensive listing of adapted equipment, see Nesbitt [1986] and Kegel [1985]):

a

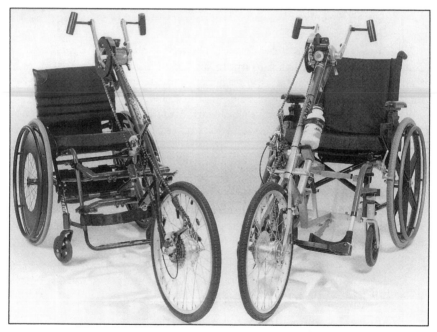

b

(continued)

Figure 9.2   Sport equipment and wheelchairs manufactured by Quickie. (a) Shadow Racers, (b) Shadow Cycle-One, (c) Shadow Quad Rugby, (d) Shadow Mach 3 (for cycling), (e) Shadow 3D (for tennis), (f) Shadow Rigid, (g) Shadow Mono-Ski, and (h) Shadow Kan Ski. Courtesy of Quickie.

c

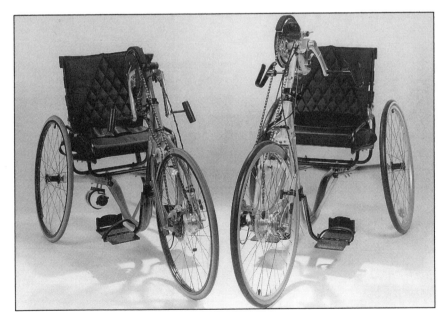

d

Figure 9.2 *(continued)*

e

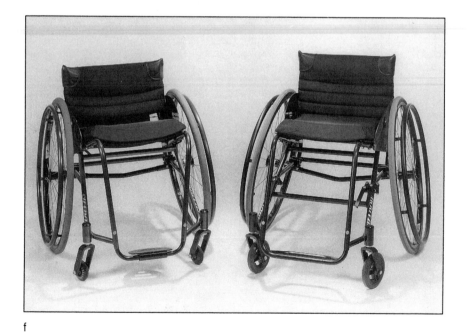

f

Figure 9.2 *(continued)*

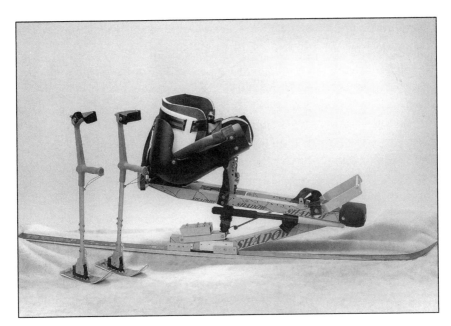

g

h

Figure 9.2 *(continued)*

- Monoski and outrigger poles for downhill skiing
- Sit-skis (or pulk) and poles/picks for winter sports
- Sledge (sleigh apparatus) and ice pick poles for ice picking (skating activity) and sledge or ice hockey
- Specially designed foot or hand prostheses for rock climbing, scuba diving, swimming, skiing, etc.
- Specially designed crutches, canes, or walkers for running, hiking, skating, skiing, soccer, etc.
- Ski-bars for four-track skiing (or learning to ski), outriggers for three- and four-track skiing
- Water Ski Bra, ski boom, hydro slide and monoski for waterskiing
- Beeping baseballs, goal balls, etc., for blind athletes
- Bowling ramp, bowling stick, ball holder, and snap handle bowling ball for physically impaired individuals
- Adapted rowing or cycling ergometers and wheelchair treadmills

a

(continued)

Figure 9.3 Examples of easily made adapted equipment. (a) Golf club adapted for use by a person in a wheelchair; (b) foot guide used by a blind person in archery. Equipment constructed by and photos courtesy of Jim Cowart.

b

Figure 9.3 *(continued)*

TECHNOLOGICAL ADVANCES

Advances in technology have greatly enhanced performances on and off the playing field. Cycling research has been applied to wheelchairs and resulted in lighter and more efficient chairs. Changes in wheelchair design have been dramatic. Various wheel sizes are available now, as well as various handrims, adjustable camber, and adjustable seat size and inclination.

Specialized equipment such as hand and foot prostheses has improved tremendously not only in design and functionality but in weight and aesthetics. Additional specialized equipment, such as skiing outriggers, monoskis, and sledges, has allowed individuals of all disabilities access to sport.

Wheelchair propulsion for movement efficiency has been studied in terms of rim diameter, stroke frequency, seat height, technique, speed, level of impairment, and event (sprint vs. distance). Results vary according to the complexity of the interaction of the variables mentioned above along with the human factor. With the decrease in the chair's mass in addition to individual adaptations of seat height, wheel camber, and handrim sizes, athletic performance has improved substantially over the years. Velocity for wheelchair ambulation has been found to be related to rapid strokes (pushes) on the handrims rather than long strokes. Hand and foot propulsion techniques have been studied in relation to athletic performances.

CONCLUDING COMMENTS

Sport opportunities are increasingly more available for and accessible to individuals with disabilities. Although opportunities are plentiful, barriers to full participation still exist. Sport and adapted equipment exist for any sport in which an individual with disability wishes to participate.

CHAPTER 10

Coaching Athletes With Disabilities

Key to the success of athletes with disabilities is training. Although some-what scarce in the past, coaches of athletes with disabilities are increasing in number. In addition, greater understanding of the application of scien-tific principles to the performance of athletes with disabilities has resulted from the intersection of research and practical experience. The various aspects of coaching outlined in this chapter are based upon general princi-ples and concepts known to work with able-bodied athletes. Where appro-priate, modifications are suggested. This is not intended to be a "how to" chapter. Rather, readers are referred to books and manuals on coaching for the specific sport and encouraged to use the information provided here in terms of understanding appropriate modifications.

TEACHING-LEARNING PROCESSES

People learn at individual rates and in individual styles. That fact cannot be ignored when working with athletes with disabilities because they have the same variability within their population as do able-bodied athletes. Thus, the approaches to teaching by coaches and learning by the athletes will be highly individual. Coaches must strive to identify the best way individual athletes learn and their preferred learning channel.

One's learning channel may be visual, auditory, a combination of both, tactile, kinesthetic, or multisensory (Rich, 1990). A visual learner needs only to see the movement several times in order to perform it. An auditory learner needs only to hear the specifics of the movement described. Some individuals have to see a movement and hear about it at concurrent times or separately. The kinesthetic channel involves manually moving through the range of motion several times so the athlete feels what the movement is like while it is being described. The tactile channel is one in which the concreteness of touching an object is utilized. Some athletes need to try several ways to initially learn a new movement. It is up to the coach and the athlete together to find the best and most efficient way for the athlete to learn a particular movement or concept. Of course, the nature of an athlete's specific disability may have an effect on which channel is chosen.

Once an individual's best mode of learning is established, the coach has a variety of teaching approaches to utilize. Among these approaches are (adapted from Rich, 1990):

- *Whole method*—An approach in which the athlete initially learns a skill all at once. This approach is appropriate when the skill is not very complex, or when the individual has difficulties in conceptual learning or is unable to put the various parts of a skill together.

- *Part-whole method*—This approach breaks down a skill into its parts. The parts are mastered individually and then combined and practiced as a whole. This approach is more suitable for individuals who can stay on-task for periods of time on small parts and not lose interest. This approach may be difficult for individuals who have trouble integrating tasks.

- *Progressive-part method*—This approach utilizes task analysis and progression. The most fundamental part of a skill is taught, and then the next part is taught. These first two parts are combined, and then the next part or two parts are presented, then practiced in combination. Eventually the entire skill is mastered.

APPLICATION OF MOTOR LEARNING PRINCIPLES

Once an athlete's best mode of learning is established and an approach is determined, the coach must then be able to apply principles of motor learning. Motor learning is the study of how individuals acquire motor skills, and these principles are also utilized with able-bodied athletes. They combine content about the psychology of learning and the role of the neurophysical domain. Rich (1990) has provided a list of motor learning principles applicable for working with individuals with disabilities:

- *Recognize that individual learning styles differ.* This aspect concerns itself with the learning channels of individuals and how best to approach learning. There is more variability among individuals with disabilities than among their able-bodied peers.

- *Neurological readiness must be attained to learn skills.* An individual's body must be neurologically as well as neuromuscularly mature. Some individuals with cognitive or motor delays are not developmentally mature enough to learn skills when others of their age are able to do so.

- *Apply the law of effect.* This means that if a learning experience is positive an individual will want to repeat that experience. Coaching an athlete with a disability means that one must be aware of an individual's level of success and try to prevent frustration. Providing a nonthreatening and socially positive environment is also beneficial.

- *Utilize positive reinforcement.* All human beings respond to positive types of reinforcement. This concept is no less true for individuals with disabilities. The ratio of positive to negative reinforcement should be from 4:1 to about 7:1 (Dunn, Morehouse, & Fredericks, 1986).

- *Understand the order in which to present skills.* This concept refers to the fact that the order of learning material is of importance as to how much a learner learns and how much is retained. Should an individual have a short attention span, it is important to present the focus of any content to the athlete early in the practice and to review it again at the very end of the lesson.

- *Learning will vary as to one's rate of acquisition.* It is a known fact that individuals will vary in how quickly they can learn a task. Beginners often show large gains in skills, while those who are highly skilled will make less obvious gains in performance. Individuals with disabilities may progress very rapidly and then plateau for several weeks.

- *Feedback is crucial to skill performance.* Immediate, meaningful, and appropriate feedback is essential for improvement in performance. This is true for any athlete and even more so for individuals with disabilities.

Verbal and nonverbal feedback and physical prompting are effective with individuals with disabilities. It is important not to overwhelm an athlete, particularly one with a cognitive disability, with constant verbal prompting; allow time for processing of information.

- *Set goals for individual and team performance.* Goal setting is a partnership between the athlete and the coach. Every athlete should be able to set realistic goals with the coach's help.

- *Transfer of previously learned skills may or may not occur.* The ability to transfer previously learned skills into different environments and to different sport skills involves a high degree of cognitive ability. For this reason, individuals with cognitive disabilities may have difficulty transferring skills from one environment or skill to another. A good coach will be able to draw similarities between skills for athletes.

- *Retention of skills is facilitated by mastery.* Athletes who practice a skill until mastery is achieved will retain more. Thus, a quality practice is important to retention because it leads to mastery. Practices for an individual with a disability may mean overlearning a skill through frequent practice. The application of these principles will make coaching athletes with disabilities more complete and enjoyable for all parties.

GENERAL PRINCIPLES OF COACHING ATHLETES WITH DISABILITIES

Coaching athletes with disabilities requires many of the same skills as coaching able-bodied athletes. A coach should treat athletes as individuals, and should understand their individual differences and their capabilities. Coaches should then maximize these qualities to the fullest so that each athlete can realize his or her potential (*Australian Coaching Council,* 1989a).

Sometimes individuals with disabilities are limited in their exposure to physical activity, coordination experiences, and fitness levels. However, the main problem facing most individuals with disabilities has been their limited opportunity at a young age to master basic movement patterns. Their confidence levels, interest, and motivation may all be affected because of this (*Australian Coaching Council,* 1989b).

Fitness programs for individuals with disabilities are available to individuals of all abilities. Researchers at the Rick Hansen Centre have developed a series of three booklets (e.g., Walsh, Holland, & Steadward, 1986) that provide individuals who use wheelchairs with specific programs about aerobic fitness, muscular fitness, and flexibility. Exercise videos are also available, as are sport instruction tapes (see Appendix G). Most physical fitness training can be adapted to individual needs and sport. Thus, access to such publications as *Sports 'n Spokes* and *Palaestra,* which regularly provide training regimens of elite athletes with a variety of disabilities, would be helpful. Specialized equipment in the form of arm ergometers, wheelchair ergometers, wheelchair rollers, adapted treadmills, and multipurpose weight machines provides countless methods and approaches for fitness training for individuals who are ambulatory and for athletes with various levels of spinal cord injuries (Paciorek & Jones, 1989).

In countries around the world various training resources are available in scientific journals, fitness magazines, rehabilitation journals, and conference proceedings. Athletes and coaches must increasingly access and utilize these resources in order to remain on the cutting edge of training and to be truly competitive.

Generic concepts of coaching can be applied for athletes with disabilities. Some of these concepts are similar for those athletes without a disability, while others call attention to special needs or concerns (*Australian Coaching Council,* 1989a, b, c, d):

- Understand that athletes with disabilities are people first and disabled second.
- Be knowledgeable of the nature and degree of disability.
- Help athletes to set realistic goals and objectives based upon your knowledge of them as individuals.
- Ask athletes for information about what they can do and how to adapt activities.
- Develop reasonable skill progressions.
- Assist athletes when requested, but do not become overbearing and smother them. It is often best to anticipate when to assist.
- Modify rules as necessary, but do not lose the essence of the activity.
- Provide consistent, reliable, and timely feedback.
- Communicate in a patient, open manner. Have athletes repeat instructions to determine whether they understand them.
- Allow athletes to experience risk, success, and failure. Do not overprotect them.
- Concentrate on what athletes can do. Do not underestimate their abilities.
- Utilize smaller groups when coaching athletes with disabilities so that the ratio of coach to athlete is lower.
- Seek solutions that match athletes' abilities and personalities.
- Coach with an open mind and do not have predetermined limits of performance.

Another consideration when coaching individuals with disabilities is attending to environmental factors that may impact upon performance. Rich (1990) has identified several environmental concerns:

- *Sound.* Sometimes sound can distract an individual's attention from tasks and thus affect movement output quality. At other times sound can be used to set a mood for practice or for assisting an individual with location of objects or direction for running.

- *Lighting.* It is important to light a gymnasium or a field so that objects and lines may be seen easily. However, some individuals may be overstimulated by too much lighting. This factor then causes them to become hyperactive and not focus on training tasks. Likewise, lowering the lighting intensity and position can have a calming effect on individuals.

- *Temperature.* Climate control of gymnasiums or outside is important for individuals with disabilities. A cool environment is preferable to one that is hot and humid. Some individuals have allergies which are activated in a hot and humid climate. A hot and humid climate will also result in a higher fluid loss rate and may impact more quickly on athletes with disabilities.

- *Organization.* The training environment should be organized for optimal practice effect. The size and color of equipment is important. A barrier-free environment is also an important consideration in organizing practices.

Gavron (1991) identified personal attributes that must be a concern of the coach when working with individuals with disabilities. One aspect is the nature, amount, and kind of medications taken. Sometimes medicines are impacted upon by exercise. For example, diabetics may have to adjust the dosage of insulin if participating in athletic events. The sun can interact with certain antibiotics and cause severe reactions. Thus, keeping an accurate record of medications and understanding drug interactions is important for an individual's health and safety. An athlete's eating habits should also concern a coach. Eating the right kinds and amounts of food is important for performance. Skipping meals can lead to hypoglycemia and fainting episodes. A poor diet can also affect muscle strength, endurance, and coordination. In activities where weight is a factor, (e.g., gymnastics, swimming, wrestling) it is important that binge eating and purging not be encouraged.

The main strategy involved when coaching athletes with disabilities revolves around knowledge of the sport content, the biomechanical and kinesiological applications, and one's professional and personal interaction with another human being.

SELECTED DISABILITIES AND SPECIFIC STRATEGIES

When working with athletes with disabilities there may be differences in coaching concepts due to one's disability and the nature of the sport in which one is involved. Thus, it is necessary to indicate specific concepts that are important to quality motor output due to an individual's disability. Coaching techniques for specific sport and recreation activities can be found in such resources as

- Hedrick, Byrnes, and Shaver (1989), *Wheelchair Basketball;*
- Grosse, Cooper, Gavron, Huber, and Stein (1991), *Sport Instruction for Individuals With Disabilities;*
- Paciorek and Jones (1989), *Sports and Recreation for the Disabled: A Resource Handbook;*
- Adams and McCubbin (1991), *Games, Sports and Exercises for the Physically Disabled;* and
- Jones (1988), *A Training Guide to Cerebral Palsy Sports.*

In addition, Special Olympics has developed coaching manuals for its sports. The disability sport groups also provide materials for their coaches and athletes (see Appendix E).

The suggestions offered here are but disability-specific modifications. Coaching techniques and training regimens used with able-bodied athletes should be used as the basis for training and suggested modifications used only as needed. Further, athletes with disabilities should also be consulted for their firsthand knowledge of effective training. See also chapter 8.

Individuals With Mental Retardation/ Developmental Disabilities

Although individuals with mental retardation have a cognitive disability, it should not be inferred that they are incapable of performing physically. In fact, if there are no secondary complications other than the diagnosis of mental retardation, there should not be any limits physiologically speaking. Thus, an individual with mental retardation has the same potential to develop physically as his or her peers. However, because of cognitive limitations and possible secondary complications, there are some specific suggestions to consider when working with individuals who are mentally retarded (Gavron, 1991; Shephard, 1990):

- Check individuals with Down's syndrome for atlanto-axial syndrome prior to participation in any sport program. If present, then eliminate activities that place pressure on the head and neck region.

- Multiple repetitions of a task are required for mastery. Practicing a pattern, skill, or series of skills in a repetitive manner is important for these individuals.

- Allow 5-10 seconds for an individual to respond to directions. There is a tendency to bombard individuals with directions. Because this is a cognitive dysfunction, these individuals need even more time to process information (Dunn, Morehouse, & Fredericks, 1986).

- Demonstration and manual manipulation through the range of motion are the most effective techniques for teaching movement. Physically assisting an individual through the range of motion provides kinesthetic feedback to the individual about the motion. This has been found to be very helpful for individuals with mental retardation.

- Use simple sequences of instructions rather than complex.

- Break tasks down into "chunks" that are sequential and have attainable goals.

- Apply behavior management strategies as needed.

- Be aware that individuals with Down's syndrome are sensitive to heat and humidity.

For those individuals with learning disabilities, some adaptations can be made in regard to coaching. These include:

- Keep directions short and concise.

- Break practice into small segments of high-intensity work.

- Identify the best learning channel for the individual.

- Utilize appropriate behavior management techniques and strategies as needed.

- Provide a structure or routine for practice.

- Provide for a nonthreatening practice environment.

- Develop balance, laterality, directionality, and coordination as needed.

Individuals With Sensory Impairments

Those individuals with hearing or vision impairments can develop into highly skilled athletes. Again, because one part of the sensory-motor integrative system is not functioning doesn't mean that everything else ceases to function. Individuals with sensory impairments can develop physiologically, strengthwise, and skillwise as do their able-bodied counterparts. Athletes with sensory disabilities have participated on the U.S.

Olympic teams in swimming, archery, and track. When working with hearing-impaired individuals, some suggestions include (Adams & McCubbin, 1991; Gavron, 1991; Shephard, 1990):

- Provide diagrams of court layouts or routes for cross-country running and locations for all support services for events.
- Utilize pictures, posters, mirrors, and videotapes for skill development.
- Develop some functional signing skills.
- Do not have athletes who are a lipreaders face you while the sun is in their eyes.
- Develop a system of hand signals for long-distance coaching (Adams & Jones, 1991).
- Work on improving balance, a major factor in quality performance output.

When working with those individuals who are visually impaired there are several specific considerations:

- Become familiar with the sport area by walking around it as with track and downhill skiing courses.
- Use voice, wooden clappers, or an automatic directional beeper for enhancing directional awareness.
- Count steps in activities where approaches are important (e.g., high jump, running long jump, vaulting).
- Use a tether or partner system when involved in running events or track and field events.
- Develop cardiovascular fitness and strength capabilities.
- Have athletes feel the shape, size, and texture of the equipment with which they will work.
- Utilize audiocassettes for instructional techniques.

Individuals With Physical Disabilities

Individuals with physical impairments will demonstrate variance in the amount of physical activity they can do (intensity), duration, frequency, and quality. Two individuals with spinal cord injuries, for example, can have a lesion at the same vertebra level and yet function in different capacities. The same is true for individuals with cerebral palsy. This is what makes the issue of classification so difficult. Although there is generalization about the level of function available, based upon research, the actual level of performance is really a matter of individual functioning. For those individuals who have a physical disability and who are ambulatory, the following suggestions are presented (Gavron, 1991; Shephard, 1990; Portia, 1990):

- Assist individuals in and out of activity positions as needed.
- Adapt positions as needed for most effective performance.
- Have amputees and crutch walkers engage in activities in which the upper torso is the primary focus of the movement.
- Teach amputees and crutch walkers who run how to fall safely.
- Develop range of motion and strength.

For those individuals who have a physical disability and utilize a wheelchair for their activity:

- Have the correct type of wheelchair for the activity.
- Adapt the wheelchair as needed for proper balance.
- Use appropriate tie-downs for wheelchair stability.
- Develop muscular strength, range of motion, and awareness of the center of gravity for activities.
- Understand that positioning may be altered due to the functioning ability of muscles (e.g., individual with cerebral palsy may push the wheelchair backwards).

Coaching athletes with disabilities requires knowledge of the sport and the disability. Having a variety of strategies going into the coaching environment is important, but it is also important to develop strategies that fit the environment and the athlete.

COACHING UNIQUE SPORTS

There are more sports for individuals with disabilities than track and field, basketball, and swimming. Perhaps one of the more unusual aspects of coaching sport for individuals with disabilities is that there are some sport experiences that have been unique to this population. Sledge hockey, sit-skiing, and quad rugby are examples of sports that have developed from adaptations of equipment and rules from able-bodied sports. Sledge hockey involves playing ice hockey on regulation-sized rinks while sitting on a metal-framed, oval-shaped vehicle that has three contact points with the ice. Helmets, gloves, pucks, and shortened sticks are used. Rules

SUE MOUCHA

At a glance:

170 trophies and medals

World Games and U.S. Sports Festival participant

Swimmer, cyclist, and track athlete

Sue Moucha has been involved with competitive sport for the past 12 years. Her participation started with support from what she labels her "sports-minded family." Sue has compiled a record of continuous achievement, from her 1982 3rd-place finish in the 100m backstroke to her 1993 2nd-place medal performances in the 100m freestyle and backstroke.

Sue has an exemplary work ethic. Her workout (5 days a week) consists of swimming 2 hours each day and running 30 minutes 3 days a week. This kind of commitment has enabled Sue to reap benefits from her efforts.

Sue says that her involvement in sport means that she "can keep a competitive edge, go after it." Sport also is a means of physical therapy and keeps her body relaxed from the effects of cerebral palsy.

Sue's suggestions to future athletes include not letting one's disability be an excuse not to practice. She also encourages persons with disabilities to practice with nondisabled athletes and to tap into the resources of nondisabled-athlete coaches.

Sue's participation extends beyond the realm of sports—her numerous civic activities in the Tampa, FL, area are well known. Sue is well educated, trains seriously, and is an excellent representative for sport and for people with cerebral palsy.

follow (for the most part) those for able-bodied ice hockey players (Paciorek & Jones, 1989).

For individuals who cannot use their legs for support, sit-skiing is but one of several forms of skiing available. Several types of sit-skis are available. Individuals who are visually impaired, hearing impaired, or developmentally handicapped utilize a "buddy" system of skiing. Amputees, postpolio hemiplegic skiers, and others with neuromuscular or neurological impairments use three- and four-track skiing. An adaptation known as a "ski bra," which ties together the front tips of skis so that they remain parallel, is often used to teach developmentally handicapped individuals as well as those with visual impairments (Paciorek & Jones, 1989).

Quad rugby combines elements of basketball and soccer while utilizing a penalty system similar to that of hockey. Quad rugby is a team sport for quadriplegics who are unable to participate in the faster game of wheelchair basketball. A volleyball is used, and the game is played in two 20-minute periods in which the goal is to pass, throw, bat, roll, dribble, or carry the ball over the opponent's goal line. Canadians, who originated the sport, have called this game "murder ball" (Adams & McCubbin, 1991; Paciorek & Jones, 1989). It is an intense physical sport.

Other competitive sport opportunities include quad tennis, sculling, beep baseball, blowdarts, cycling, lawn bowling, weight lifting, and table tennis. There are more. What is important is that a coach understands the content of the sport and is able to communicate clearly and effectively with an athlete. To become familiar with any of the unique sports for individuals with disabilities, coaches must utilize the resources of various journals, sport guides, and disability sport magazines that are available worldwide (Appendix I).

CONCLUDING COMMENTS

Competent coaches are critical to the continued improvement of athletic performance of people with disabilities. Knowledge of sport and appropriate adaptations by disability are prerequisites to success. This chapter provided an overview of the fundamentals of working with individuals with disabilities and their application to sport.

CHAPTER 11

Event Management

This chapter reviews the management aspects of a sport event for individuals with disabilities. Brief discussions of the needs for fielding a team for international competition and the particulars of major international competitions are also included.

MANAGING THE SPORT EVENT

Whether a recreation or sport event of small or large proportions, two things are essential for its success: planning and organization. No matter the size, location, or ability of the participants, these two elements are critical for the event to be a success in the perceptions of the participants, the public, and the sponsors. There may, of course, be some additional needs and concerns if the population/participant focus is individuals with disabilities. However, generally there are more commonalities for event management for individuals with disabilities and their able-bodied counterparts than differences.

Initial Planning

One of the most important aspects of planning a recreational or sporting event is to conceptualize the idea. This means talking through the idea, its purpose, and theme in an open, creative, and nonthreatening environment. This process may, at first, bring out a multitude of ideas that may appear to conflict but in actuality serve as a cleansing and focusing function.

A steering committee should consist of an external consultant from the world of business who can objectively answer questions concerning the feasibility of sponsorship and marketing. This person may be from a major business in the community or the chamber of commerce. Other members of the steering committee should include an athlete, a representative from a sporting organization, and someone with experience in field operations for recreational or sporting events. If working with a nearby university or local parks department, a representative from that entity should also be included. But this committee should remain small and manageable.

During the brainstorming sessions, which may last weeks or months, the steering committee should ask the questions suggested in Table 11.1. Another activity of the steering committee may be to engage a consultant to conduct a feasibility study. This study may explore the following questions (adapted from Jackson & Schmader, 1990):

- What type of event is most appropriate?
- What kind of weather is necessary?
- What is the competition in terms of established events in the nation or region?
- Does demographic research indicate that there is a target population?
- What is the attitude of the target population toward a proposed event?
- What kinds of facilities and services are needed?
- What is the nature of community support for the event?
- Has the community supported such events in the past?
- What is the history and potential for financial backing from community businesses?

Additional content may be specified in the consultant's contract. That is, the feasibility study may be as in-depth as the committee specifies in view of the amount of lead time available and the cost. The cost for such

Table 11.1 Questions and Activities for Steering Committee's Agenda

Question	Action
Who can assist us and in what capacity?	Generate a list of names and tentative areas of responsibility.
	Employ a professional consultant.
	Identify potential financial backers.
What kind of events will be held and what kind of facilities do we need?	Identify nature of event: single (swim meet) or multiple sport meet.
	Identify facilities available.
	Identify accessibility issues.
When is this event held?	Timing is absolutely critical: are any other events close to the date?
	Sponsor support lead time.
Where is the event to be held?	Identify facilities.
	Identify lodging potential.
	Identify transportation accessibility.
How do we go about organizing working committees and ancillary services?	Identify the kinds of committees needed and their specific tasks.

Note. This process serves to initially provide some sort of structure for the event. Another purpose is to begin to recruit volunteers to serve on the various committees. It is so much easier to recruit volunteers and backers when the event has a theme, title, logo, and colors. This process lets others know that there is a focus and an accountable group steering the activity.

an undertaking is in proportion to the degree of sophistication of the study and must be a part of the steering committee's first fundraising efforts. Such an activity as a feasibility study should be conducted with enough lead time so that fundraising and financial backers have anywhere from 3 months to a year or two to commit to the event (Jackson & Schmader, 1990). The results of the feasibility study should be utilized throughout the planning and organizing process.

Structure and Organization

After the initial planning stage and when the results of the feasibility study are positive, the organization and structure for the event can be formalized. Either a steering committee of 3-8 members or a board of directors consisting of 10-15 people may be formed. The role of each member on the steering committee or board of directors should be identified. Jackson and Schmader (1990, p. 26) suggested that a board of directors consist of the following:

> Administrative officer from a company to serve as a chair and to coordinate events.
>
> Bank officer or someone with financial acuity about borrowing or lending money.
>
> Public relations, marketing, or advertising expert.
>
> Certified accountant or comptroller.
>
> Leader from the cultural arts community.
>
> Professional tourism, travel, or leisure industry representative.
>
> Law enforcement representative.
>
> Salesperson.
>
> Attorney.
>
> Official from the city or parks department.

The board could also include a medical authority or local emergency medical services representatives. An individual who is experienced with equipment necessary for the conduct of the event may also be appointed at this time or identified later on as the content of the event is specifically identified.

After the board of directors is appointed, the next step is to develop a specific table of organization (TO). This is the result of thinking through and *anticipating* what is needed to run the event in as flawless a manner as possible. The directors must be careful not to overextend themselves by volunteering in too many other aspects of the event. Their job is to delegate to other competent people specific tasks that need to be accomplished for the event to function efficiently. In addition, directors serve as resources for problem solving and dispensing accurate information (see Figure 11.1).

Committees and Functions

Jackson and Schmader (1990, pp. 27-31) identify a number of committees that are necessary for effective event management. All of the following positions need experienced people who are willing to give of their time and expertise so that the best and smoothest possible running of the

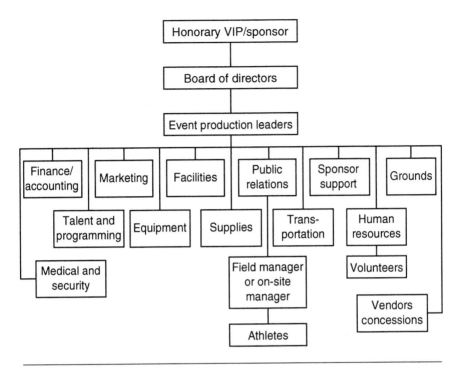

Figure 11.1   An organizational schema for events.

event may be experienced by the participants, coaches, and the spectators. Suggested committees and a brief description of suggested responsibilities follow:

1. *Event production committee*—all committee chairs meet to exchange information on a regular basis and to identify insurance needs for the board of directors.
2. *Transportation committee*—smooth routing of all participants to and from events; acquisition of donated vehicles, drivers, signs for directions; interface with law enforcement representative; special needs for specific venues (e.g., golf carts), and parking.
3. *Talent and program scheduling committee*—entertainment programming, parades, opening and closing ceremonies, celebrities, and workshops.
4. *Sponsorship support committee*—provides financing for the event by selling ad space or renting space to vendors.
5. *Accounting committee*—monetary control, prepare financial statements, IRS status.
6. *Vendors or concessions*—food, beverages, souvenirs, licenses to conduct business, trademark patents, and logo licenses.

7. *Facilities, equipment, and supplies*—securing facilities, purchasing disposable supplies, and purchasing, renting, or borrowing equipment.

8. *Maintenance committee*—grounds, litter control, garbage removal, sanitary conditions.

9. *Human resources committee*—volunteers and paid labor.

10. *Marketing committee*—media relations, advertising, promotions, ticketing, and programs.

11. *Decorations committee*—signs, posters, and banners.

Many of these major committees will have specific subgroups. For example, the marketing committee will have a subgroup for press credentials and one for advertising, which will interface with the sponsorship support committee and the promotions committee. The facilities, equipment, and supplies committee will be divided into the three subgroups, which all must interface with the maintenance committee. The talent and program scheduling committee will need separate subgroups for the opening and closing ceremonies and possibly another subgroup just for awards. Specific job tasks and functions should be identified for each committee and subgroup so that duplication is avoided.

Other committees suggested by Wyness (1984) include a *security committee* and a *medical emergencies committee*. A *technical or electronic committee* would be appropriate to take care of all P.A. system needs, lighting, and computer support needs. A *housing committee* is appropriate for those events lasting more than one day that involve large numbers of participants and VIPs. In many instances, a *VIP committee* is formed in very large events just to see to all their needs (e.g., lodging, transportation, meals, and equipment for clinics).

The Event Venue Field Manager

The event venue field manager is quite possibly the key to running a smooth schedule and successful event; one should be appointed for each sporting event. In track and field this person is identified as the clerk of the course, while in swimming this person is the meet manager.

This person should have organizing skills and patience, be knowledgeable about the rules of the event and how it is organized, understand the organization of the entire workings and know where to refer people who have questions or complaints, and, above all, must communicate well with people so that things are resolved quickly and quietly. The event venue field manager is really the quality control inspector for running any venue. Should the event venue manager have any questions, he or she should be able to contact the head of any major committee by radio to get information quickly and accurately. This reduces confusion. Having a roving troubleshooter on the field at all times is also a good strategy.

This person should be clearly identified so that coaches and venue managers may receive assistance.

EVENT MANAGEMENT FOCAL POINTS FOR INDIVIDUALS WITH DISABILITIES

Several focal points need to be addressed when staging an integrated or segregated event for individuals with disabilities. The particular areas of emphasis include (a) physical accessibility to housing, sport or activity venues, eating establishments, and transportation, and (b) medical support needs to address the effects of weather, cultural differences, the nature of a particular disability and the effects of training, and media exposure.

The one experience that can frustrate any participant in a recreational or sporting event is that of physical barriers. When considering housing or hotel/motel accommodations, it is necessary to ascertain the specific nature of accessibility. Because housing units are built at different times, the laws governing accessibility are different. What is accessible to one person may be inaccessible to another. Acquiring a specific list of accessible features is helpful, as is a personal tour of the lodging. Some considerations in declaring a lodging accessible include the following:

- Wide doorways.
- Elevators.
- Entrances to bathrooms are wide enough for wheelchairs, and there is space to maneuver the wheelchair once in the bathroom.
- Showers and bathtubs are wheelchair high for easy transferability.
- Ramps are available wherever there are different levels.
- Signs in Braille or large print.
- Emergency system (e.g., lights, horns).

Access to sport and activity venues must also be accommodating. Bleachers should have areas specifically for individuals with disabilities. The paths that lead to a venue need to be paved and free of cracks or other debris that would impede a person in a wheelchair or a visually impaired person. Basketball courts should have an area set aside for individuals in wheelchairs that is within five feet of the end line. Fields of play for soccer, softball, or track and field should be of the highest quality so that individuals will not step into holes or sink into mud. Additional parking space for individuals whose vehicles are so designated should be made available. Should there not be any parking within a reasonable distance, then alternate means of transportation should be made available for those who need it (e.g., use of golf carts). These are little things, but they do impact upon both participants' and spectators' impressions of an event.

Another important concern for participants and spectators alike is access to eating establishments within the community. Such accessibility issues as large-print menus, willingness to fix special diets (low fat, low salt, low cholesterol, and low sugar), accessible bathrooms, and wide doorways are important. Entering a restaurant by the back door is not accessibility! Another concern would be to sensitize service personnel to speak directly to individuals with disabilities. Attending to these aspects will certainly attract repeat business.

Transportation for participants must be available. This is especially true for a multiday, large event in which athletes, coaches, and support staff are housed in dormitory settings such as those of a university campus or motel settings in town. The distance from housing to sport venues must be taken into account. Contestants should not have to plan to walk for 30 minutes to get to a venue. Should long distances from housing to sport venues be a concern, then alternative means of transportation must be provided. The most common method is that of using buses or vans. A daily schedule of times and stop points should be posted in conspicuous places and included in the information packet for athletes and coaches. Ramps may have to be built so that individuals in wheelchairs have access to buses. Volunteers should be recruited for major stop points to assist in offloading individuals as needed. Finally, the use of golf carts for short distances and emergency troubleshooting are other ways to assist.

Some of the most important aspects of event management concern the organization and information of the efforts of the participants. This translates into who participates in what event, which heat at what time, and what day. Having the support staff to run computer programs is an absolute necessity. Getting information to venue heads is essential if a reasonable time schedule is to be met. This is particularly true if staying outside in prolonged heat or cold may be detrimental to an individual with a specific type of disability. The U.S. Cerebral Palsy Sports Association has a computer program for event managers that is comprehensive and easy to use.

It is important to avoid using inappropriate methods for providing participant information. An example is the use of a plastic wrist band which may have the events listed for a particular individual (similar to a hospital band) or the wearing of a participant number with all sorts of identifying information on the back of it. Using a picture ID, similar to other athletic events, on a chain around the neck is more appropriate.

Prior to the actual event, organizers should

- obtain necessary licenses, permits for the grounds.
- determine fees necessary for special events or entertainment.
- acquire appropriate insurance coverage for all, including volunteers.
- secure signed agreements for vendors (concessions) and souvenir sales.
- develop a written plan for police assistance and security measures.
- develop a list of assistants, their job assignments, and their work schedules.
- secure contract for health and maintenance services (Wyness, 1984).

MEDICAL SUPPORT NEEDS

Organizers for any sporting event, regardless of its size, must take into account the medical needs of both the spectators and the athletes. Martinez (1991) has identified the needs for spectator care being concerned with planning: Planning for large events should include evacuation strategies in the event of sudden natural disaster or terrorism, disaster response structure (incident command structure), roles and responsibilities of various medical personnel, and supply resources and storage. Additionally, medical responders should be prepared for dehydration from alcohol, insect stings, cardiac and diabetic events, seizures, allergies, and pedestrian injuries. Other recommendations for spectator care include the following:

- Clear directional signs.
- Clean floor surfaces.
- Adequate lighting.
- Handrails to prevent falls.
- Easily identifiable first-aid signs.
- Padding for temporary structural hazards.
- Environmental and weather conditions should be anticipated, and medical personnel should be familiar with stadium design (Carlson, 1992).

Martinez (1991) further recommends that an *incident command system* (ICS) be established for handling multiple spectator injuries. Briefly, ICS is a system by which a senior officer in law enforcement or a firefighter takes command of a multiple persons injury situation by coordinating resources, site safety, security, and communications so that a command structure develops on-scene. "In particular the medical division would have four components activated: triage, treatment, morgue, and transport. Medical personnel should understand their assignments beforehand and report to a predetermined station in the event of a multiple injury situation" (Martinez, 1991, p. 43).

The care and treatment of athletes with disabilities generally follow those recommendations for able-bodied athletes. That is, any event should have medical staff support in proportion to the number of participants and venues. Medical staff support can mean personnel such as certified athletic trainers, physical therapists, first responders, EMTs, paramedics, or physicians. Additionally, the local hospital community should be notified of the event, the number of individuals expected, and the nature of their disability. This linkage is necessary to assist the hospital, for example, in identifying persons who can interpret for the hearing impaired or for international competitors. The local fire department should also be notified and involved in the planning inasmuch as their ambulance service may play a role in transporting individuals to the hospital. The input from the fire department is especially critical in establishing entrance and exit points from various parts of the games site.

The overall planning for medical support services should be overseen by a physician, preferably one who is familiar with emergency medicine and with individuals with disabilities. It is preferable that this physician work with the facility manager (Carlson, 1992, p. 142). The plan for medical services should be established so that all participants, coaches, and medical support staff know where to go for assistance. This is also true for those who run the sport venues and organize volunteers. Knowing where to go in an emergency will save time, which could be critical in treatment. Thus, clear signs for first-aid stations are an absolute necessity. It is also helpful if all medical support personnel wear a distinctive color, hat, or uniform. Medical information in the form of where first-aid stations are located, how to obtain assistance during the day and after hours, and where hospitals are located should be made available to all coaches, participants, and parents in the coach's handbook and other materials routinely distributed to all prior to the event.

Medical supplies should include various kinds of insulin for individuals with diabetes, antiseizure medications, and allergy medications. Various straps for positioning individuals with spinal cord injuries or cerebral palsy may also be helpful. Access to a current *Physicians Desk Reference for Drugs* (PDR) would be another useful item available to key first aid stations because many individuals with disabilities are taking several kinds of medication at once.

Information about each athlete and the specific nature of the disability along with any medications or allergies should be with every coach at all times or entered into a computerized system to ensure instant access. Because of the interactions of certain drugs or allergies to certain substances it is important that this information be available to medical support staff. This is especially true for those individuals who are speech impaired or nonverbal. Another concern from a medical point of view is the effect of climate and cultural changes on international athletes. Sometimes extreme changes in either can trigger seizures or allergic reactions.

When working with athletes with disabilities, there is still a possibility that all are not equally trained in terms of physiological conditioning. This factor may cause some problems at the conclusion of an event rather than during it. It is therefore helpful to find out the exact nature of the event in which a person was participating and whether they had trained adequately; this may impact the nature of the medical crisis. Other aspects that may cause problems include (a) the weather (in cold rainy weather, for example, asthmatics may have trouble breathing and amputees may develop hypothermia more easily) and (b) prostheses, which may need repair and may cause blistering or other soft tissue types of injury. Thus, including prosthesis and wheelchair repair resources as part of the medical support team is recommended.

From an administrative standpoint, some aspects of medical support services will interface with other areas. For example, a communications system is needed strictly for medical support services. Communications must be available from the field to a central point (e.g., hospital or physician in charge) and to the fire department for transportation needs. Transportation must be established not only during the day for events but also during the evening if participants are housed in university dorms. Emergency routing must be identified by law enforcement agencies and emergency personnel. Supplies and access to supplies must be arranged so that all aid stations are well stocked. The medical support staff need to have a system of command established for each shift and to identify the roles and responsibilities of various personnel. All of this planning should occur prior to the event and should be evaluated after its conclusion (Martinez, 1991).

Media and Individuals With Disabilities

Media exposure is another important aspect of event management. Any event should have a public relations specialist or a complete press center, although one or two people may handle smaller events. A press center should be large enough to hold press representatives, phone lines, computers, tables, food, and preassembled press kits. However, even the best equipped media center cannot make sure that individuals with disabilities are treated as hard news or sport stories. Often the stories are classified as human interest rather than as legitimate sport stories. The only avenue open is to present the most professional press releases possible and run the media operations as if the event were for able-bodied athletes. The atmosphere of the press center imparts a sense of what is going on to the media, and they will take their cue from it. Emphasize that these individuals are athletes first and disabled second.

ANATOMY OF INTERNATIONAL SPORT EVENTS

In planning and implementing a sport event for athletes with disabilities, it is important to be cognizant of, and perhaps model, the program provided at the major international competitions for athletes with disabilities (e.g., Paralympics, Paralympics for the Mentally Handicapped, World Games for the Deaf, Special Olympics International). Although these are very complex undertakings, the following information is provided as examples of those things that can be included as an integral part of a sport event for athletes with disabilities.

All of these aforementioned competitions include grandiose opening and closing ceremonies. Opening ceremonies have typically included

- a march of athletes;
- colorful displays of logos and mascots;
- parade of flags;
- official welcomes by host country government officers and official representatives of sport organizations (e.g., IOC, IPC, IFs);
- the athletes' oath;
- official anthems and other musical presentations;
- lighting of the torch; and
- various forms of entertainment including fireworks, celebrities, and the like.

With similar activities, closing ceremonies tend to continue this festive nature of the competition and the celebration of athletic performance and include the passing on of the games to representatives from the site of the next games and extinguishing of the "Olympic" flame. Opening and closing ceremonies are held in large arenas or stadia that can accommodate (tens of) thousands of spectators, athletes, coaches, officials, etc. (Souvenir books are usually produced to commemorate the games.)

In addition to the sport program offered at each of these international competitions, social and cultural programs are offered for spectators as well as athletes and coaches. These often include games rooms, social tents, evening dances and performances, collector pins trading centers, food booths, and souvenir vendors. T-shirts, pins, buttons, pens, sportswear, postcards, commemorative stamps and postmarks, hats, visors, etc., are often offered for sale during the competitions. In addition, official photographers make pictures of competitors and events available for purchase.

Usually a "newspaper" of the games is published daily. In such papers are the results of competitions held the day before, medal count standing, feature articles on selected athletes or sport leaders, and so on. For these international competitions, a media center is centrally located. Reporters from around the world are provided with press credentials and given space, typewriters, and phones to facilitate media coverage. In addition, official press releases are written daily. Often representatives of the media (news reporters for print and visual media, reporters for sport magazines like *Palaestra* or *Sports 'n Spokes*) are supplied with pertinent written information about the games, profiles of selected athletes, list of contacts, etc., as well as gifts, film, and free development.

These competitions require that attendees receive appropriate credentials primarily for security reasons and logistics. Among the categories used for badges are the following: athletes, coaches, officials, press, invited guests (VIPs), officers, national delegates, medical staff, organizing committee, volunteers. The type of badge obtained often carries with it restrictions on access to the various venues of the games.

Medical services for athletes and spectators at major international competitions are provided in a variety of ways. For example, an area for prosthesis and wheelchair repair is provided at the Paralympics. This area is not only staffed by experts but also includes space and equipment necessary for self-repair. In addition, first aid stations and medical emergencies areas are dispersed throughout the grounds. These facilities and services are accessible to all.

In addition to the athletic competitions and social programs, opportunity and space for classification, athlete certification, official meetings, coaches and athlete training workshops, and drug testing are commonly provided. Scientific congresses may also be included before the games (e.g., the Paralympic Scientific Congress preceding the 1996 Paralympic Games in Atlanta).

The athletes and coaches are housed in an Athletes' Village (Paralympic Village). These tend to be areas reserved for athletes and coaches. Included in these villages are restaurants, residences, religious services, television, library, cinema, information centers, discotheque, game rooms, and commercial services such as public telephones, post office, hairdressers, travel agency, bank and automatic tellers, photographic services, and florist (*Guide of the Barcelona '92 IX Paralympic Games*, 1992).

FIELDING A NATIONAL TEAM
FOR INTERNATIONAL COMPETITION

It takes a concerted effort by many people to field a national team for international competitions. Preparations are actually begun years in advance, but most of the work is accomplished during the months preceding the competitive event. The logistics of fielding a team include selecting the athletes and coaches, identifying support staff, selecting the chef de mission (person in charge) and board of directors, coordinating the disability sport organizations, and securing necessary financial support.

CONCLUDING COMMENTS

The most important aspect of event management is planning and anticipation (Wyness, 1984). Entire books written on event management detail the kinds of committees needed and the functions of each. This chapter has provided an overview of event management and highlighted those things necessary to consider when planning and implementing a recreation or sport event for individuals with disabilities. A glimpse was included of the complexity of fielding a national team for major international competitions as well as the anatomy of selected international events.

PART III

Issues in Sport
and Disability

CHAPTER 12

Research and Athletes With Disabilities

Research about sport and individuals with disabilities has evolved along with the disability sport movement. The early years saw research focused on rehabilitation or on growth and development of individuals with physical and mental disabilities (DePauw, 1985a; Huber, 1984; Lindstrom, 1984; Lipton, 1970; Rarick, Dobbins, & Broadhead, 1976), whereas the post–World War II efforts focused on programming. The modern era of disability sport research started in the late 1970s.

EARLY RESEARCH EFFORTS

In the 1960s, emphasis was placed upon physical fitness parameters (strength, flexibility, weight) of those with mental retardation, as well as perceptual-motor development and social development (Broadhead, 1986; DePauw, 1986b; Dunn, 1987; Pyfer, 1986; Stein, 1983). During the 1970s research was conducted on exercise physiology and biomechanics (De-Pauw, 1988; Gass & Camp, 1979; Zwiren & Bar-Or, 1975). The exercise physiology research was confined to understanding disabled athletes' levels of fitness or conditioning and their response to exercise, whereas the biomechanics research was focused on wheelchair propulsion. Subjects included wheelchair users, individuals with postpolio, and spinal cord injured individuals. Since the 1970s, research has increased significantly and has become sport and disability specific as well as discipline oriented and performance based (DePauw, 1988). For an excellent overview of research, see Shephard (1991).

USOC COMMITMENT TO RESEARCH

A commitment to disability sport research was formalized in 1985 when the United States Olympic Committee (USOC) agreed with the Committee on Sport for the Disabled (COSD) to establish a special subcommittee concerning research on sport for the disabled.

This research subcommittee interviewed coaches, athletes with disabilities, and professionals in the field of recreation and adapted physical education and came up with seven areas of concern:

Effects of training and/or competition

Selection and training of coaches, volunteers, officials

Technological advances in sport research

Sociological/psychological aspects of sport

Differences/similarities between disabled and nondisabled athletes

Demographics of sport for the disabled

Legal, philosophical, and historical bases for sport (DePauw, 1988, p. 293)

As a result of this survey, over 70 different topics were identified. These topics were meant to be a starting point for the next generation of researchers.

IPC COMMITMENT TO RESEARCH

In 1993, the IPC established a sport science committee as an indication of its commitment to sport science research and the advancement of knowledge about Paralympic sport. In April 1994, a seminar on sport science and athletes with disabilities was held at the German Olympic Institute in Berlin. In attendance were the members of the IPC Sport Science Committee and representatives from the International Federation of Adapted Physical Activity. The IPC committee was chaired by Dr. Gudrun Doll-Tepper from the Free University of Berlin.

As a result of the seminar, the mission, goals, and objectives for the IPC sport science committee were established. In addition, guidelines for research conducted at Paralympic Games and world championships were developed, guidelines for the conduct of the Paralympic Congress and International Symposium were proposed, and a plan for preparing a Paralympic research agenda was prepared. Initial efforts for setting a research agenda included the development of selected position statements, a monograph series on Paralympic sport, an international directory of sport scientists, and a database of research on disability sport.

SUMMARY OF SELECTED RESEARCH FINDINGS

Of value to understanding and reading the sport and disability research literature are articles/abstracts contained in the *Adapted Physical Activity Quarterly, Completed Research in Health, Physical Education, Recreation, and Dance*, and *Abstracts of Research Presentations at the American Alliance for Health, Physical Education, Recreation, and Dance Convention*. Other publications include *Physical Educator, Palaestra, Physician and Sportsmedicine, Research Quarterly for Exercise and Sport, Rehabilitation Yearbook, Journal of Teaching Physical Education, Medicine and Science in Sport and Exercise*, and selected special education journals. For a listing of selected periodicals about sport and disability sport, see Appendix I. The Sport Information Resource Clearinghouse has published two comprehensive bibliographies on disability sport research. In addition, a database for research on wheelchair sport has been established by the British Wheelchair Sports Foundation and the Department of Physical Education, Sport Sciences, and Recreation Management at Loughborough University, Loughborough, England.

Generalizations about the results of research in physical education and sport for individuals with disabilities should be avoided or at least interpreted cautiously because of the individualistic and preliminary nature of some of the research. The diversity of the disabled population and the small number of subjects limit generalization capability. On the other hand, a synthesis and summation of completed research could provide a knowledge base for and about disability sport, indicate trends, and identify further research needs.

Biomechanics

Wheelchair propulsion for movement efficiency has been studied in terms of rim diameter, stroke frequency, seat height, technique, speed, level of impairment, and event (sprint vs. distance) (Higgs, 1983, 1986; Sanderson & Sommer, 1985; York & Kimura, 1986). Results are varied due to the complexity of the interaction of the variables mentioned above along with the human factor. With the decrease in the mass of the chair in addition to individual adaptations of seat height, wheel camber, and handrim sizes, athletic performance has improved substantially over the years. Velocity for wheelchair ambulation has been found to be related to rapid stroking (pushes) on the handrims rather than long strokes. Hand and foot propulsion techniques have been studied in relation to athletic performances of individuals with disabilities.

Studies of gait performance of elite athletes with disabilities include the effect of prosthetic design on amputee performance (Enkola, Miller, & Burgess, 1982; Gandee, Datta, Chatterjee, & Roy, 1973; Kegel, Burgess, Starr, & Daly, 1981). Visually impaired athletes' running and walking gaits have also been studied (Arnhold & McGrain, 1985; Dawson, 1981; Gorton & Gavron, 1987; Pope, McGrain, & Arnhold, 1986). Biomechanical gait studies in running and racewalking have also been conducted with individuals with developmental disabilities and cerebral palsy (Gorton & Gavron, 1987; Skrotsky, 1983). Steadward and colleagues from the Rick Hansen Centre have studied the kinematics of wheelchair propulsion.

Biomechanics research has been conducted both in the field and in laboratory settings. There is a need to replicate studies in both environments to increase the subject pool and improve accuracy in generalizing the results for application for the athletes and coaches. Biomechanical research may lead to better-designed wheelchairs and mono-skis and to improved performance in all sport areas.

Classification

Classification of athletes with disabilities for competition has been a long-standing controversy. On one hand, the goal of classification seems to be to enable each competitor, regardless of severity of impairment, to compete in a fair manner with others of similar ability/disability (a more medically based classification system). On the other hand, the goal of classification based upon functional ability applied to sport is to provide for meaningful athletic competition based upon ability, not disability, and thus tends to eliminate the more severely impaired from elite athletic competition. This latter goal of classification has emerged as a result of the administrative problem and logistics of numerous classes for competitions: more than 70 100m races by gender and disability type—3 for blind, 8 for cerebral palsy, 9 for amputee, 6 for les autres, 7 for wheelchair users, and 42 for spinal cord (below C6) injured males and females (Higgs, Babstock, Buck, Parsons, & Brewer, 1990).

Wheelchair basketball, swimming and track and field have been at the forefront of the classification controversy (Brasile, 1990a, 1990b; Gehlsen & Karpuk, 1992; Richter, Adams-Mushett, Ferrara, & McCann, 1992). The medical versus functional issues can be found in the literature from 1979 onward (Lindstrom, 1985; McCann, 1979; Thiboutot, 1986; Weiss & Curtis, 1986).

The results of research conducted on classification have been mixed, and these are often undertaken and reported based upon the differing goals identified above. Differences found in athletic performances in track and field by gender, distance, and class of athletes (Coutts & Schultz, 1988; Ridgeway, Pope, & Wilkerson, 1988; Wicks, Oldridge, Cameron, & Jones, 1983) have been used to support the need for classification for fairness. On the other hand, the findings reported by Higgs et al. (1990), as well as Gorton and Gavron (1987), support a reduction in the number of classifications. (For more information on classification, see chapter 7.)

Coaches

Because the number of sporting events and opportunities has increased so dramatically during the past several years, the problem of finding enough coaches continues. DePauw and Gavron (1991) found that athletes with disabilities have, for the most part, practiced on their own until recently. And although the literature for able-bodied sport is replete with studies on coach role conflict, burnout, gender issues, and role modeling (Capel, Sisley, & Desertrain, 1987; Decker, 1986; Knoppers, 1987; Whitaker & Molstead, 1988), there is a paucity of research available about coaches for athletes with disabilities (DePauw & Gavron, 1991).

That there is a need for the study of coaches, officials, and volunteers is not disputed. DePauw (1986b) summarized the areas of needed study as identified by the research subcommittee of the Committee on Sports for the Disabled (COSD) of the United States Olympic Committee (USOC). Specifically, broad topics were identified as "the training, selection, effectiveness, evaluation, and the advisability of volunteers versus paid staff" (DePauw, p. 294). Some of the research topics put forth included

a. comparing the performance of athletes when coached by volunteers, trained able-bodied coaches, and specific sport experts,

b. effectiveness of various coaches' training programs,

c. development of coaching certification for coaches of disability sport,

d. development of training programs for coaches of youth sport, and

e. profiling the background and training of current coaches.

As the sport movement for individuals with disabilities moves forward, the role of the coach becomes significant. DePauw and Gavron (1991) studied 155 coaches of disability sport and found the following:

- Approximately 71% of the coaches were between the ages of 20 and 40.
- Only 16% of the coaches were themselves disabled.
- Over 85% of the coaches held college degrees.
- Many of the coaches indicated that they had coached able-bodied athletes longer than athletes with disabilities.
- Over 75% of the coaches had attended a workshop on coaching techniques, but only 56% had attended workshops on coaching athletes with disabilities.
- The amount of time they actually coached varied by sport and association.
- More males than females tended to be involved in coaching.

This study indicates a need for more coaches who are better trained and who have access to practice facilities and time for practice. They also need more training via workshops or the certification route. Athletes with disabilities should be encouraged to become trained coaches. The importance of coaches and athletes with hearing impairments is demonstrated by the fact that initial involvement in Deaf sport usually results from contact with its coaches and athletes (Stewart, McCarthy, & Robinson, 1988).

Exercise Physiology

Although differences exist, athletes with disabilities exhibit responses to exercise similar to those of able-bodied athletes. Generally, the "true" differences found are caused by differences in functional muscle mass resulting from paralysis, amputation, or osteoporosis in paralyzed limbs and the severity of the physical impairment. Differences might be caused by difficulties of comprehension, motivation, or mechanical inefficiency related to specific types of impairment (e.g., mental retardation, cerebral palsy) (Shephard, 1990). In these cases, it remains unclear whether the differences in physiological responses are caused by differences in physiological functioning or in assessment techniques.

As would be expected, wheelchair athletes who compete in track and swimming events have larger maximum oxygen intake than those who compete in strength events. Regular physical activity by wheelchair athletes can increase cardiac stroke volume; paraplegic athletes have been shown to experience greater increases than do quadriplegics (Shepherd, 1990).

Training regimens for elite athletes with disabilities should include principles and practices followed by able-bodied athletes with adaptations as needed. Although a specific disability may affect the degree of intensity, duration, and frequency of exercise, there is enough evidence to suggest that physiological training effects can be achieved with individuals with disabilities (Burke, Auchinachie, Hayden, & Loftin, 1985; Cameron, Ward, & Wicks, 1978; Coutts, Rhodes, & McKenzie, 1983; Coutts & Steryn, 1987; Cowell, Squires, & Raven, 1986; Shephard, 1990). In times of practical application, it may be necessary to change or adapt body position or the number of repetitions and sets. It is also important to adjust the direction, especially for those individuals who can only propel the chair backwards (e.g., person with severe cerebral palsy).

Other exercise physiology studies have been conducted with below-knee and above-knee amputees (Davis, Shepard, & Jackson, 1981; Ryser, Erickson, & Calahan, 1988), hearing impaired athletes (Lewis, Higam, & Cherry, 1985), individuals with cerebral palsy (Birk et al., 1983; Birk et al., 1984; McCubbin & Shasby, 1985), and developmentally handicapped athletes (Rimmer & Kelly, 1991). In all instances there were not enough studies to generalize nor were numbers of subjects robust. Additional research in this area would further benefit those athletes and coaches who seek state-of-the art training regimens.

Female Athletes With Disabilities

Few investigations could be found in which gender-specific or gender-neutral phenomena were studied. Sherrill and Rainbolt (1987) found that female cerebral palsied athletes exhibited "normal" rather than high or low self-actualization profiles. DePauw and Gavron (1991) found that more males than females coached for international competitions. In a cross-cultural comparison of athletes from the United States, Great Britain, and Japan reported by Fung (1992), male disabled athletes were found to enter sport for reasons of achievement and obtaining status, whereas female disabled athletes were motivated more by friendship.

In a study of the Profile of Moods States (POMS), French, Henschen, and Horvat (1985) found that 62 female wheelchair basketball players exhibited the "iceberg" profile: high vigor and low tension, depression, anger, fatigue, and confusion. In comparison between male and female wheelchair athletes, Horvat, French, and Henschen (1986) found that females scored significantly higher on depression, anger, fatigue, and confusion and lower on vigor. In additional studies, gender differences were found for blind athletes by Mastro, Sherrill, Gench, and French (1987) but not for athletes with cerebral palsy (Canabal, Sherrill, & Rainbolt, 1987; Goodbrand, 1987). Specifically, male blind athletes were found to exhibit the iceberg profile, whereas the elite female blind athletes did not.

Virtually unstudied is the experience of females with disabilities and sport. Although both male and female athletes with disabilities have been studied, males are included more frequently, and in some instances sex differences are ignored. Gender, as a specific variable, has yet to be systematically investigated in the disability sport literature (DePauw, 1994).

As previously noted there is a paucity of research concerning girls and women by disability and by sport. Research questions abound about gender differences in physical parameters (physiological, biomechanical), locus of control, self-determination, satisfaction, and peak experience. By studying the uniqueness of female athletes with disabilities, it may be possible to understand how to encourage more participation as well as to strive for better sport performances.

Sport Injuries and Sports Medicine

Injuries during sport participation and competition found among athletes with disabilities are similar to sport injuries common to able-bodied athletes. The frequency of a selected injury (e.g., blisters from wheelchair propulsion) may vary depending on the specific disability.

In order of frequency, these injuries include soft tissue injuries (sprains, strains, muscle pulls, tendinitis), blisters, lacerations/abrasions/cuts, pressure sores, temperature regulation disorders, fractures, and head and face injuries (Curtis, 1982; Bloomquist, 1986).

Simulated conditions in the laboratory setting need to be studied as well as field-based settings for injury mechanisms related to heat, humidity, cold, snow, or rain by disability and sport. Prevention and treatment of sport injuries need to be further addressed.

Further study on the effect of prescribed drugs also needs to be undertaken, especially if those drugs are on the ban list for athletes at the national or international level. Drug testing of athletes with disabilities and its full ramifications for competition is an area of scientific investigation currently being initiated.

Finally, athletic trainers need to understand the needs of elite athletes with disabilities and be trained to understand the etiology of disability and its effects on motor output. To assist in these areas, a national sport injury registry has been established, similar to the one existing for able-bodied athletes (Ferrara, 1990).

Sport Psychology/Sport Sociology

Research in the psychosocial dimension of athletes with disabilities is in the "exploratory stage of inquiry" (Sherrill, 1990, p. 357). Interdisciplinary research efforts as well as research conducted from a theoretical framework are needed to move research into its next phase. Goodling and Asken (1986a) identified the lack of research in this area and the fact that many conclusions are not scientifically founded.

More similarity than difference has been reported in studies comparing athletes with disabilities and able-bodied athletes on psychological parameters. Consistently, the iceberg profile (below-average tension, depression, anger, fatigue, and confusion; above-average vigor) has been reported with wheelchair athletes and visually impaired athletes. Athletes with disabilities have also demonstrated similar responses to failure/success and measures of anxiety as seen with able-bodied peers.

Of all the studies conducted on mood states of athletes with disabilities, the majority of the samples exhibited the iceberg profile regardless of gender, type of sport, level of skill, and sport setting (Sherrill, 1990). As a result, it appears as if disabled athletes are more similar than different when compared to able-bodied athletes during training and competition.

Sport socialization (the process through which one enters sport) among athletes with disabilities has received some attention in the research literature. Sport socialization has been found to be different when comparing blind and cerebral palsy athletes with able-bodied athletes. In contrast to able-bodied athletes, the family and home were found not to be of primary importance for blind and CP athletes (Lugo, Sherrill, & Pizarro, 1992; Sherrill, Rainbolt, Montelione, & Pope, 1986). Blind students tended to rate their physical education teacher and their school as more important. For wheelchair athletes in the VIII Pan Am Games, self-motivation, disabled friends, and physical educators were the three leading factors for facilitating sport participation (Gavron, 1989).

Disabled athletes (wheelchair, cerebral palsied, blind) were found to hold the same perceptions, cognitive behaviors, and psychological profiles as able-bodied athletes. Self-concept varied depending on one's level of physical ability.

Cross-cultural comparisons regarding sport participation by athletes with disabilities are virtually nonexistent. Fung (1992) discovered significant differences among athletes with disabilities from United States, Great Britain, and Japan in terms of motive factors of fitness, team atmosphere, and excitement and challenge. These differences were similar to those among able-bodied athletes and most likely related to the sociocultural and sociopolitical content of a given country rather than differences between able-bodied and disabled athletes. For example, in a study of Chinese disabled athletes, the physical education teacher was found to be the primary socializing agent for sport (Wang & DePauw, 1991). On the other hand, no differences were found among Swedish athletes and their socialization into sport by disability status (with or without disability) (Johansson & DePauw, 1991).

Technology

Advances in technology over the years have greatly enhanced and contributed to the improved performances of athletes with disabilities on and off the playing field. Cycling research has been applied to wheelchairs and resulted in lighter and more efficient chairs. Various wheel sizes are available now as well as various handrims, adjustable camber, and adjustable seat size and inclination (Brubaker, 1984; Brubaker & McLaurin, 1982; Engel & Hildebrandt, 1974; Floyd, Gutmann, Noble, Parks, & Ward, 1966; Hale, 1988; Higgs, 1983, 1992; Smith, 1990; Walsh, Manchiori, & Steadward, 1986; Wirta, Golbranson, Manson, & Calvo, 1990).

Specialized equipment such as hand and foot prostheses has improved tremendously not only in design and functionality but in weight and aesthetics. Additional specialized equipment has allowed individuals of all disabilities access to sport, including devices for the hearing-impaired and visually impaired. Skiing outriggers, mono-skis, and sledges have allowed select physically disabled athletes to participate in sport.

TRENDS IN DISABILITY SPORT RESEARCH

Research since the 1980s has been geared toward understanding the scientific bases of performance, physiological as well as mechanical. Psychological and sociological factors (e.g., state anxiety, motivation, socioeconomic factors, sport socialization) affecting individuals with disabilities were studied for nearly the first time just recently. The application of technology to the motor performance of athletes with disabilities took the form of research on movement efficiency through wheelchair design, adapted equipment, and prostheses design. Sport has been studied in terms of the effects of training, sport injuries, selection and training of coaches, sociological/psychological aspects of sport, and the physiological and biomechanical principles of sport performance.

The classification systems used in disability sport have also been studied. Most recently, cross-cultural comparisons have been undertaken.

Athletes of all ages with all types and degrees of physical, sensory, and learning impairments have been studied. Although studies have used both male and female subjects, relatively few have focused on females. Since the 1980s, the sport research, which was once more specific to the disability, has been conducted with emphasis on specific sports (e.g., road racing, wheelchair basketball, sprinting, volleyball, javelin, skiing) as well as by disability. The subdivisions of disabled sport research have become increasingly more distinct and fall along disciplinary lines (e.g., sport sociology, sport psychology, biomechanics). These trends are expected to continue into the next century, as there are still many unanswered questions in these areas.

When taken collectively, several trends have emerged out of the research conducted on individuals with disabilities. In general, the findings have tended to support ability more than disability, more similarities with able-bodied peers than differences, and performance rather than description of motor ability. Relative to disability sport, the research has become sport specific, disability specific, designed for enhancing performance, and discipline oriented (e.g., sociology, exercise physiology) (DePauw, 1988).

FUTURE RESEARCH DIRECTIONS

Research efforts must continue in support of athletes with disabilities and their involvement in sport. Research is needed in the following areas (adapted from DePauw, 1988):

- Movement efficiency—research on the mechanical and physiological factors underlying performance including wheelchair design, adapted sport equipment, and applied technology;

- Sport performance—research on the effectiveness of training regimens and coaching techniques, appropriate classification systems, application of sound principles of sport physiology, biomechanics, psychology, and nutrition for enhancing performance and injury prevention;

- Sport initiation—research on the reasons for and the extent of participation in sport and participation in youth sport programs, recreation, and leisure activities;

- Effects of sport—research on the values of and specific sociological, psychological, and physical benefits of participation and competition upon functional capacity for sport and activities of daily living; and

- Influences upon sport—research on the historical, philosophical, legal, and societal factors influencing sport and athletes with disabilities.

Inasmuch as very little sport research has been conducted which reported (included) females with disabilities, an important step is the identification and inclusion of disabled women athletes in research investigations in the areas mentioned above. As appropriate, gender differences, as well as gender-specific and gender-neutral phenomena, should be examined relative to sport and disability.

Ethnicity, race, and class and their relation to disability sport have not been studied. Inasmuch as sport is a social institution, societal issues and factors such as ethnicity, class, and culture and their intersection with gender and disability would be important to understanding the sporting arena and those who participate.

In April 1994, the International Paralympic Committee and the International Federation of Adapted Physical Activity cosponsored an international seminar on research directions for sport and disability, which resulted in a new research agenda.

CONCLUDING COMMENTS

Research on athletes with disabilities is critical to the future of disability sport. Increased understanding of the scientific basis of performance and the application for athletes with disabilities will lead to increased athletic performance.

CHAPTER 13

Females With Disabilities in Sport

Throughout history, various segments of society have experienced exclusion. Included among these "marginalized" groups are women, certain racial and ethnic groups, individuals with disabilities, those in lower social classes, gays, lesbians, bisexuals, and so on. Because of marginalization, disabled women have often found themselves in double jeopardy (Holcomb, 1984). The sporting world for females with disabilities is no exception.

The books that have been written about individuals with disabilities in sport (e.g., Guttmann, 1976; Paciorek & Jones, 1989; Sherrill, 1986; Stewart, 1991; van Hal, Rarick, & Vermeer, 1984; Vermeer, 1986) have made little or no mention of diversity such as race, ethnicity, or gender. The first to include women with disabilities were writers of women-in-sport books (e.g., Cohen, 1993; Hult & Trekell, 1991) and Stewart (1991), who discussed gender and race issues in Deaf sport. Inasmuch as this book provides an overview of sport and disability, this chapter is intended to outline the progress and accomplishments of girls and women with disabilities in the context of sport.

Although the disability sport literature contains very little reference to gender, let alone to differing ethnic backgrounds or issues of class, sexual orientation, religion, or cultural context, it is a well-acknowledged fact that one's sport experience varies dependent upon one's specific frame(s) of reference (e.g., Birrell, 1988; Boutilier & SanGiovanni, 1983; Theberge, 1985). This chapter is but an initial attempt to explore gender as one of the various interacting factors influencing sport participation by individuals with disabilities.

Although researchers have recently included females athletes with disabilities in their studies, research on females athletes as well as studies of gender are very limited. The only known comprehensive survey of females with disabilities and their participation in sport and physical activity was conducted in Canada in the late 1980s. With support from the Fitness Canada Women's Program, the Canadian Federation of Sport Organizations for the Disabled surveyed girls and women with physical disabilities throughout Canada between 1986 and 1988. The results indicated the following (excerpted from *Physical Activity and Women With Disabilities: A National Survey*, n.d.):

1. Current levels of physical activity were insufficient.

2. Physical activity was at least somewhat important or very important.

3. Awareness of the physical activity opportunities available was limited.

4. They preferred to participate in organized noncompetitive or recreationally competitive activities.

5. Very few were satisfied with the type of activities available.

6. Participation in physical activity was mostly self-initiated but also influenced by family and friends.

7. They participated for pleasure and fun, to feel better, to relax and reduce stress, and to improve or maintain fitness.

8. Barriers to participation included time constraints, inaccessible facilities, transportation problems, and lack of available information; disability and medical concerns were not primary barriers.

9. Increased participation could occur through facilities closer to home, accessible facilities, knowledgeable instructors, partners for participation, and more information on programs for women with disabilities.

10. They did not prefer segregated participation by gender and/or disability; integrated settings were fine.

HISTORICAL PERSPECTIVES

Women with disabilities had to fight for their right to be included in the arena of sport (Hedrick & Hedrick, 1991; Karwas & DePauw, 1990). Thus, their history is difficult to trace separately from the history of disability sport (DePauw, 1994), and references to persons with disabilities in sport have tended to be made as a group regardless of gender, specific type of impairment, ethnicity, and so on. Further, the actual narratives were more applicable to the experiences of disabled men (mostly wheelchair users) than disabled females.

Given that disability sport is actually relatively young (DePauw, 1986c, 1990a; Steadward & Walsh, 1986), it follows that girls' and women's participation in sport is an even newer phenomenon. With a few notable exceptions, the inclusion of females with disabilities in the sport world began in the 1960s, and sport has become increasingly more accessible in the 1990s.

Throughout its history, disability sport has tended to be disability specific. As a result, a chronology tends also to be outlined in terms of a given disability grouping. Table 13.1 is a brief overview of the involvement of girls and women with disabilities in sport by three general disability groupings. This chronology is admittedly not all-inclusive and represents primarily a North American perspective. It does include all milestones and accomplishments that could be identified.

Deaf/Hard-of-Hearing

Under the auspices of the CISS (International Committee on Deaf Sport), Deaf males and females were given the opportunity to compete in the first World Games for the Deaf in 1924. Since then, participation at the international and national competitions for the Deaf has remained at approximately one fourth to one third female.

The governance structure of Deaf sport has been male dominated in the United States as well as internationally. Specifically, all CISS presidents have been men and the prominent leadership positions have also been held by men. In the late 1980s, CISS elected a woman to its Executive Committee before the IOC saw fit to do so (Steward, 1991, p. 7).

In the United States, two Deaf women assumed leadership positions in the late 1980s. The American Athletic Association of the Deaf (AAAD) elected its first woman to serve as secretary-treasurer, Shirley Platt from

Table 13.1 Chronology of Women With Disabilities in Sport

Date	Event
1924	First International Silent Games (Paris); women among competitors.
1935	U.S. sends Deaf men and women to compete at IV World Games for the Deaf.
1952	Liz Hartel (postpolio) wins silver medal in dressage at Summer Olympics representing Denmark.
1957	First U.S. National Wheelchair Games (Adelphi College, New York); women among competitors.
1960	First International Games for Disabled (Paralympics) in Rome; women among the competitors.
1968	International Special Olympics founded by Eunice Kennedy Shriver; first competition held in Chicago.
1974	First Women's National Wheelchair Basketball Tournament.
1976	UNESCO conference establishes right of all individuals with disabilities to participate in physical education and sport.
1977	First female wheelchair entrant to the women's division of Boston Marathon (3:48:51).
1979	USOC Handicapped in Sports Committees formed, chaired by Kathryn Sallade (AAAD).
1980	Olympics for Disabled (Paralympics) is held in Arnhem, The Netherlands. Cerebral palsy athletes—males and females—(ambulatory) are included for the first time.
1982	Linda Downs, Class 5 CP athlete, finishes New York Marathon in 11 hours, 15 minutes.
	Karen Farmer, a single-leg amputee, attends college on athletic scholarship for women's track at Eastern Washington University.
	Blind women compete for the first time in the World Goal Ball Championships at Butler University in Indianapolis.
1983	First International Women's Wheelchair Tournament is held in France.
1984	Neroli Fairhall (N.Z.) is first wheelchair athlete to meet eligibility and compete in Olympics (women's archery).
	First wheelchair races as exhibition events for 1984 Olympics (1,500m is won by Paul Van Winkle at Belgium in 3:58.50; 800m is won by Sharon Rahn Hedrick in 2:15.50).

Date	Event
1984	First full-length article in commercial magazine, *Runner's World*, about female disabled athlete: Linda Downs for the 1982 New York Marathon.
1985	The 1985 U.S. Olympic Sports Festival includes athletes with disabilities for the first time: 16 females and 26 males.
	Sharon Hedrick wins the Southland Olympic Award.
1987	Candace Cable wins the Boston Marathon for the fifth time (Andre Viger wins for the 3rd time; John Brewer wins the Quad Division for the 7th time).
1988	Winter Olympics in Calgary include exhibition events (three-track Alpine, blind Nordic) for males and females.
	Summer Olympics (South Korea) include wheelchair races as exhibition events (1,500m for men; 800m for females); Sharon Hedrick wins second gold medal in Olympics Wheelchair 800m (2:11.49).
1989	Seven females and seven males are named the first winners of U.S. Disabled Athletes of the Year Award.
1990	Shirley Platt becomes the first female (Deaf) executive secretary of AAAD.
	Dr. Donalda Ammons is appointed the first Deaf female director of the World Games for the Deaf U.S. team.
	Diana Golden, three-track skier, signs sponsorship agreement with Subaru and also becomes official spokesperson for the ChapStick Challenge for Disabled Skiers.
1991	Jean Driscoll becomes the first athlete with a disability to win the Sudafed Female Athlete of the Year Award.
	Sue Moucha attends as the first athlete with a disability at the International Olympic Academy in Greece.
	Jan Wilson becomes the first coordinator, disabled sport programs, United States Olympic Committee.
1992	Connie Hansen and Candace Cable become the only two women to compete in all Summer Olympic exhibition events to date.

Utah, and Dr. Donalda Ammons from Washington, D.C., became the first women to chair the United States World Games for the Deaf Team Committee.

Physical Impairments

In 1944, organized sport opportunities for individuals with physical impairments emerged in conjunction with the creation of the Spinal Injuries Centre of the Stoke Mandeville Hospital in England. Its development marked the beginning of wheelchair sports as part of the rehabilitation of war veterans by hospital administrator Sir Ludwig Guttmann. Four years later, 13 men and 3 women (all patients at the hospital) competed in wheelchair archery at what would become the first Stoke Mandeville Games.

In contrast to the inclusion of females in Stoke Mandeville, the early days of wheelchair basketball around the world provided opportunities for men only. From the initiation of wheelchair basketball in the mid-1940s, it took over 20 years for women to be included. In 1968, the Paralympics in Tel Aviv formally introduced women's wheelchair basketball, and since then, it has been included on the program of the International Stoke Mandeville Games (1970), the Pan American Wheelchair Games (1971), the European Championships (1974), and the World Cup Championships (1990).

Although U.S. women participated in the 1968 Paralympics, the National Wheelchair Basketball Association (NWBA) did not end its discriminatory practice of prohibiting women from participating until 1974 (Hedrick & Hedrick, 1991). The next year, the first women's national tournament was held.

As international competitions for athletes with disabilities prior to the 1960s were only for Deaf individuals and wheelchair users (primarily spinal cord injured), additional sport associations were formed and competitions organized to include individuals with other physical impairments. Inasmuch as women had already broken through, the newly developed organizations such as International Sports Organization for the Disabled (ISOD), Cerebral Palsy–International Sports and Recreation Association (CP–ISRA), International Blind Sports Association (IBSA), the International Coordinating Committee (ICC), and the International Paralympic Committee (IPC) provided opportunities for both men and women from the outset.

Today, approximately one third of the athletes in international competitions are women. Similar to the able-bodied sport world and the CISS, men hold the leadership positions. A notable exception is Elizabeth Dendy from Great Britain, who served as the first and only president of CP–ISRA and, in that capacity, presided over the ICC's last meeting. In addition, she has the distinction of being the only female to date to serve as a member of the IPC.

KAREN FARMER-LEWIS

At a glance:

Track and field athlete

Collegiate scholarship

National athlete of the year, U.S. Amputee Athletic Association

National and international medal winner

World and U.S. record holder

Karen Farmer-Lewis's resume looks just like any typical elite athlete's—state, national, and international competition, medal performances, and athletic scholarships. As one looks further, the extent of this record becomes quite impressive, beyond the "typical." Karen has earned 14 world records in track and field events ranging from discus, shot put, javelin, and long jump to the 100m, 200m, and 400m dashes. These world records are also U.S. records. That Karen is both female and a congenital amputee is significant in terms of her accomplishments on and off the field. Karen was born in Harbor City, CA, without a right tibia and with a deformed right foot.

Karen is also unique in that she still competes in both able-bodied and disability sport competitions. Karen states, "Sport continues to be a great part of my life." Her support comes from her husband and children. Her advice for youngsters is to go for it! "Don't let anyone take your dreams away. Believe in yourself. Create your own goals."

Karen Farmer-Lewis was a national athlete of the year in 1984 (USAAA) and the only disabled athlete recognized by the U.S. Women's Sports Federation Award as an up-and-coming athlete in 1985. She is a certified therapeutic recreation professional, an elite athlete, and a quality human being.

Mental Impairments

Special Olympics International (SOI) and the International Sports Federation for Persons with Mental Handicap (INAS–FMH) have always provided sport opportunities for mentally retarded males and females. A fairly equitable distribution of male and female athletes participate in their national and international competitions. The leadership positions for both groups are male dominated with the notable exception of Eunice Kennedy Shriver, SOI founder.

WOMEN WITH DISABILITIES IN THE OLYMPICS

Very few women with disabilities have participated in both the Summer and Winter Olympic Games. One example is Liz Hartel (postpolio), who won a silver medal in dressage in 1952. The most visible has been Neroli Fairhall, representing New Zealand, who competed in archery during the 1984 Olympics in Los Angeles. As a fully accepted Olympian, she competed in her wheelchair.

Male and female athletes with disabilities competed in their first exhibition events at the 1984 Winter Olympics in Sarajevo and the 1984 Summer Olympics in Los Angeles. The two exhibition events selected for the Summer Olympics were the 800m wheelchair race for women and the 1,500m wheelchair race for men. These events were continued in Seoul in 1988 and Barcelona in 1992. As for the Winter Olympic Games, Alpine and Nordic skiing events for blind and physically disabled athletes were offered in Sarajevo (1984) and Calgary (1988), but not in Albertville (1992). Diana Golden, a single-leg amputee, became the most celebrated female disabled skier in Calgary.

In the United States, male and female disabled athletes participated in the 1985 National Sport Festival (now called Olympic Sport Festivals). Since then, men and women across all disability groupings have competed regularly at the annual (except Olympic year) Olympic Sport Festivals.

WOMEN WITH DISABILITIES AND SELECTED COMPETITIVE OPPORTUNITIES

The Boston Marathon, which included wheelchair athletes as early as 1974, is considered the premier road racing/marathon event for athletes with disabilities. The first female wheelchair competitor was Sharon Rahn

JEAN DRISCOLL

At a glance:

Wheelchair racer

Congenital spina bifida

World record holder in Boston Marathon, 10K, and 800m

Women's Sport Foundation Amateur Sportswoman of the Year, 1991

An outstanding racer, Jean Driscoll of Milwaukee has been involved in competitive sport since 1983. Her list of accomplishments in road racing and track accounts for a significant number of medal performances at the regional, national, and international levels. Her academic record and list of awards also read like a Who's Who.

Between 1990 and 1993, Jean held the course and world record for the Boston Marathon. Her 1993 time was 1:34:50. Jean was also a world record holder in the 10K at 23:46, and her 800m world record is 1:56 min. Additionally, Jean owns course records for various road races in Illinois, Ohio, and the 1992 Barcelona Paralympics. Her regimen of training 2-4 hours per day, 6-7 days a week, has definitely paid off.

Jean's involvement in competitive sport started late in life. "Sport was always a void in my life. I didn't own a wheelchair until I was 15 years old, and I didn't participate in wheelchair sports until I was 16 years old." Her advice to young people with disabilities is to get involved, balance school achievements and sports, and regard sport as fun.

Jean states, "Sport has changed my life. It has taught me time management and organizational skills. I have developed self-confidence, something that was missing as a child. Success in sport has created opportunities I never dreamed would come my way"—such as meeting the president of the United States. Not bad for someone who was told as a child that she would be "just a secretary."

Hedrick. She entered the race in 1977 and won with a time of 3:48:51. Since then, the times have decreased dramatically (see Figure 3.3). The gap between the winning times for women and for men has narrowed over the years; in 1990 the time for the men's division was 1:29:53 and for the women's division, 1:43:17. Although the performances have improved, the number of female competitors remains relatively low (only three or four each year).

Since the first running (wheeling) of the Boston Marathon, wheelchair divisions for competition in other marathons (e.g. Montreal, Japan, Los Angeles, Long Beach) and other road races (e.g. Lilac Bloomsday Run, Wheels of Fire, Gasparilla, Ouantas Oz) have been developed. Male and female Americans have been able to compete professionally, earning up to $7,000 per race.

Sport opportunities for athletes with disabilities in the United States have been expanded beyond selected community recreation and sport programs into collegiate programs. Individuals with physical impairments at the University of Illinois and Wright State University, and Deaf athletes at Gallaudet University have been provided with collegiate sport experiences, including athletic scholarships (see Appendix H). Although these sport opportunities have been available to women, the numbers favor men.

CONCLUDING COMMENTS

Although much progress appears to have been made, women and disabled individuals have long been excluded from sport (Birrell, 1988; DePauw, 1994). Parallels between the women's and disability sport movements have been identified (Karwas & DePauw, 1990). The parallels include specific cultural and attitudinal similarities (Mastro, Hall, & Canabal, 1988), medical restrictions to participation in sport, legal mandates for nondiscrimination and equal opportunity, socialization via and into sport, involvement of professional organizations (e.g., AAHPERD) and the USOC, basketball as the first sport for women and disabled athletes, the Boston Marathon for breaking into the able-bodied sport world, and common barriers to sport participation. Among these barriers are the lack of school or community programs, role models, coaches, and accessibility (Grimes & French, 1987).

Perhaps the single greatest barrier to equity in sport for female athletes with disabilities is the historical model of sport. As the domain of the elite and the masculine, sport has played a significant role in preserving the patriarchal social order (Hall, 1985) and the gender segregation and inequality found in other realms of social life (Theberge, 1985, p. 193).

The "masculinity" of sport has had the effect of excluding women from full participation (e.g., Birrell, 1988; Felshin, 1974; Theberge, 1985). Similarly, the "physicality" of sport has tended to exclude individuals with disabilities (DePauw, 1994; Hahn, 1984). Body concept and objectification of one's body, as topics found within both the disability and women's movements, gain greater significance within the context of sport.

In opposition to the "exclusive" nature of sport, the disability sport movement championed the inclusion of athletes with disabilities in the sporting world. Disabled men and women fought together for their collective right to participate in sport. These efforts have changed sport significantly since the early 1900s.

Even though disabled women did not initially have to fight their battle alone, their struggle is not yet over. The additional barriers being faced by disabled women who actively seek sport competitions can, and will, be overcome so that women of tomorrow will have greater opportunities than their foremothers. As the future of sport including and for athletes with disabilities unfolds, women with disabilities will be found not only among the athletes, but as coaches, administrators, trainers, officials, and spectators. They, in turn, will serve as role models for aspiring youth. As barriers are eliminated, sport programs for disabled women will become increasingly more available and accessible.

CHAPTER 14

Sport in the 21st Century

Disability sport has come a long way since its beginnings in the late 19th century. Not only have sport and society changed but so has sport for and including individuals with disabilities.

Throughout history, and especially in the 20th century, individuals with disabilities have experienced increasingly greater inclusion and acceptance within society (DePauw, 1986c). As a result, they have also been able to experience selective inclusion and acceptance in the sport world. Although doors are opening, they have not been opened without resistance. In these instances, the openings have occurred as a result of federal legislation and/or political pressures.

Throughout the world, disability sport programs have been shaped by the interaction of given societal factors (e.g., political, economic, sociohistorical, sociocultural). Regardless, the trend is one of inclusion. Internationally, athletes with disabilities have experienced selected inclusion within the Olympic arena (e.g., exhibition events at the Summer and Winter

Olympics, use of term *Paralympics*). In keeping with the trend, athletes with disabilities will find themselves with increasingly more opportunities to compete with able-bodied athletes.

ISSUES OF SPORT AND DISABILITY

The future of disability sport is not yet fully charted. There are still many issues and controversies facing this sport movement which will not be easily resolved. Given the assumption of progressive inclusion, disability sport must address at least three major issues:

a. sport by ability or by disability,

b. sport for participation or for competition, and

c. integrated or separate sport competitions (DePauw, 1990a).

Each of these issues can be expressed along a continuum and should not be viewed as representing a dichotomy (see Figure 14.1).

Generally speaking, the continuum of sport by disability/ability represents the emphasis placed upon classification for sport competition by disability (e.g., visual impairment, level of amputation, severity of cerebral palsy, level of spinal cord lesion) and by ability (e.g., without regard to disability, cross-disability classification). Regarding sport for participation/competition, the issue revolves around the perceived primary purpose of the sporting event (e.g., Special Olympics for participation, Paralympics for competition). As for integrated or separated

---

Sport by ability (emphasis on sport)

Sport by disability (emphasis on disability)

Sport for participation

Sport for competition

Segregated sport (sport only for individuals with disabilities, sport by specific disability)

Integrated sport (cross-disability sport, sport with able-bodied athletes)

Figure 14.1   Factors influencing the future of sport for individuals with disabilities.

competitions, the continuum includes integration defined as competition with able-bodied persons as well as competitions with other persons with disabilities (cross-disability) and segregation as separate competitions for those with disabilities (Paralympics) or by specific disability grouping (Special Olympics International, World Games for the Deaf). In addition, this continuum includes the notion of separate events for athletes with disabilities within a competition for able-bodied athletes.

Disability sport is a rather complex entity constructed by interaction of these three continua with the sociohistorical and sociocultural context of a specific cultural setting (e.g., country, disability grouping). We believe that the future of sport will be described relative to these three issues and applied within the specific cultural context.

INTEGRATION OF ATHLETES WITH DISABILITIES

Athletes with disabilities will be increasingly found competing with able-bodied athletes. Internationally as well as nationally, recent efforts have been extended in this direction.

One instance was the formation of the IPC International Committee on Integration of Athletes with a Disability (ICI) in November 1990 by a "group of Canadians who envisioned the inclusion of selected full medal events for athletes with disabilities in major international competitions" (Merklinger, 1991, p. 8). Specifically targeted were the Olympic Games and the Commonwealth Games. This was later renamed the Commission for Inclusion of Athletes with a Disability (CIAD). Rick Hansen, a Canadian who completed the Man in Motion World Tour, accepted the IPC invitation to chair this committee. According to its June 1993 progress report, the CIAD's goals were as follows:

1. Develop a lobbying strategy for the inclusion of selected full medal events for athletes with disabilities initially within the Olympic Games and Commonwealth Games

2. Increase the awareness and understanding of the appropriateness of the inclusion of selected full medal events for athletes with disabilities into major international competitions

3. Facilitate the successful conduct of selected full medal events included into major international competitions

4. Develop a model process for the inclusion of selected full medal events for athletes with disabilities into major international events

5. Establish formal linkages and effective liaisons with appropriate entities

6. Gain interest and financial support for the CIAD and its objectives

RICK HANSEN

At a glance:

National and international marathoner

Man in Motion, around-the-world tour

Medal winner at international level

Rick Hansen of Canada is probably best known for his monumental around-the-world tour by wheelchair. This tour enabled millions of people from around the world to see that a person who was a posttraumatic paraplegic and who used a wheelchair for ambulation was not limited in meeting challenges. His following and reception along his travels are well documented, and his ability as a fundraiser and motivating speaker is widely known.

Rick started out in competitive sport in 1980 at the Orange Bowl Marathon in Miami. Since then he has won 19 international wheelchair marathons, including races in Japan, Hawaii, and North America. More than a one-dimensional athlete, Rick has also competed nationally for teams in basketball, volleyball, tennis, and racquetball. Rick has used his expertise and experience to coach able-bodied and youth with disabilities. He is a worldwide spokesperson for including individuals with disabilities in able-bodied sport.

The CIAD concentrated its efforts on the 1994 Commonwealth Games in Victoria, BC. In April 1991, the Commonwealth Games Federation (CGF) agreed to include six exhibition events in the 1994 games. The events finally selected were Men's Open Wheelchair Marathon, Men's Open 800m wheelchair race, Men's 100m Freestyle Class S9, Women's 100m Freestyle Class S9, Men's Visually Impaired Lawn Bowling Singles, and Women's Visually Impaired Lawn Bowling Singles.

In the summer of 1992, the Commonwealth Games Federation granted athletes with disabilities greater inclusion in the 1994 Games. Athletes would also receive distinctive medals, be allowed to live in the Athletes' Village, receive full athlete accreditation, participate fully in the opening and closing ceremonies, and wear their countries' national team uniforms.

Although progress has been made toward integrating athletes with disabilities into major international sport competitions, much work is still clearly needed. The CIAD efforts will continue specifically in the quest for inclusion in future Olympic Games (e.g., 1996 Summer Olympic Games in Atlanta and 1998 Winter Olympic Games in Nagano, Japan, and beyond). It is likely that discussions between the IPC and the IOC as well as within the IPC will continue for a number of years until the issues surrounding inclusion are resolved.

The question of integrating athletes with disabilities into international competitions can only be answered as the issues facing athletes with disabilities identified throughout the book are not only acknowledged but specifically addressed. For example, in order to have gained the progress identified above, disability sport must have been viewed as being for competition, not participation, and the primary emphasis must have been upon sport by ability, not disability. Inasmuch as disability remains an important factor (for both the CIAD and the Olympic Games organizers), the events selected will be limited to selected athletes with disabilities, specific disabilities in particular.

In support of inclusion (integration), Hedrick and Hedrick (1993) questioned the current organizational structure of disability sport as one of promoting segregation. Alternatively, they proposed that "the current segregation model must be gradually replaced by one wherein adapted sports become legitimate members with the mainstream NGBs" (pp. 14-15). Landry (1992) also called for integrating and streamlining the various structures of the disability sport movement into one international governing body (e.g., IPC) as the means for accepting athletes with disabilities and disability sport throughout the world.

FUTURE TRENDS

Societal attitudes toward sport participation and competition by athletes with disabilities have changed significantly over the past half-century. The "original" rehabilitation purpose through sport has given way to sport for sport's sake and competition for competition's sake.

Disability sport of the 21st century will not only be shaped by the political, social, and economic factors of a given cultural context but will continue to be influenced by the Olympic sport movement. Classification issues, drug testing, technological advances, improved training techniques, and sports medicine will continue to be factors in the development of elite disability sport. Characteristics that will describe disability sport in the next century will include the following (adapted from DePauw, 1990a; DePauw, 1994):

- A vertical structure of sport with extensive developmental sports programs for individuals with disabilities leading toward a national and international level competitive structure for elite athletes with disabilities

- Establishment of multidisability national and international sport organizations as the governing bodies for disability sport with strong links to and within the national and international sport structure (organized more by sport than by disability)
- Increasing emphasis on high levels of athletic excellence and high standards for performance
- Increasing specialization within sport among athletes with disabilities and fewer athletes being able to participate in multiple events
- Classification and competitions becoming more sport specific and ability oriented than disability specific
- Increasing numbers of individuals with disabilities (adults, youth, seniors) participating in sport at all levels
- Increasing equity in sport opportunities for girls and women with disabilities, and increasing concern for issues of race, gender, and class
- Increasing numbers of athletes with disabilities included within the sport world including major international competitions such as the Olympic Games and world championships
- Greater inclusion of persons with disabilities within the structure of disability sport as well as coaches, officials, and administrators
- Increased public awareness and acceptance of athletes with disabilities and of sport as a viable option for youth

SPORT, SOCIETY, DISABILITY, AND THE 21ST CENTURY

Convergence of the sports movement for athletes with disabilities with the Olympic sports movement was inevitable (Landry, 1992). As a result of international competitions for athletes with disabilities (e.g., Paralympics, World Games for the Deaf, Special Olympics), sport is no longer the sole prerogative of able-bodied athletes.

What once was exclusively the domain of those free of physical impairments—sport, and society's view of sport—has now been altered for more inclusion and greater acceptance of individuals with disabilities. Although sport remains a forum for the expression of physical prowess, strength, endurance, and grace, society's view has been expanded to include athletes using wheelchairs and those with other physical, mental, or sensory impairments.

If accurate, the trend of "progressive inclusion and acceptance" would result in the integration of persons with disabilities into sport. Critical to acceptance of this trend, or assumption, is an understanding of what is meant by integration, or inclusion. What is advocated here is "true" accessibility to sport or the reconstruction of sport as an institution that allows individuals with disabilities (e.g., as a marginalized group) an informed choice about sport participation (DePauw, 1994).

"Real" inclusion (integration) means that individuals (e.g., with disabilities, of racial or ethnic minority backgrounds, women) have the same choices afforded those of the dominant culture (e.g., white, male, able-bodied). Having access to sport should not imply that all individuals with disabilities will opt for, or desire, participation (or competition) with able-bodied persons. It means having the choice. Inclusion of individuals with disabilities in sport is having "choice" and not being excluded solely because of a condition of one's being. Integration does not mean that competition and participation with able-bodied individuals is preferred; rather it means having the option to choose to compete in a segregated setting (e.g., Deaf Sport, wheelchair basketball).

Throughout history, sport has remained a somewhat exclusive or elite institution. As such, sport is socially constructed. But with the inclusion of individuals with disabilities within the boundaries of sport, a partial deconstruction of sport has begun. Inasmuch as women have succeeded in entering the sporting arena, athletes with disabilities will, too. As for the beginning of the 21st century, individuals with disabilities will remain in the margins of sport. The selection of those athletes with disabilities who are "accepted" into sport will be influenced by society's view of sport as masculine/feminine and physical and based upon type and severity of impairment as well as by one's gender, race, and social class.

CONCLUDING COMMENTS

Athletes with disabilities today have a far greater number of opportunities for sport participation and competitions than in the first half of the 20th century. In turn, they will have greater options in the 21st century. Sport of tomorrow will be an avenue of socialization for youth with disabilities in the same way that sport serves the youth of today. Sport for and including individuals with disabilities is a movement whose time has come.

APPENDIX   A

Selected Paralympic Records

Sport event	Paralympic record	Olympic record
Athletics		
Men's high jump (one leg amputee)	1.96m (A. Bolt, CAN)	2.44m
Men's 100m (amputee)	11.63 (T. Volpentes, USA)	9:86
Men's 800m (wheelchair)	1:40.63 (S. Hollenbeck, USA)	1:41.71
Men's 1,500m (arm amputee)	3:54.61 (J. Conde, SPA)	3:29.46
Men's 1,500m (wheelchair)	3:16.24 (M. Pitz, GER)	
Women's 1,500m (wheelchair)	3:45.23 (C. Hansen, DEN)	3:52.47
Men's 5,000m (wheelchair)	11:10.41 (H. Frei, SUI)	12:58.39
Marathon (wheelchair)	1:27.53 (H. Frei, SUI)	2:06.50
Weight lifting	602 lbs (K. Brownfield, USA)	
Javelin	59.38 m	
Swimming (blind)		
Women's 50m freestyle	29.32 (T. Zorn, USA)	24.79
Men's 50m freestyle	26.58 (J. Morgan, USA)	21.91
Women's 100m butterfly	1:07.07 (E. Scott, USA)	58.62
Men's 100m backstroke	1:09.23 (J. Morgan, USA)	53.98
Women's 200m backstroke	2:31.13 (T. Zorn, USA)	2:07.06
Men's 200m medley	2:22.97 (J. Morgan, USA)	2:06.76

APPENDIX B

List of Abbreviations

AAAD	American Athletic Association of the Deaf
AAC	Athletes Advisory Council
ADA	Americans With Disabilities Act
AK	Above-knee amputation
BK	Below-knee amputation
CFSOD	Canadian Federation of Sport Organizations for the Disabled
CISS	International Committee of Sports for the Deaf
COSD	Committee on Sports for the Disabled
CP	Cerebral Palsy
CP-ISRA	Cerebral Palsy International Sport and Recreation Association
DAAA	Dwarf Athletic Association of America
DSO	Disabled Sport Organization
DS/USA	Disabled Sports USA
IBSA	International Blind Sport Association
ICC	International Coordinating Committee
IF	International Federation (international sport governing body)
IFSD	International Fund Sport Disabled
INAS-FMH	International Sports Federation for Persons With Mental Handicap
IOA	International Olympic Academy
IOC	International Olympic Committee
IPC	International Paralympic Committee
ISMWSF	International Stoke Mandeville Wheelchair Sports Federation
ISOD	International Sports Organization for the Disabled
LA	Les Autres

NASCP	National Association of Sport for Cerebral Palsy
NGB	National Governing Body (category of member in USOC)
NHSRA	National Handicapped Sports and Recreation Association
NOC	National Olympic Committee
NWAA	National Wheelchair Athletic Association
NWBA	National Wheelchair Basketball Association
OOC	Olympic Organizing Committee
RESPO DS-DI	Recreational Sports Development and Stimulation Disabled International
SCI	Spinal Cord Injury
SOD	Sport Organization for the Disabled
SOI	Special Olympics International
USABA	United States Association for Blind Athletes
USCPAA	United States Cerebral Palsy Athletic Association
USLASA	United States Les Autres Sport Association
USCO	United States Olympic Committee
USOTC	United States Olympic Training Center
WC	Wheelchair
WGD	World Games for the Deaf

APPENDIX C

Outdoor Recreation Activities for Individuals With Disabilities

ACCESSIBLE CAMPING IN SELECTED NATIONAL PARKS

ALASKA

Denali National Park and Preserve
Denali Park
Accessible sites near accessible toilets are reserved for use by disabled campers at Riley Creek, Savage, Teklanika, and Wonder Lake campgrounds.

ARIZONA

Grand Canyon National Park
Grand Canyon
Six accessible tent/RV sites near wheelchair-accessible rest rooms are available at Mather. Wheelchair-accessible rest rooms are provided at Desert View.

Organ Pipe Cactus National Monument
Ajo
Wheelchair-accessible rest rooms are available.

CALIFORNIA

Death Valley National Monument
Death Valley
The Sunset area has 16 accessible sites near wheelchair-accessible rest rooms.

Furnace Creek and Mesquite Springs have wheelchair-accessible rest rooms.

Sequoia National Park
Three Rivers
Lodgepole has accessible rest rooms, and Potwisha has an accessible site near accessible rest rooms.

COLORADO

Mesa Verde National Park
Six accessible campsites are located near wheelchair-accessible rest rooms.

Rocky Mountain National Park
Estes Park
Moraine Park, Glacier Basin, and Timber Creek have wheelchair-accessible rest rooms. An accessible back-country site, Handi-camp, has an accessible rest room.

FLORIDA

Everglades National Park
Homestead
Each campground has one site reserved for people with disabilities,

FLORIDA (*continued*)

next to a wheelchair-accessible rest room. One back-country site, Pearl Bay Chickee, is accessible.

Gulf Islands National Seashore
Gulf Breeze

Several campsites near a wheelchair-accessible rest room are held for disabled campers until at least noon each day.

GEORGIA

Chickamauga and Chattanooga National Military Park
Fort Oglethorpe

One accessible group-campground is located near an accessible toilet.

KENTUCKY

Mammoth Cave National Park
Mammoth Cave

Two accessible sites at Headquarters Campground, located near accessible rest rooms, are held until 6:00 p.m.

each day during the camping season for disabled campers.

MAINE

Acadia National Park
Bar Harbor

Both campgrounds have a few wheelchair-accessible sites near accessible rest rooms.

NORTH CAROLINA

Blue Ridge Parkway
Asheville

All campgrounds have at least two wheelchair-accessible sites near accessible rest rooms.

VIRGINIA

Prince William Forest Park
Triangle

Both campgrounds have wheelchair-accessible sites and rest rooms. One whole section of accessible cabins and rest rooms in the group-camping area is available.

ACCESSIBLE OUTDOOR RECREATION AND WILDERNESS EXPERIENCES

The following programs offer outdoor recreation and wilderness experiences for individuals with disabilities. The groups served are identified in parentheses; PI—physical impairment, VI—visual impairment, D/HI—deaf and hearing impairment, MR—mental retardation. The abbreviation Integ stands for integrated programs (with able-bodied persons).

Alaska Handicapped Sports and Recreation Association (PI, VI)
Girdwood, AK

All Outdoors, Inc. (all)
Redmond, OR

Alternate Mobility Adventure Seekers (all)
Boise State University
Boise, ID

Aspen BOLD (Blind Outdoor Leisure Dev.) (VI)
Aspen, CO

Boy Scouts of America (scouting for the handicapped) (all)
Irving, TX

Capable Partners (Integ)
St. Louis Park, MN

Colorado Outdoor Education Center for the Handicapped (all)
Breckenridge, CO

Cooperative Wilderness
Handicapped Outdoor Group
(C.W. HOG) (PI, VI, D/HI)
Pocatello, ID

Courage Center (PI, VI, D)
Golden Valley, MN

Eden Wood Camping and Retreat
Center (MR)
Eden Prairie, MN

Environmental Traveling
Companions (all)
San Francisco, CA

Girl Scouts of the USA
(girls with disabilities) (all)
New York, NY

Maine-Niles Association
of Special Recreation (all)
Niles, IL

Minnesota Outward Bound School (PI)
Long Lake, MN

Northeast DuPage Special
Recreation Association
(PI, Integ)
Wood Dale, IL

Paraplegics in Independent Nature
Trips (PI)
Bedford, TX

Recreational Challenges for the
Disadvantaged Outfitter Guide
(PI)
Pierce, ID

Shared Outdoor Adventure
Recreation (SOAR) (all)
Portland, OR

Veterans on the Lake (PI)
Ely, MN

Vinland National Center (all)
Loretto, MN

Voyageur Outward Bound
(PI, D/HI, VI)
Minnetonka, MN

Wilderness Inquiry
(Integ)
Minneapolis, MN

SKI PROGRAMS

ALASKA
Challenge Alaska
Anchorage

CALIFORNIA
National Handicapped Sports
of Orange County
La Habra

Tahoe Handicapped Ski School
Truckee

COLORADO
Aspen Handicapped Skiers
Association
Snowmass Village

Breckenridge Outdoor Ed. Center
Breckenridge

Durango/Purgatory Handicapped
Sports Association
Durango

National Sports Center
for the Disabled
Winter Park

IOWA
Sundown Handicapped Skiers
Dubuque

MASSACHUSETTS
New England Handicapped Sports
  Association
Chelmsford

MICHIGAN
Michigan Handicapped Sports
  & Recreation Association
Rochester Hills

MINNESOTA
Courage Alpine Skiers
Golden Valley

Courage Duluth
Duluth

NEW MEXICO
Lovelace/Sandia Peak Ski Program
Albuquerque

NEVADA
Northern Nevada Ski School
  for the Disabled
Incline Village

NEW YORK
Disabled Ski Program
  at Ski Windham
Windham

OREGON
Shared Outdoor Adventure
  Recreation (SOAR)
Portland

UTAH
Park City Handicapped Sports
Park City

VERMONT
Vermont Handicapped Ski
  and Sports Association
Brownsville

WASHINGTON
Skiforall
Seattle

APPENDIX D

International Disability Sport Organizations

Cerebral Palsy–International Sport and Recreation Association (CP–ISRA)
9 Kingswood Rd.
London, England W4 5EU

Comité International des Sports des Sourds (CISS)
826 Locust Dr.
West River, MD 20778

Federation Equestre International (FEI)
Schosshaldenstrassee, 32
24, ave. Mon-Repos
BP 157
CH-1000 Lausanne 5, Switzerland

Federation Internationale Amateur de Cyclisme (FIAC)
Via Cassia 490
I-00 189 Rome, Italy

Federation Internationale de Basketball (FIBA)
Kistler hofstrasse 168
Postfach 700607
81306 Munich, Germany

Federation Internationale de Canoe (FIC)
G. Massala, 59
I-50134 Florence, Italy

Federation Internationale d'Escrime (FIE)
32 Rue de la Boetie
F-75008 Paris, France

Federation Internationale de Football Association (FIFA)
Hitzigweg 11
Postfach 85
CH-8030 Zurich, Switzerland

Federation Internationale de Gymnastique (FIG)
10, rue des Oeuches
Case Postale 359
CH-2740 Moutier 1, Switzerland

Federation Internationale de Handball (FIH)
Lange Gasse 10
CH-4052 Basel, Switzerland

Federation Internationale des Luttes Associees (FILA)
3, ave. Ruchornet
CH-1003 Lausanne, Switzerland

Federation Internationale de Natation Amateur (FINA)
9, ave. de Beaumont
CH-012 Lausanne, Switzerland

Federation Internationale de Roller Skating (FIRS)
Rambla Cataluna, 80 (piso 1), 08008
Barcelona, Spain

Federation Internationale de Ski (FIS)
Blochstr. 2
CH-3653 Oberhofen, Switzerland

Federation Internationale de Softball
(ISF)
321 N. West End Ave.
Lancaster, PA 17603

Federation Internationale de Tennis
(FIT)
Palliser Rd.
Barons Ct.
London W14 9EN England

Federation Internationale
de Volleyball (FIVB)
12, ave. de la Gare
CH-1001 Lausanne, Switzerland

International Amateur
Athletic Federation (IAAF)
17, rue Princesse Florestine
BP 359
MC-98007 Monaco Cedex, Monaco

International Blind Sports
Association (IBSA)
c/o Quevodo 1
28014 Madrid, Spain

International Sports Federation
for Persons With Mental Handicap
(INAS–FMH)
c/o Bernard Atha
USKA
13-27 Brunswick Place
London, England N1 6DX

Peter Burwash International
Special Tennis Programs (PBISTP)
2203 Timberloch Place, Suite 126
The Woodlands, TX 77380

International Paralympic Committee
c/o Secretariat
Res. Lodewijk 1, Abdijbekestraat 4B
8200 Brugge, Belgium

International Skating Union
(ISU)
Postfach
CH-7270 Davos-Platz, Switzerland

International Sport Organization
for the Disabled (ISOD)
Ferrez 16
28008 Madrid, Spain

International Stoke Mandeville
Wheelchair Sports Federation
(ISMWSF)
2165 Lamartine St.
Sherbrooke, Quebec
Canada J1J 4R3

International Table Tennis
Federation (ITTF)
53 London Road
St. Leonards-on-the-sea
E. Sussex TN37 6AY, England

International Weightlifting
Federation (IWF)
Rosenburg HP.U.L.
Postafiok 614
1374 Budapest, Hungary

International Wheelchair
Road Racers Club, Inc.
c/o Joseph M. Dowling
30 Myano Ln., Box 3
Stamford, CT 06902

International Wheelchair Aviators
Bill Blackwood, Secretary
1117 Rising Hill
Escondido, CA 92029

Recreational Sports Development
and Stimulation Disabled
International (RESPO DS–DI)
P.O. Box 263
8440 AG Heerenveen
The Netherlands

APPENDIX E

U.S. and Canadian Disability Sport Organizations

NATIONAL SPORT ASSOCIATIONS: U.S.

Access to Sailing
19744 Beach Blvd., Ste. 340
Huntington Beach, CA 92648

Aircraft Owners and Pilots
Association (AOPA)
421 Aviation Way
Frederick, MD 21701

Amateur Softball Association
(ASA)
2801 N.E. 50th St.
Oklahoma City, OK 73111

American Amateur Racquetball
Association (AARA)
1685 W. Uintah
Colorado Springs, CO 80904-2921

American Athletic Association
of the Deaf (AAAD)
3607 Washington Blvd., No. 4
Ogden, UT 84403-1737

American Blind Bowling Association
c/o Alice Hoover
411 Sheriff
Marcer, PA 16137

American Bowling Congress (ABC)
Women's International Bowling
Congress (WIBC)
5301 South 76th St.
Greendale, WI 53129

American Canoe Association (ACA)
7432 Alban Station Rd., Suite B226
Springfield, VA 22150

American Canoe Association
Disabled Paddlers Committee
c/o Lynne Andrus
9107B Rockcrest Circle
Austin, TX 78704

American Horse Shows Association
(AHSA)
220 E. 42nd St., Suite 409
New York, NY 10017-5876

American Water Ski Association
(AWSA)
799 Overlook Dr.
Winter Haven, FL 33884

American Water Ski Association
Rhonda VanDyk
Disabled Ski Committee
13009 Seven Mile Road NE
Belding, MI 48809

**American Wheelchair Bowling
Association (AWBA)**
3620 Tamarack Dr.
Redding, CA 96003

**American Wheelchair Table Tennis
Association (AWTTA)**
23 Parker St.
Port Chester, NY 10573

**Aqua Sports Association
for the Physically Challenged**
830 Broadway, Ste. 10
El Cajon, CA 92021

Disabled Sports USA (DS/USA)
Kirk Bauer, Executive Director
451 Hungerford Dr., Suite 100
Rockville, MD 20850

**Dwarf Athletic Association
of America (DAAA)**
c/o Janet Brown
418 Willow Way
Lewisville, TX 75067

**Eastern Amputee Athletic
Association**
Jack Graff, President
Mike Donals, Vice President
2080 Ennabrock Road
North Bellmore, NY 11710

52 Association for the Handicapped
(Skiing-Blind, Amputee)
350 5th Ave., Suite 1829
New York, NY 10018

Goal Ball Championships
c/o United States Association
for Blind Athletes (USABA)
33 N. Institute St.
Colorado Springs, CO 80903

Handicapped Scuba Association (HSA)
7172 W. Stanford
Littleton, CO 80123

International Wheelchair Aviators
1117 Rising Hill
Escondido, CA 92029

**National Amputee Golf Association
(NAGA)**
Bob Wilson, Executive Director
P.O. Box 1228
Amherst, NH 03031-1228

**National Archery Association
of the United States (NAA)**
1 Olympic Plaza
Colorado Springs, CO 80909-5778

**National Association of
Handicapped Outdoor Sportsmen,
Inc. (NAHOS)**
R.R. 6, Box 33
Centralia, IL 62801

**National Beep Baseball Association
(NBBA)**
Dr. Ed Bradley, President
9623 Spencer Highway
LaPorte, TX 77571

**National Foundation of Wheelchair
Tennis (NFWT)**
Brad Parks, Executive Director
940 Calle Amanecer, Suite B
San Clemente, CA 92673

**National Handicap Motorcyclist
Association (NHMA)**
315 West 21 St., Ste. 5B
New York, NY 10011

National Ocean Access Project
P.O. Box 10726
Rockville, MD 20849-0726

**National Rifle Association
(NRA)**
1600 Rhode Island Ave., NW
Washington, DC 20036

**National Strength and Conditioning
Association (NSCA)**
P.O. Box 81410
Lincoln, NE 68501

National Wheelchair Athletic
Association
3595 E. Fountain Boulevard
Suite L-1
Colorado Springs, CO 80910

National Wheelchair Basketball
Association (NWBA)
110 Seaton Building
University of Kentucky
Lexington, KY 40506

National Wheelchair Racquetball
Association
2380 McGinley Rd.
Monroeville, PA 15146

National Wheelchair Shooting
Federation (NWSF)
102 Park Ave.
Rockledge, PA 19046

National Wheelchair Softball
Association (NWSA)
Jon Speake, Commissioner
1616 Todd Ct.
Hastings, MN 55033

North American Riding for the
Handicapped Association (NARHA)
Bill Scebbi, Executive Director
Box 33150
Denver, CO 80233

POINT (Paraplegics On Independent
Nature Trips)
4144 N. Central Expy., Ste. 515
Dallas, TX 75204

Professional Association of Diving
Instructors
1251 E. Dyer Rd., No. 100
Santa Ana, CA 92705

Skating Association for the Blind and
Handicapped (SABAH)
548 Elmwood Ave.
Buffalo, NY 14222

Ski for Light, Inc.
1455 W. Lake Street
Minneapolis, MN 55408

Special Olympics International
(SOI)
1350 New York Ave. NW
Suite 500
Washington, DC 20005

United States Amateur Confederation
of Roller Skating (USACRS)
P.O. Box 6579
Lincoln, NE 68506

United States Association for Blind
Athletes (USABA)
33 N. Institute St.
Colorado Springs, CO 80903

United States Cerebral Palsy Athletic
Association (USCPAA)
34518 Warren Rd., Suite 264
Westland, MI 48185

United States Cycling Federation
(USCF)
1750 E. Boulder St.
Colorado Springs, CO 80909

United States Deaf Tennis
Association (USDTA)
c/o American Athletic Association
for the Deaf (AAAD)
3607 Washington Blvd., No. 4
Ogden, UT 84403-1737

United States Diving (USD)
Pan American Plaza
201 S. Capitol Ave., Ste. 430
Indianapolis, IN 46225

United States Fencing Association
(USFA)
1750 East Boulder St.
Colorado Springs, CO 80909

United States Figure Skating
Association (USFSA)
20 First St.
Colorado Springs, CO 80906

U.S.A. Gymnastics (USA Gym)
201 S. Capitol Ave., Suite 300
Indianapolis, IN 46225

United States International
Speedskating Association (USISA)
P.O. Box 16157
Rocky River, OH 44116

United States Les Autres Sports
Association (USLASA)
1101 Post Oak Blvd., Suite 9-486
Houston, TX 77056

United States Organization
for Disabled Athletes (USODA)
c/o John Hurley
143 California Ave.
Uniondale, NY 11553-1131

United States Parachute Association
(USPA)
1440 Duke St.
Alexandria, VA 22314

United States Powerlifting Federation
(USPF)
1013 S. Fayetteville St.
Asheboro, NC 27203-6809

United States Quad Rugby
Association (USQRA)
1605 Mathews St.
Ft. Collins, CO 80525

United States Skiing (USSA)
P.O. Box 100
Park City, UT 84060

United States Disabled Ski Team
(USDST)
P.O. Box 100
Park City, UT 84060

United States Soccer Federation
(USSF)
1801-1811 S. Prairie Ave.
Chicago, IL 60616

United States Swimming (USS)
1 Olympic Plaza
Colorado Springs, CO 80909

United States Table Tennis
Association (USTTA)
1 Olympic Plaza
Colorado Springs, CO 80909

United States Taekwondo Union
(USTU)
1750 East Boulder St., Ste. 405
Colorado Springs, CO 80909

United States Team Handball
Federation (USTHF)
1750 East Boulder St.
Colorado Springs, CO 80909

United States Tennis Association
(USTA)
1212 Avenue of the Americas
New York, NY 10036

United States Volleyball Association
(USVBA)
3595 E. Fountain Blvd.
Colorado Springs, CO 80910-1740

United States Weightlifting
Federation (USWF)
1 Olympic Plaza
Colorado Springs, CO 80909

United States Wheelchair Weightlifting
Federation (USWWF)
Bill Hens
39 Michael Place
Levittown, PA 19057

U.S. Sailing
P.O. Box 209
Newport, RI 02840

U.S.A. Basketball
5465 Mark Dabling Blvd.
Colorado Springs, CO 80918-3842

The USA Karate Federation
(USAKF)
1300 Kenmore Blvd.
Akron, OH 44314

U.S.A. Wrestling (USAW)
6155 Lehman Dr.
Colorado Springs, CO 80918

US Association of Disabled Sailors
Southern California Chapter
Mike Watson, P.O. Box 15245
Newport Beach, CA 92659

United States Blind Golfer's
Association
  3094 Shamrock St. N.
  Tallahassee, FL 32308

United States Deaf Skiers
Association
  c/o Sandra McGee
  130 Rosewood Pl.
  Bridgeport, CT 06610

US Rowing Association
  Adaptive Rowing Committee
  201 S. Capitol Ave., Ste. 400
  Indianapolis, IN 46225

USA Track and Field
  P.O. Box 120
  Indianapolis, IN 46206

Wheelchair Motorcycle Association
(WMA)
  Dr. Eli Factor
  101 Torrey St.
  Brockton, MA 02401

NATIONAL SPORT ASSOCIATIONS: CANADA

Alberta Sledge Hockey and Ice
Picking Association
  Medicine Hat, AB

Canadian Association for Disabled
Skiing
  Banff, AB

Canadian Blind Sports Association
(CBSA)
  Ottawa, ON

Canadian Electric Wheelchair
Hockey Association
  Willowdale, ON

Canadian Wheelchair Sports
Association
  Gloucester, ON

Ontario Wheelchair Sports
Association (OWSA)
  North York, ON

Ottawa-Carleton Sledge Hockey
and Ice Picking Association
  Nepean, ON

Sport for the Physically Disabled
  Ottawa, ON

DISABLED SPORTS USA (DS/USA), FORMERLY NATIONAL HANDICAPPED SPORTS (NHS) REGIONAL CHAPTERS

ALASKA
  Access Alaska
  Fairbanks

  Alpine Alternatives
  Anchorage

  Challenge Alaska
  Anchorage

CALIFORNIA
  CalSTAR
  Berkeley

  Mother Lode Chapter
  Camp Connell

  NHS, Northern California Chapter
  Truckee

CALIFORNIA (*continued*)
NHS of Fresno
Fresno

NHS of Orange County
La Habra

NHS of Southern California
Redondo Beach

San Diego Adventurers
Encinitas

CONNECTICUT
Connecticut Handicapped Ski Foundation
South Windsor

COLORADO
Aspen Handicapped Skiers Association
Snowmass Village

Breckenridge Outdoor Education Center for the Handicapped
Breckenridge

Challenge West
Colorado Springs

Children's Hospital Handicapped Sports Program
Denver

Colorado Discover Ability
Mesa

Crested Butte Physically Challenged Skier Program
Mount Crested Butte

Durango/Purgatory Handicapped Sports Association
Durango

Golf 4 Fun
Englewood

National Sports Center for the Disabled
Winter Park

Rocky Mountain Handicapped Sportsmen's Association
Lakewood

DISTRICT OF COLUMBIA
National Ocean Access Project
Washington

Nation's Capital Chapter
West River

FLORIDA
NHS, South Florida Chapter
Coral Gables

GEORGIA
NHS, Atlanta Chapter
Clarkston

IDAHO
Association for Handicapped Recreation, Inc.
Coeur d'Alene

Recreation Unlimited, Inc.
Boise

ILLINOIS
Chicagoland Handicapped Skiers
Wheaton

R-I-Ckiers (Rehabilitation Institute of Chicago)
Chicago

INDIANA
Calumet Region Chapter
East Chicago

Greater Indianapolis Chapter Handicapped Skiing
Indianapolis

Special Outdoor Leisure Opportunities, Inc.
South Bend

IOWA
Sundown Handicapped Skiers
Dubuque

MARYLAND
Baltimore Adaptive Recreational Sports
Towson

MASSACHUSETTS,
NEW HAMPSHIRE, MAINE
New England Handicapped
Sports Association
Chelmsford

MICHIGAN
Michigan Handicapped Sports and
Recreation Association
Rochester Hills

Cannonsburg Challenged Skier
Association
Grand Rapids

MINNESOTA
Courage Alpine Skiers
Minnetonka

Twin Ports Flyers
Duluth

MONTANA
Dream-Big Mountain Disabled Ski
Program
Kalispell

I Am Third Foundation dba Eagle
Mount
Bozeman

NEVADA
Lakeside Chapter, City
of Las Vegas
Las Vegas

Northern Nevada Ski School
for the Disabled
Incline Village

NEW HAMPSHIRE
Northeast Passage Outing Club
Salem

NEW MEXICO
Lovelace/Sandia Peak Ski Program
Albuquerque

NEW YORK
NHS of New York
Endwell

Disabled Ski Program
of Ski Windham
Albany

NORTH CAROLINA
YMCA Wake County Inc.
Raleigh

OHIO
Three Trackers of Ohio
Akron

OREGON
Flying Outriggers Ski Club
Portland

Mount Hood Handicap Ski
Association, Inc.
Portland

Shared Outdoor Adventure
Recreation
Portland

PENNSYLVANIA
Deutsch Institute Applied Research
Center
Scranton

Good Shepherd Rehabilitation
Hospital
Allentown

The Philadelphia Area
Handicapped Skiing Club
Ardmore

Three Rivers Adaptive Sports
Pittsburgh

SOUTH CAROLINA
Palmetto Players
Irmo

TEXAS
Southwest Wheelchair Athletic
Association
Houston

UTAH
Park City Handicapped Sports
Association
Park City

UTAH (*continued*)
Paul Hill Adaptive Sports
Association
American Forks

Utah Handicapped Skiers
Association
Roy

VERMONT
Vermont Handicapped Ski
and Sports Association
Brownsville

VIRGINIA
Woodrow Wilson Rehabilitation Ctr.
Fisherville

WASHINGTON
Seattle Handicapped Sports
& Recreation Association
Seattle

WEST VIRGINIA
The Challenge Athletes
of Silver Creek, West Virginia
Slatyfork

NATIONAL WHEELCHAIR ATHLETIC ASSOCIATION CHAPTERS

Appalachian WAA
Harrisburg, PA

Central States WAA
Indianapolis, IN

Dixie WAA
Grayson, GA

Far West WAA
San Jose, CA

Hawaii WAA
Honolulu, HI

Michigan WAA
Sterling Heights, MI

Mid-Atlantic WAA
Fisherville, VA

New England WAA
Plympton, MA

North Central WAA
Marshall, MN

Southwest WAA
Houston, TX

Sunshine WAA
Tampa, FL

Tri-State WAA
Whitestone, NY

WHEELCHAIR SPORTS USA

American Wheelchair Table Tennis
Association
Port Chester, NY

Archery Sports Section
West Sunbury, PA

National Wheelchair Shooting
Federation
San Antonio, TX

United States Wheelchair Weightlifting Federation
Levittown, PA

U.S. Wheelchair Swimming
Middleboro, MA

Wheelchair Athletics of the USA
Houston, TX

SPECIAL OLYMPICS INTERNATIONAL

Special Olympics International (SOI) has chapters throughout the United States and U.S. Territories, including American Samoa, Guam, and the Virgin Islands.

SOI also offers programs in numerous countries around the world. For further information on these programs, contact the Washington, DC, SOI office, or the appropriate regional director (Africa, Asia/Pacific, Caribbean, Europe, or Latin America).

International Regional Directors

Programs are offered in the following countries:

Antigua	Macao
Argentina	Mexico
Australia	Monaco
Austria	Nepal
Bahamas	New Zealand
Barbados	Nicaragua
Belgium	Nigeria
Bermuda	Norway
Bolivia	Panama
Brazil	Paraguay
Canada	People's Republic of China
Chile	Peru
Chinese Taipei	The Phillippines
Colombia	Poland
Costa Rica	Portugal
Cuba	St. Kitts-Nevis
Cyprus	St. Lucia
Denmark	St. Vincent and the Grenadines
Ecuador	San Marino
El Salvador	The Seychelles
France	Sierra Leone
Ghana	Singapore
Gibraltar	South Korea
Greece	Spain
Grenada	Suriname
Guatemala	Switzerland
Honduras	Tanzania
Hong Kong	Thailand
India	Trinidad/Tobago
Ireland	Tunisia
Israel	Turkey
Italy	United Kingdom
Jamaica	Uruguay
Japan	Venezuela
Jordan	West Germany
Kenya	Yugoslavia
	Zimbabwe

APPENDIX F

Selected National Disability Sport Organizations Worldwide (Except United States)[1]

AFGHANISTAN
Blinderinstitut Kabul
Kabul

ALGERIA
Federation Sports pour
Handicapes et Inadaptes
Algiers

ARGENTINA
Servicio Nacional de Rehabilitacion
Capital Federal BS AS

AUSTRALIA
Australian Deaf Sports
Federation LTD
East Melbourne

Australian Paralympic Federation
Avalon Beach

AUSTRIA
Osterreichischer
Vienna

Osterreichischer Gehörlosen-
Sportverband
Wien

BAHAMAS
Bahamas Paraplegic Association
Nassau

STATE OF BAHRAIN
Bahrain Disabled Sports
Committee
Manama

BANGLADESH
National Games for Disabled
Association
Dhaka

Bangladesh Deaf Sports
Federation
Dhaka

BELGIUM
B.S.V.G.
Brussels

Royale Federation Sportive
des Sourds de Belgique
Waregem

---

[1]Addresses for these organizations can be obtained from the IPC.

BOLIVIA
Organizacion Deportiva
   Para Ciegos
La Paz

BRAZIL
Brazilian Paralympic Committee
Brazilia

Confedercao Brasileira Desportiva
   Dos Surdos
Rio de Janiero

BULGARIA
Bulgarian Council for Physical
   Culture & Sports
Sofia

Union of the Deaf in Bulgaria
Sofia

BURMA
The Blind School
Rangoon

CAMEROON
Ministere des Affairs Sociales
Yaounde

CANADA
Canadian Federation of Sports
   Organizations for the Disabled
Gloucester

Canadian Federation of Sports
   Organizations for the Disabled
Federation canadienne
   des organizations de sport
   pour handicapes
Ottawa

Canadian Amputee Sports
   Association
Association canadienne des sports
   pour amputee
Ottawa

Canadian Association for Disabled
   Skiing
Association canadienne des sports
   pour skiers handicapes
Ottawa

Canadian Blind Sports Association
Association canadienne des sports
   pour aveugles
Ottawa

Canadian Wheelchair Sports
   Association
Association canadienne des sports
   en fauteuil roulant
Ottawa

Canadian Deaf Sports Association
L'association des sports des sourds
   du Canada
Vancouver

CHILE
Federacion de Deportistas Lisiados
Santiago

CHINA
All China Sports Federation
   International Department
Beijing

COLOMBIA
Federacion de Deportes
Bogota

Federacion Colombiana Deportiva
   de Sordos
Cali

COSTA RICA
Asociacion de Ciegos
San Jose

Asociacion Deportiva Nacional
   de Sordos de Costa Rica
San Jose

CUBA
Federacion de Deportes
Havana 4

CURACAO
Sport Gehandicapten
Willemstad

CYPRUS
Cyprus Paraplegic Organisation
Nicosia

CZECHOSLOVAKIA
Sports Organisation for the
Disabled
Prague

Svaz Neslysicich Sportovcu
CTSV
Prague

DENMARK
Dansk Handicap Idraets-Forbund
Brøndby

Dansk Dove-Idraetsforbund
Copenhagen

DOMINICAN REPUBLIC
Organizacion De Deportes
Santo Domingo

ECUADOR
Federacione Deportiva
Guayaquil

EGYPT
Egyptian Sports for Disabled
Cairo

EL SALVADOR
Centro de Rehabilitacion para
Ciegos "Eugenia de Duenas"
San Salvador

ETHIOPIA
Ethiopian National Association
of the Blind
Addis Ababa

FAROE ISLANDS
Itrottasamband Fyri Brekad
Torshavn

FIJI
The Principal Fiji School
for the Blind
Suva

FINLAND
Finnish Association of Sports
for the Disabled
Helsinki

Suomen Kuurojen
Espoo

FRANCE
Federation Francaise Handisport
Paris

Federation Sportive des Sourds
de France
Paris

GERMANY
Deutscher Behinderten
Sportverband
Duisburg

Deutscher Gehörlosen
Sportverband
Essen

GHANA
Wenchi Secondary School
Wenchi

GREECE
Spinal Injuries Association
of Greece
Athens

Hellenic Athletic Association
of the Deaf
Athens

GUATEMALA
Union de Minusvalidos
Colonia Miraflores

HONG KONG
Hong Kong Sports Association
for the Physically Handicapped
Kowloon

Hong Kong Sports Association
of the Deaf
Kowloon

HUNGARY
Sports Federation for Disabled
Budapest

Hallasserultek Testnevelesi
Essportbizottsaga
Budapest

ICELAND
Sport Association for the Disabled
in Iceland
Reykjavik

ICELAND *(continued)*
Iceland Deaf Sport Club
Reykjavik

INDIA
Indian Council of Sports
for the Disabled
Calcutta

All India Sports Council of India
New Dehli

INDONESIA
Indonesian Foundation
for the Promotion of Sports
for the Disabled
Surakarta

IRAN
Sports Federation for Disabled
Tehran

Deaf Sports Federation
Islamic Republic of Iran
Tehran

IRAQ
Iraqi Federation of Sport
for the Disabled
Baghdad

IRELAND
Irish Wheelchair Association
Dublin

Irish Deaf Sports Association
Dublin

ISRAEL
Israel Sports Association
for the Disabled
Tel Aviv

Sport Organisation of the Deaf
in Israel
Tel Aviv

ITALY
Federazione Italiana Sport
Handicappati
Rome

Federazione Sport Silenziosi
D'Italia
Rome

JAMAICA
Jamaica Paraplegic Association
Kingston

JAPAN
Japanese Sports Association
for the Disabled
Tokyo

Japan Athletic Association
of the Deaf
Tokyo

JORDAN
Sports Federation
for the Handicapped
Amman

KENYA
Kenya Paraplegic Sports
Association
Nairobi

KOREA
Korea Sports Association
for the Disabled
Seoul

Korea Deaf Sports Federation
Seoul

KUWAIT
Kuwait Club for the Disabled
Hawalli

LEBANON
Lebanese Blind Worker's
Association
Beirut

LIBYA
Libyan Federation of Sports
for the Disabled
Tripoli

LIECHTENSTEIN
Liechtensteinischer
Invalidenverband
Vaduz

LUXEMBOURG
Federation Sportive
Luxembourgeoise des
Handicapes Physiques
Mersch

MACAU
Associacao Recreativa
des Deficientes
Macau

MADAGASCAR
Institut des Aveugles de Loharano
Antsirabe

MALAYSIA
Perstuan Orang-Orang, Cacat
Anggota Malaysia
Kuala Lumpur

MALI
Association Malienne pour la
Promotion Sociale des Aveugles
Bamako

MALTA
Physically Handicapped
Rehabilitation Fund
Paola

MAURITIUS
Mauritius Handisports Red.
Beau Bassin

MEXICO
Federacion Mexicana de Deportes
Sobre Silla de Ruedas
Y Rehabillitados
Mexico City

Asociacion Deportiva Silente
de Mexico, A.C.
Mexico City

MOROCCO
Royal Moroccan Federation
of Sports for the Disabled
Rabat

MOZAMBIQUE
Instituto Nacional para Deficientes
Visuais de Beira
Beira

NETHERLANDS
S.V.G.N.
Utrecht

Koninklijke Nederlandse Doven
Sport Bond
Amsterdam

NEW ZEALAND
The New Zealand Paraplegic and
Physically Disabled Federation
Hamilton

New Zealand Deaf Amateur
Sports Association
Christchurch

NAIMEY
Association Nationale
des Aveugles
Balafon

NICARAGUA
Centro de Rehabilitacion
Managua

NIGERIA
Sports Association for the
Disabled
Sabo, Yaba

NORWAY
Norges Handicap
Rud

Norges Dove-Idrettsforbund
Oslo

OMAN
Ministry of Social Affairs
Muscat

PAKISTAN
National Training Centre
for Disabled Persons
Islamabad

PANAMA
Asociacion Nacional de Deportes
para Ciegos
Panama City

PAPUA NEW GUINEA
Port Moresby General Hospital
Boroka

PERU
Union Nacional de Ciegos
Lima

POLAND
Zrzeszenie Sportowe
Spoldzielcsosci Pracy
Warsaw

Polski Zwiazek Gluchych
Warsaw

PORTUGAL
Associacao Portuguesa
de Paralesia Cerebral
Coimbra

Associacao Portuguesa de Surdos
Lisbon

PUERTO RICO
Asociacion Deportivea de Sillas
de Ruedas
San Juan

SAUDI ARABIA
Vocational Rehabilitation Centre
for Handicapped
Riyadh

SCOTLAND
Scottish Council For Spastics
Edinburgh

SENEGAL
Union Nationale des Aveugles
du Senegal
Jhies

SEYCHELLES
Sports Association for the
Disabled
Victoria

SINGAPORE
Singapore Sports Council
for the Disabled
Singapore

SOUTH AFRICA
South African Sports Association
for the Physically Disabled
Somerset West

South African Deaf Sports
Federation
Pretoria

SPAIN
Federacion Espanola de Deportes
para Minusvalidos
Madrid

Comite Espanol de Deportes
Silenciosos
Madrid

SRI LANKA
National Association of Sports
for Disabled
Moratuwa

SUDAN
The Sudanese Society for Disabled
Khartoum

SWAZILAND
Swaziland National Society
for the Handicapped
Mbabane

SWEDEN
SHIF
Farsta

Sveriges Dovas
Nyhamnslage

SWITZERLAND
Swiss Paralympic Committees
Kriens

Schweizerischer Gehörlosen
Sportverband SGSV
Grub/AR

SYRIA
Syrian Sports for Disabled
Damascus

TAIWAN
Sports Organization for Disabled
Taipei

TANZANIA
Sports Association for the Disabled
Dar es Salaam

THAILAND
The Sports Association for the
Disabled of Thailand
Bangkok

TRINIDAD AND TOBAGO
Society for Disabled
Port-of-Spain

TUNISIA
Federation Tunisienne des Sports
Pour Handicapes
Tunis

TURKEY
Altan Enguclu
Ankara

Turkiye Sagir-Dilsiz Spor
Kulupleri Federasyonu
Istanbul

UNITED KINGDOM
British Paralympic Association
Croydon

British Sports Association
for the Disabled
Aylesbury

Central Council of Physical
Rehabilitation
London

British Council of Physical
Education
Liverpool

PHAB (Physically Handicapped
Able Bodied)
London

The Spastics Society
London

Royal National Institute for the
Blind
London

British Amputees Sports
Association
Redhill

British Association for Sporting
and Recreational Activities
of the Blind
London

British Deaf Sports Council
Bradford

British Deaf Sports Council
Carlisle

British Paraplegic Sports Society
Aylesbury

United Kingdom Sports Association
for People with Mental
Handicap
London

Special Olympics UK
London

British Ski Club for the Disabled
Warminster

British Disabled Water Ski
Assocation
Ashtead

UNITED KINGDOM *(continued)*
Riding for the Disabled Association
Kenilworth

BSAD Water Sports Division
East Sussex

Association of Swimming Therapy
Sandbach

National Association of Swimming
Clubs for the Handicapped
Brighton

Wheelchair Dance Association
Tonbridge

USSR
USSR Federation for Disabled
Moscow, Russia

All-Russian Federation of Deaf
Sports
Moscow, Russia

URUGUAY
Organizacion Deportiva de Sordos
del Uruguay
Montevideo

Organizacion Deportiva de Sordos
del Uruguay
Montevideo

VENEZUELA
Fundacion Amigos de Ciegos
Maracaibo

Federacion Venezolana
Polideportiva de Sordos
Caracas

VOLTA
Association des Aveugles
Burkina Faso
Ougadougou

YUGOSLAVIA
Savez Za Sport I Rekreaciju
Invalida Jugoslavija
Belgrade

Savez Gluvih I Naluvih
Jugoslavije
Belgrade

ZAMBIA
Zambia National Federation
of the Blind
Lusaka

ZIMBABWE
The Zimbabwe Association
for the Disabled
Bulawayo

APPENDIX G

Videos and Films on Disability Sports[1]

WHEELCHAIR SPORTS

"Advanced Wheelchair Tennis"

"Ball Bearings and Bent Spokes"

"Basketball Classification"

"Choosing Victory"

"Classification of Wheelchair Athletes"

"Introduction to Wheeling and Long-Distance Road Racing"

"Reach for the Stars"

"Sharing Is Caring"

"Tennis in a Wheelchair"

"USABA Summer Sports Coaches/Officials Training Video"

"USABA Winter Sports Adaptations"

"Wheelchair Basketball"

FITNESS

"Fit Is for Everyone"

"Keep Fit While You Sit"

"MS Workout"

"Nancy's Special Workout for the Physically Challenged"

"Sit and Be Fit"

"Theracise"

"Wheelchair Aerobics"

"Wheelercise"

[1]For information on how to obtain any of these videos or films, contact a national DSO or *Sports 'n Spokes*.

WINTER SPORTS

"Escape to Ski"

"Mono-Ski Instruction"

"Sled Skiing for the Handicapped"

"Snow Dance"

COMPETITION

"1985 Boston Marathon"

"1985 National Wheelchair Games"

"30th National Wheelchair Games"

"34th Wheelchair Basketball Championships"

KOSAD—"Human Victory"

"Los Angeles Olympics Wheelchair Track Events"

"Pan American Wheelchair Games"

GENERAL SPORT

"Beginnings—Images of Excellence"

"Challenge Golf"

"Challenged Equestrians: The Use of the Horse for Special Populations"

"Crossbar"

"Freedom in Depth"

"Goal Ball: An Instructional Video"

"Here I Am"

"Introduction to Sailing for the Disabled"

"Never Say Never"

"The Terry Fox Mobile Clinic Presentation"

"Truly Exceptional: Carol Johnston"

APPENDIX H

Colleges and Universities With Scholarships for Individuals With Disabilities

ARIZONA

Arizona State University
Tedde Scharf, Director
Disabled Student Resources
Matthews Center, Room 143
Tempe, AZ 85287-3202

University of Arizona
Dr. Kent Kloepping, Director
David Corsi Outreach Counseling
  Service Center for Disability
  Relations and Resources
Second Street and Cherry
Tucson, AZ 85721

The U of A's wheelchair-sports programs include basketball, track, rugby, tennis, road racing, swimming, fitness, and weight training.

COLORADO

University of Colorado-Boulder
Ruth Fink, Director
Office of Services for Disabled Students
331 Willard
Campus Box 107
Boulder, CO 80309-0107

DELAWARE

Goldey-Beacom College
Jane Lysle, Director of Financial Aid
4701 Limestone Road
Wilmington, DE 19808

ILLINOIS

Southern Illinois University
  at Carbondale
Kathleen Plesko, Coordinator
Disabled Student Services
Woody Hall, B-150
Carbondale, IL 62901

University of Illinois
Dean Michael Ellis, Interim Director
Division of Rehabilitation
  Education Services
1207 South Oak Street
Champaign, IL 61820

The university provides comprehensive training and competitive programming in men's and women's wheelchair basketball, racing, quad rugby, and a wheelchair-tennis program.

IOWA

Iowa State University
Joyce Packwood, Coordinator
Services for Students with Disabilities
210 Student Services
Ames, IA 50011

NEW JERSEY

College of St. Elizabeth (for women)
Donna Yamanais, Dean of Admissions
and Financial Aid
2 Convent Road
Morristown, NJ 07960

NEW YORK

Hofstra University
Karin Spencer
Director, Programs for the Higher
Education of the Disabled
University Advisement Office
Hempstead
Long Island, NY 11550

OHIO

Kent State University
Janet Filer, Coordinator
Disabled Student Services
Michael Schwartz Center, Rm. 181
Kent, OH 44242-0001

Wright State University
Stephen Simon, Director
Jean Denney, Director of Intramural
Sports
E186 Student Union
Dayton, OH 45435

The campus has built a tunnel system that connects all major campus buildings, including one dorm. Students can travel in a climate-controlled environment. Wheelchair programs include men's intercollegiate wheelchair basketball, women's wheelchair basketball, wheelchair tennis, wheelchair softball, quad rugby, tandem biking, downhill skiing, aquatics, fitness, adapted intramurals and recreation, and wheelchair football. About 75% of all disabled students at Wright State University participate in one or more of the athletics programs.

Michael Emrick Scholarship
Up to five awards are given each year to students participating in adapted athletics or intramurals and recreation.

Wright State University Campus Scholarship
This award (the number given varies) goes each year to students participating in adapted athletics or intramurals and recreation.

Dan Byrnes Wheelchair Basketball Scholarship
Two awards are given each year, one each to a male and female wheelchair-basketball athlete.

SOUTH CAROLINA

Francis Marion College
Scott Brown
Financial Aid Director
Box 100547
Florence, SC 29501

SOUTH DAKOTA

South Dakota School of Mines and Technology
Michelle Spindler
Assistant Director of Financial Aid
501 East St. Joseph Street
Rapid City, SD 57701-3995

TEXAS

Texas A&M University
Molly Georgiades
Scholarship and Employment
Administrator
Student Financial Aid Office
College Station, TX 77843-1257

University of Houston
Caroline Gergely, Director
Handicapped Student Services
4800 Calhoun
Student Services Center, Rm. 307
Houston, TX 77204-3243

The school has an adapted physical education program and a wheelchair-basketball team, the Rolling Cougars.

The University of Texas-Arlington
Jim Hayes, Director
Office for Students With Disabilities
LL University Center
Box 19355
Arlington, TX 76019

Andrew David Beck Memorial Wheelchair Scholarship

This award is given to a wheelchair athlete in the tennis, quad rugby, track and field, swimming, table tennis, or air weapons program.

Wheelchair Athletic Scholarship

This award is given to an incoming freshman recruited for the basketball team. The student must maintain a 2.0 GPA and full-time status.

VIRGINIA

Old Dominion University

Nancy Olthoff
Director of Disabilities Services
1050 Webb Center
Norfolk, VA 23529

APPENDIX I

Periodicals on Physical Education, Sport, and Recreation for Individuals With Disabilities[1]

Accent on Living

Adapted Physical Activity Quarterly

American Journal of Art Therapy

American Journal of Physical Medicine

American Rehabilitation

Archives of Physical Medicine and Rehabilitation

Bulletin of Prosthetics Research

Canadian Abilities Foundation

Clinics in Sports Medicine

Committee on Recreation and Leisure Newsletter

Disabled USA

Exceptional Children

Exceptional Child Education Resources

Exercise and Sports Science Review

The Gold Rush

Itinerary Magazine

Journal of Leisurability

Journal of Pediatric Exercise Science

Journal of Physical Education and Sport

Journal of Physical Education, Recreation and Dance

Journal of Rehabilitation

LTD Travel

Mainstream

MCTRH Newsletter

Medicine and Science in Sports and Exercise

The National Hookup
A monthly newsletter of indoor sports.

National Wheelchair Athletic Association Newsletter

---

[1]Addresses for these periodicals may be found in *Ulrich's International Periodical Directory* (33rd ed.), published by Bowker.

New World Magazine

Orthotics and Prosthetics

Palaestra

Paraplegia Life

Paraplegia News

Physical Therapy

Physician and Sportsmedicine

Rehabilitation Gazette

Rehabilitation Literature

Special Recreation Digest

Sports Medicine

Sports 'n Spokes

Strategies

Teaching Exceptional Children

Therapeutic Recreation Journal

Together—News for the
Rehabilitation Community

Update

Note: Newsletters are available from disability sport organizations as well.

References

Adams, R.C., & McCubbin, J.A. (1991). *Games, sports and exercises for the physically disabled* (4th ed.). Philadelphia: Lea & Febiger.

Adelson, E., & Fraiberg, S. (1974). Gross motor development in infants blind from birth. *Child Development*, **5**, 114-126.

Adeoja, T.A. (1987). Psychological and social problems of physical disability: State of the art and relevance to physical education. In M.E. Berridge & G.R. Ward (Eds.), *International perspectives on adapted physical activity* (pp. 25-31). Champaign, IL: Human Kinetics.

Alexander, M.J. (1984). Analysis of the high jump technique of an amputee. *Palaestra*, **1**, 19-23, 44-48.

American Academy of Orthopedic Surgeons. (1991). *Athletic training and sports medicine*. Park Ridge, IL: Author.

American Alliance for Health, Physical Education, Recreation and Dance. (1975). *Annotated bibliography in physical education, recreation, and psychomotor function of mentally retarded persons*. Reston, VA: Author.

American Alliance for Health, Physical Education, Recreation and Dance. (1976). *Involving impaired, disabled, and handicapped persons in regular camping programs*. Reston, VA: Author.

American College of Sports Medicine. (1990). The recommended quantity and quality of exercise for developing and maintaining fitness in healthy adults. *Medicine and Science Sports Exercise*, **22**, 265-274.

Ammons, D. (1986). World Games for the Deaf. In C. Sherrill (Ed.), *Sport and disabled athletes* (pp. 65-72). Champaign, IL: Human Kinetics.

Anderson, S.C. (1980). Effectiveness of an introduction to therapeutic recreation courses on students' attitudes toward the disabled. *Leisurability*, **7**, 13-16.

Andrew, G.M., Reid, J.G., Beck, S., & McDonald, W. (1979). Training of the developmentally handicapped young adults. *Canadian Journal of Applied Sport Sciences*, **4**, 289-293.

Appenzeller, H. (1983). *The right to participate*. Charlottesville, VA: Michie.

Arnhold, R.W., & McGrain, P. (1985). Selected kinematic patterns of visually impaired youth in sprint running. *Adapted Physical Activity Quarterly*, **2**, 206-213.

Asken, M.J. (1990). The challenge of the physically challenged: Delivering sport psychology services to physically disabled athletes. *Sport Psychologist*, **5**, 370-381.

Asken, M.J., & Goodling, M.D. (1986a). Sport psychology I: An undeveloped discipline from among the sport sciences for disabled athletes. *Adapted Physical Activity Quarterly*, **3**, 312-319.

Asken, M.J., & Goodling, M.D. (1986b). Sport psychology II: The basic concepts of readiness and concentration. *Sports 'n Spokes*, **12**, 22-24.

Asken, M.J., & Goodling, M.D. (1986c). Sport psychology III: Techniques for performance enhancement and competitive stress management. *Sports 'n Spokes, 12,* 27-29.

Asmussen, E., & Poulsen, E. (1966). A battery of physiological tests applied to two different groups of handicapped persons. *Communications of Testing and Observation Institute, 13,* 1-13.

Atlanta Paralympic Organizing Committee. (n.d.). *The triumph of the human spirit.* Atlanta, GA: Author.

Aufsesser, P.M. (1982). Comparison of the attitudes of physical education, recreation, and special education majors toward the disabled. *American Corrective Therapy Journal, 36,* 35-41.

Australian Coaching Council. (1989a). Coaching athletes with disabilities. *Sports Coach, 12*(4), 6-8.

Australian Coaching Council. (1989b). *Amputee athletes: Coaching athletes with disabilities.* Canberra, NSW: Australian Sports Commission.

Australian Coaching Council. (1989c). *Coaching athletes with disabilities: Hearing impaired athletes.* Canberra, NSW: Author.

Australian Sports Commission. (1989d). *Intellectual disabilities: Coaching athletes with disabilities.* Canberra, NSW: Author.

Australian Sports Commission. (1993). *Coaching athletes with disabilities: General principles.* Canberra, NSW: Author.

Axelson, P., & Castellano, J. (1990). Take to the trail . . . Everything you wanted to know about off-road wheelchairs. *Sports 'n Spokes, 16,* 20-24.

Barker, R.G., Wright, B.A., & Gonick, H.R. (1983). Adjustment to physical handicap and illness: A survey of the social psychology of physique and disability. *Social Science Research Council Bulletin, 5*(55), 5.

Barrish, M.B., & Ndungane, E. (1988). Sport for the physically disabled in South Africa. *Journal of the International Council for Health, Physical Education, and Recreation, 25,* 13-15, 27.

Beal, O.P., Glaser, R.M., Petrofsky, J.S., Smith, P.A., & Fox, E.L. (1981). Static components of handgrip muscles for various wheelchair propulsions. *Federation Proceedings, 40,* 497.

Beasley, C.R. (1982). Effects of a jogging program on cardiovascular fitness and work performance of mentally retarded adults. *American Journal of Mental Deficiency, 86,* 609-613.

Berg, K. (1970). Effect of physical training of school children with cerebral palsy. *Acta Paediatrica Scandinavica,* (Suppl. 244), 27-33.

Beuter, A.C. (1983). Effects of mainstreaming on motor performance of intellectually normal and trainable mentally retarded students. *American Corrective Therapy Journal, 37,* 48-52.

Bicknell, J. (1972). Riding for the handicapped. *Outdoors, 3*(3), 33.

Biering-Sorensen, F. (1980). Classification of paralyzed and amputee sportsmen. In H. Natvig (Ed.), *Proceedings of the First International Medical Congress on Sports and the Disabled* (pp. 44-54). Oslo, Norway: Royal Ministry of Church and Education, Office of Youth and Sport.

Bird, P.J., & Gansneder, B.M. (1979). Preparation of physical education teachers as required under Public Law 94-142. *Exceptional Children*, **45**, 464-466.

Birk, T., Gavron, S., Ross, S.E., Hackett, K., Boullard, K., Olson, R., & Gosling, R. (1983). *Physiological profiles of three women from the 5th International Cerebral Palsy Games*. Paper presented at the 4th International Symposium in Adapted Physical Activity, London.

Birk, T., Gavron, S., Ross, S.E., Hackett, K., Boullard, K. & Olson, R. (1984). *Relationship of perceived exertion and heart rate response during exercise testing in wheelchair users*. Paper presented at American Alliance of Health, Physical Education, Recreation and Dance, April 8, 1983, Minneapolis.

Birk, T.J., & Birk, C.A. (1987). Use of ratings of perceived exertion for exercise prescription. *Sports Medicine*, **4**, 1-8.

Birrell, S.J. (1988). Discourses on the gender/sport relationship: From women in sport to gender relations. In K.B. Pandolf (Ed.), *Exercise and Sport Sciences Reviews* (pp. 459-502). New York: Macmillan.

Birrer, R.B. (1984). The Special Olympics: An injury overview. *Physician and Sportsmedicine*, **12**, 95-97.

Blair, S., Kohl, H., & Goodyear, N. (1987). Rates and risks for running and exercise injuries: Studies in three populations. *Research Quarterly for Exercise and Sport*, **58**, 221-228.

Bloomquist, L.E. (1986). Injuries to athletes with physical disabilities: Prevention implications. *Physician and Sportsmedicine*, **14**, 96-105.

Bobath, B. (1971). Motor development: Its effect on general development and application to the treatment of cerebral palsy. *Physiotherapy*, **57**, 526-532.

Bonace, B., Karwas, M.R., & DePauw, K.P. (1992). *Sport and marginalized individuals*. Paper presented at the National Girls and Women in Sport Symposium, October 1992, Slippery Rock, PA.

Boutilier, M.A. & SanGiovanni, L. (1983). *The Sporting Woman*. Champaign, IL: Human Kinetics.

Boyd, J. (1967). Comparison of motor behavior in deaf and hearing boys. *American Annals of the Deaf*, **112**, 598-605.

Braginsky, D.D., & Braginsky, B.M. (1971). *Hansels and Gretels: Studies of children in institutions for the mentally retarded*. New York: Holt, Rinehart & Winston.

Brandmeyer, G.A., & McBee, G.F. (1985). Social status and athletic competition for the disabled athlete: The case of wheelchair road racing. In C. Sherrill (Ed.), *Sport and disabled athletes* (pp. 181-188). Champaign, IL: Human Kinetics.

Brasile, F.M. (1986). Wheelchair basketball skills proficiencies versus disability classification. *Adapted Physical Activity Quarterly*, **3**, 6-13.

Brasile, F.M. (1990a). Performance evaluation of wheelchair athletes: More than a disability classification level issue. *Adapted Physical Activity Quarterly*, **4(7)**, 289-297.

Brasile, F.M. (1990b). Wheelchair sports: A new perspective on integration. *Adapted Physical Activity Quarterly*, 4(7), 3-11.

Brasile, F.M. (1992). Inclusion: A developmental perspective—A rejoinder to examining the concept of reverse integration. *Adapted Physical Activity Quarterly*, 9, 293-304.

Brattgard, S.O. (1970). Energy expenditure and heart rate in driving a wheelchair ergometer. *Scandinavian Journal of Rehabilitation and Medicine*, 2, 143-148.

Brenes, G., Dearwater, S., Shapera, R., LaPorte, R.E, & Collins, E. (1986). High-density lipoprotein cholesterol concentrations in physically active and sedentary SCI patients. *Archives of Physical Medicine and Rehabilitation*, 67, 445-450.

Broadhead, G.D. (1986). Adapted physical education research trends: 1970-1990. *Adapted Physical Activity Quarterly*, 3, 104-111.

Brouha, L., & Korbath, H. (1967). Continuous recording of cardiac and respiratory functions in normal and handicapped persons. *Human Factors*, 9, 567-571.

Brubaker, C. (1984). Determination of the effects of mechanical advantage on propulsion with hand rims. *Wheelchair Mobility 1982-3*, pp. 1-3.

Brubaker, C., & McLaurin, C. (1982). Ergonomics of wheelchair propulsion. *Wheelchair III*, pp. 22-42.

Brud, R., & Grass, K. (1987). Strapping to enhance athletic performance of wheelchair competitors with C.P. *Palaestra*, 3, 28-32.

Bruin, M.I. de, & Binkhorst, R.A. (1982). Motor proficiency traits of deaf children. *Research Quarterly*, 53, 236-238.

Buell, C. (1979). Association for blind athletes as seen by a blind sportsman. *Journal of Visual Impairment and Blindness*, 73, 412-413.

Bulbulian, R., Johnson, R., Bruber, J., & Darabos, B. (1987). Body composition in paraplegic male athletes. *Medicine and Science in Sports and Exercise*, 19, 195-210.

Burgess, E.M., & Rappoport, A. (n.d.) *Physical fitness: A guide for individuals with lower limb loss*. Washington, DC: Veteran's Health Administration.

Burke, E.J., Auchinachie, J.A., Hayden, R., & Loftin, J.N. (1985). Energy cost of wheelchair basketball. *Physician and Sportsmedicine*, 13(3), 99-105.

Burkett, L.N., Chisum, J., Cook, R., Norton, B., Taylor, B., Ruppert, K., & Wells, C. (1987). Construction and validation of a hysteresis brake wheelchair ergometer. *Adapted Physical Activity Quarterly*, 4, 60-71.

Butterfield, S.A. (1986). Gross motor profiles of deaf children. *Perceptual and Motor Skills*, 62, 68-70.

Butterfield, S.A. (1991). Physical education and sport for the deaf: Rethinking the least restrictive environment. *Adapted Physical Activity Quarterly*, 8, 95-102.

Byrens, D.P. (1983). *Analysis of the competitive wheelchair stroke*. Unpublished master's thesis, University of Alberta.

Cameron, B.J., Ward, G.R., & Wicks, J.R. (1978). Relationship of type of training to maximum oxygen uptake and upper-limb strength in male paraplegic athletes. *Medicine and Science in Sports and Exercise*, 9, 58.

Canabal, M., Sherrill, C., & Rainbolt, W. (1987). Psychological mood profiles of elite cerebral palsied athletes. In M. Berridge & G. Ward (Eds.), *International perspectives on adapted physical activity* (pp. 157-163). Champaign, IL: Human Kinetics.

Canadian Association for Health, Physical Education and Recreation/L'Association canadienne pour la santé l'education physique et le loisir. (1988). *Jasper talks: Strategies for change in adapted physical activity in Canada*. Ottawa, ON: Author.

Capel, S.A., Sisley, B.L., & Desertrain, G.S. (1987). The relationship of role conflict and role ambiguity to burnout in high school basketball coaches. *Journal of Sport Psychology*, **9**, 106-117.

Carlson, L. (1992). Spectator medical care. *Physician and Sportsmedicine*, **20**(1), 141-142, 144.

Carter, M.J., Van Andel, G., & Robb, G. (1985). *Therapeutic recreation: A practical approach*. St. Louis: Times Mirror/Mosby.

Cauette, M., & Reid, G. (1985). Increasing the work output of severely retarded adults on a bicycle ergometer. *Education and Training of the Mentally Retarded*, **20**, 296-304.

Ceccotti, F.S. (1984). Wheelchair sport injuries: An athletic training approach. *Paraplegia News*, pp. 29-30.

Chawla, J.C., Bar, C., Creber, I., Price, J., & Andrews, B. (1977). Techniques for improving the strength and fitness of spinal cord injured patients. *Paraplegia*, **17**, 185-189.

Clark, G., French, R., & Henderson, H. (1985). Teaching techniques that develop positive attitudes. *Palaestra*, **2**, 14-17.

Clark-Carter, D.D., Heyes, A.D., & Howarth, C.I. (1986). The efficiency and walking speed of visually impaired people. *Ergonomics*, **29**, 779-789.

Clark-Carter, D.D., Heyes, A.D., & Howarth, C.I. (1987). The gait of visually impaired pedestrians. *Human Movement Science (Amsterdam)*, **3**(6), 277-282.

Clarke, H.H., & Clarke, D.H. (1963). *Developmental and adapted physical education*. Englewood Cliffs, NJ: Prentice-Hall.

Clarke, K.S. (1966). Caloric costs of activity in paraplegic persons. *Archives of Physical Medicine and Rehabilitation*, **47**, 429-435.

Clarke, K.S. (1986). Perspectives for the future of the disabled in sport. *Adapted Physical Activity Quarterly*, **3**, 152-155.

Clinkingbeard, J.R., Gersten, J.W., & Hoehn, D. (1964). Energy cost of ambulation in traumatic paraplegia. *American Journal of Physical Medicine*, **43**, 157-165.

Coaching disabled athletes: The role of NSA. (1985). *Coaching Director*, **1**(2), 7-10.

Cocoran, P.J. (1980). Sports medicine and the physiology of wheelchair marathon racing. *Orthopedic Clinics of North America*, **11**, 697-716.

Cohen, G.L. (1993). *Women in Sport*. Newbury Park, CA: Sage.

Comité International des Sports des Sourds. (1975-1985). *CISS handbook*. Washington, DC: Gallaudet University.

Cooke, R.E. (1984). Atlantoaxial instability in individuals with Down's syndrome. *Adapted Physical Activity Quarterly*, **1**, 194-196.

Cooper, M.A. (1988). The computer as a tool in coaching disabled athletes. *Palaestra*, **4**, 30-32, 35.

Cooper, M.A., Sherrill, C., & Marshall, D. (1986). Attitudes toward physical activity of elite cerebral palsied athletes. *Adapted Physical Activity Quarterly*, **3**, 14-21.

Copeland, R., & Sherrill, C. (1986). Colors seen best by visually impaired athletes: Implications for coaching. *Abstracts of Research Papers. 1986 AAHPERD Convention*. Reston, VA: American Alliance of Health, Physical Education, Recreation and Dance.

Corbett, J.L., Frankel, H.L., & Harris, P.J. (1971). Cardiovascular responses to tilting in tetraplegic man. *Journal of Physiology (London)*, **215**, 411-413.

Coutts, K.D. (1988). Heart rates of participants in wheelchair sports. *Paraplegia*, **26**, 43-49.

Coutts, K.D., Rhodes, E.C., & McKenzie, D.C. (1983). Maximal exercise responses of tetraplegics and paraplegics. *Journal of Applied Physiology*, **55**, 479-482.

Coutts, K.D., Rhodes, E.C., & McKenzie, D.C. (1985). Submaximal exercise responses of tetraplegics and paraplegics. *Journal of Applied Physiology*, **59**, 237-241.

Coutts, K.D., & Schutz, R.W. (1988). Analysis of wheelchair track performances. *Medicine and Science in Sports and Exercise*, **20**(2), 188-194.

Coutts, K.D., & Steryn, J.L. (1987). Aerobic and anaerobic power of Canadian wheelchair athletes. *Medicine and Science in Sports and Exercise*, **19**, 62-65.

Cowan, J. (1993). Brave in the attempt. *Olympian*, **19**, 23.

Cowell, L.L., Squires, W.G., & Raven, P.B. (1986). Benefits of aerobic exercise for the paraplegic: A brief review. *Medicine and Science in Sports and Exercise*, **18**, 501-508.

Coyle, C.P., & Kenney, W.B. (1990). Leisure characteristics of adults with physical disabilities. *Therapeutic Recreation Journal*, **24**(4), 64-73.

Cratty, B.J., Cratty, I.J., & Cornell, S. (1986). Motor planning abilities in deaf and hearing children. *American Annals of the Deaf*, **131**, 281-284.

Crews, D., Wells, C.L., Burkett, L., & McKeenman-Hopkins, V. (1982). A physiological profile of four wheelchair marathon racers. *Physician and Sportsmedicine*, **10**, 134-143.

Crocker, P.R.E. (1993). Sport and exercise physiology and research with individuals with physical disabilities: Using theory to advance knowledge. *Adapted Physical Activity Quarterly*, **10**, 324-335.

Curtis, K.A. (1981a). Wheelchair sports medicine: Part 1. *Sports 'n Spokes*, **7**.

Curtis, K.A. (1981b). Wheelchair sports medicine: Part 2. Training. *Sports 'n Spokes*, **7**, 21-22.

Curtis, K.A. (1982). Wheelchair sports medicine: Part 4. Athletic injuries. *Sports 'n Spokes*, **7**, 20-24.

Curtis, K.A. (1991). Sport-specific functional classification for wheelchair athletes. *Sports 'n Spokes,* **17**(2), 45-47.

Curtis, K.A., & Dillon, D.A. (1985). Survey of wheelchair athletic injuries: Common patterns and prevention. *Paraplegia,* **23,** 170-175.

Daignault, L. (1990). Integration battle heats up at Commonwealth Games. *Abilities,* **1,** 6-7.

Dal-Monte, A., Faina, M., Maglio, A., Sardella, G., & Guide, G. (1982). Cardiotele-metric and blood lactate investigations in paraplegic subjects during several sports activities. *Journal of Sports Medicine and Physical Fitness,* **22,** 172-184.

D'Alonzo, B.J. (1976). Rights of exceptional children to participate in interscholastic athletics. *Exceptional Children,* **43,** 86-92.

Dattilo, J. (1985). An alternative method to studying individuals with disabilities: Single subject research. *Leisure Information Quarterly,* **1**(12), 11.

Davies, E. (1975). *Adapted physical education* (3rd ed.) New York: Harper & Row.

Davis, G.M., Kofsky, P.R., Shephard, R.J., & Jackson, R.W. (1981). Classification of psycho-physiological variables in the lower-limb disabled. *Canadian Journal of Applied Sport Sciences,* **6**(3), 141.

Davis, G.M., Shephard, R.J., & Jackson, R.W. (1981). Cardiorespiratory fitness and muscular strength in the lower-limb disabled. *Canadian Journal of Applied Sport Sciences,* **6,** 159-165.

Davis, G.M., Shephard, R.J., & Ward, G.R. (1984). Alterations of dynamic strength following forearm crank training of disabled subjects. *Medicine and Science in Sports and Exercise,* **16,** 147.

Davis, R., & Ferrara, M. (1991). *Training profiles of elite wheelchair athletes.* Paper presented at the 8th International Symposium of Adapted Physical Activity, Miami.

Dawson, M. (1981). A biomechanical analysis of gait patterns of the visually impaired. *American Corrective Therapy Journal,* **35,** 66-71.

Decker, J.I. (1986). Role conflict of teacher/coaches in small colleges. *Sociology of Sport Journal,* **3,** 356-365.

Dendy, E. (1978). Recreation for the disabled people—What do we mean? *Physiotherapy,* **64,** 290-297.

DePauw, K.P. (1985a). History of sports for individuals with disabilities. *Able Bodies,* **4,** 1, 3.

DePauw, K.P. (1985b). USOC's commitment to sports for individuals with disabilities. *Palaestra,* **1,** 6.

DePauw, K.P. (1986a). Horseback riding for individuals with disabilities: Programs, philosophy, and research. *Adapted Physical Activity Quarterly,* **3,** 217-226.

DePauw, K.P. (1986b). Research on sport for athletes with disabilities. *Adapted Physical Activity Quarterly,* **3,** 292-299.

DePauw, K.P. (1986c). Toward progressive inclusion and acceptance: Implications for physical education. *Adapted Physical Activity Quarterly,* **3,** 1-5.

DePauw, K.P. (1988). Sport for individuals with disabilities: Research opportunities. *Adapted Physical Activity Quarterly*, **5**, 80-89.

DePauw, K.P. (1990a). Sport, society and individuals with disabilities. In G. Reid (Ed.), *Problems in movement control*. North Holland: Elsevier Science.

DePauw, K.P. (1990b). PE and sport for disabled individuals in the United States. *Journal of Physical Education, Recreation and Dance*, **61**, 53-57.

DePauw, K.P. (1990c). Teaching and coaching individuals with disabilities: Research findings and implications. *Physical Education Review*, **13**, 12-16.

DePauw, K.P. (1994). A feminist perspective on sport and sports organizations for persons with disabilities. In R.D. Steadward, E.R. Nelson, & G.D. Wheeler (Eds.), *VISTA '93—The Outlook*. Edmonton, Alberta: Rick Hansen Centre.

DePauw, K.P., & Clarke, K.C. (1986). Sports for disabled U.S. citizens: Influence of amateur sports act. In C. Sherrill (Ed.), *Sport and disabled athletes* (pp. 35-50). Champaign, IL: Human Kinetics.

DePauw, K.P., & Doll-Tepper, G. (1989). European perspectives on adapted physical activity. *Adapted Physical Activity Quarterly*, **6**, 95-99.

DePauw, K.P., & Gavron, S.J. (1991). Coaches of athletes with disabilities. *Physical Educator*, **48**, 33-40.

DePauw, K.P., & Rich, S. (1993). Paralympics for the mentally handicapped. *Palaestra*, **9**, 59-64.

Dodds, A.G., & Carter, D.D.C. (1983). Memory for movement in blind children: The role of previous visual experience. *Journal of Motor Behavior*, **15**, 343-352.

Doll-Tepper, G., & DePauw, K.P. (1989). COSD forum: Sport for the disabled in the Federal Republic of Germany. *Palaestra*, **5**, 6, 13.

Donaldson, G.W., & Swan, M.D. (1979). *Administration of eco-education*. Reston, VA: American Alliance of Health, Physical Education, Recreation and Dance.

Dreisinger, T.E., & Londeree, B.R. (1982). Wheelchair exercise: A review. *Paraplegia*, **20**, 20-34.

Dummer, G., Ewing, M., Halbeck, R., & Overton, S. (1986a). *Achievement motivation, coping processes, and sports participation of athletes with physical handicaps: A brief report*. Unpublished manuscript.

Dummer, G., Ewing, M., Halbeck, R., & Overton, S. (1986b). Cognitive reactions of athletes with cerebral palsy to success and failure in sports competition. *Abstracts of Research Papers. 1986 AAHPERD Convention*, 219. Reston, VA: American Alliance for Health, Physical Education, Recreation and Dance.

Dunn, J.M. (1987). The state-of-the-art of research concerning physical education for handicapped children and youth. In L. Bowers, S. Klesius, & B. Price (Eds.), *Proceedings of the CIVITAN—I'M SPECIAL NETWORK International Conference on Physical Education and Sport for Disabled Persons*. Tampa, FL: University of South Florida.

Dunn, J.M., Morehouse, J.W., & Fredericks, H.D. (1986). *Physical education for the severely handicapped*. Austin, TX: Pro-Ed.

Effgen, S.K. (1981). Effect of an exercise program on the static balance of deaf children. *Physical Therapy*, **61**, 873-877.

Eitzen, D.S., & Sage, G.H. (1986). *Sociology of North American sport*. Dubuque, IA: Brown.

Ellis, M.K., & Darby, L.A. (1993). The effect of balance on the determination of peak oxygen consumption for hearing and nonhearing athletes. *Adapted Physical Activity Quarterly*, **10**, 216-225.

Emes, C. (1978). Physical work capacity of wheelchair athletes. *Research Quarterly*, **48**, 209-212.

Engel, B.T. (1992). *Therapeutic riding programs: Instruction and rehabilitation*. Durango, CO: Barbara Engel Therapy Services.

Engel, R., & Hildebrandt, G. (1974). Wheelchair design: Technological and physiological aspects. *Proceedings of the Royal Society of Medicine*, **67**, 409-411.

Enkola, R.M., Miller, D.I., & Burgess, E.M. (1982). Below-knee amputee running gait. *American Journal of Physical Medicine*, **62**(2), 66-84.

European charter for sport for all: Disabled persons. (1987). Strasbourg, France: Council of Europe.

Felshin, J. (1974). The triple option . . . for women in sport. *Quest*, **21**, 36-40.

Ferrara, M. (1990). *Sports injuries to disabled athletes*. Paper presented at the USODA meeting, Tampa, FL, February 1990.

Ferrara, M., & Davis, R. (1990). Injuries to elite wheelchair athletes. *Paraplegia*, **28**, 335-341.

Floyd, W.F., Guttmann, L., Noble, C.W., Parks, K.R., & Ward, J. (1966). A study of the space requirements of wheelchair users. *Paraplegia*, **4**, 24-37.

Frederick, K.L. (1991). *A comparison of rural and urban parent perceptions of elementary multihandicapped students' leisure activities*. Unpublished master's thesis, Bowling Green State University.

French, R., Henschen, K., & Horvat, M. (1985). The psychological characteristics of female wheelchair basketball players. *Abstracts of Research Papers*. Reston, VA: American Alliance of Health, Physical Education, Recreation and Dance.

Fung, L. (1992). Participation motives in competitive sports: A cross-cultural comparison. *Adapted Physical Activity Quarterly*, **9**, 114-122.

Gandee, R., Datta, S.R., Chatterjee, B.B., & Roy, B.N. (1973). Performance evaluation of amputee prosthesis systems in below-knee amputees. *Ergonomics*, **16**, 797-810.

Gandee, R., Winningham, M., Deitchman, R., & Narraway, A. (1980). The aerobic capacity of an elite wheelchair marathon racer. *Medicine and Science in Sports and Exercise*, **12**, 142.

Gass, G.C., & Camp, E.M. (1979). Physiological characteristics of trained Australian paraplegic and tetraplegic subjects. *Medicine and Science in Sports and Exercise*, **11**, 256-259.

Gavron, S. (1989). *Early play and recreational experiences of elite athletes with disabilities of the VII Pan Am Games*. Paper presented at the VII International Symposium in Adapted Physical Activity, Berlin, June 1989.

Gavron, S.J. (1991). Track and field for all persons. In S. Grosse, C. Cooper, S. Gavron, J. Huber, & J. Stein (Eds.), *Sport instruction for individuals with disabilities* (pp. 217-234). Reston, VA: American Alliance of Health, Physical Education, Recreation and Dance.

Gavron, S., & DePauw, K. (1989). National coaches of disabled skiing: A background survey. *Journal of Applied Research in Coaching and Athletics, 4*(1), 17-34.

Gehlsen, G.M., & Karpuk, J. (1992). Analysis of the NWAA swimming classification system. *Adapted Physical Activity Quarterly, 9,* 141-147.

General and Functional Classification Guide. Barcelona: COOB 92, S.A. Paralympic Division.

Gessaroli, M.E., & Robertson, D.G.E. (1980). Comparison of two wheelchair sprint starts. *Canadian Journal of Applied Sport Sciences, 5*(4), 202.

Gibbons, S.L., & Bushakra, F.B. (1989). Effects of Special Olympics participation on the perceived competence and social acceptance of mentally retarded children. *Adapted Physical Activity Quarterly, 6,* 40-51.

Gibson, P.M. (1979). Therapeutic aspects of wilderness programs: A comprehensive literature review. *Therapeutic Recreation Journal, 3*(3), 21-33.

Giddens, A. (1977). *Studies in social and political theory.* New York: Basic Books.

Gilstrap, T., & Sherrill, C. (1989). Personality profiles of elite blind female athletes. *Palaestra, 6,* 21-23, 31-33.

Glaser, R.M., & Collins, S.R. (1981). Validity of power output estimation for wheelchair locomotion. *American Journal of Physical Medicine, 60,* 180-189.

Glaser, R.M., Foley, D.M., Laubach, L.L., Sawka, M.N., & Suryaprasad, A.G. (1979). Exercise test to evaluate fitness for wheelchair activity. *Paraplegia, 16,* 341-349.

Glaser, R.M., Laubach, L.L., Foley, D.M., Barr, S.A., & Suryaprasad, A.G. (1978). Interval training program for wheelchair users (Abstract). *Medicine and Science in Sports, 10,* 54.

Glaser, R.M., Sawka, M.N., Brune, M.F., & Wilde, S.W. (1980). Physiological responses to maximal effort wheelchair and arm crank ergometry. *Journal of Applied Physiology, 48,* 1060-1064.

Goffman, E. (1963). *Stigma: Notes on the management of spoiled identity.* Englewood Cliffs, NJ: Prentice-Hall.

Goodbrand, S. (1987). *A comparison of the psychological mood profiles of elite cerebral palsied athletes and cerebral palsied nonathletes.* Unpublished master's thesis, McGill University, Montreal.

Gorton, B., & Gavron, S. (1984). A biomechanical analysis of the running patterns of mentally retarded boys and girls in the 50-meter dash. In A. Brown (Ed.), *Adapted physical activities: Proceedings of the Fourth International Symposium in Adapted Physical Activity* (pp. 98-114). Bodmin, Cornwall: Hartnoll.

Gorton, B., & Gavron, S.J. (1987). A biomechanical analysis of the running pattern of blind athletes in the 100-m dash. *Adapted Physical Activity Quarterly, 4,* 192-203.

Grant, J., & Pryke, G. (1987). The organization of disabled sport. In R. Lockwood (Ed.), *Physical Education and Disability* (pp. 209-213). Parkside, Australia: Australian Council for Health, Physical Education, and Recreation.

Greenwood, C.M., Dzewaltowski, D.A., & French, R. (1990). Self-efficacy and psychological well-being of wheelchair tennis participants and wheelchair non-tennis participants. *Adapted Physical Activity Quarterly, 7*(1), 12-21.

Grimes, P.S., & French, L. (1987). Barriers to disabled women's participation in sport. *Journal of Physical Education, Recreation and Dance, 58*, 24-27.

Grosse, S., Cooper, C., Gavron, S., Huber, J., & Stein, J.U. (Eds.). (1991). *Sport instruction for individuals with disabilities: The best of practical pointers.* Washington, DC: American Alliance of Health, Physical Education, Recreation and Dance.

Gueth, V., Abbink, F., Theysoin, H., & Heinrichs, W. (1977). Kinesiologic and electromyographic methods for functional analysis of the muscles of the hip and trunk. *Journal of Human Movement Studies, 3*, 110-119.

Guttmann, L. (1971, July 16). Sport for the disabled. *Times Educational Supplement,* pp. 31-32.

Guttmann, L. (1976). *Textbook of sport for the disabled.* Oxford: HM & M.

Hahn, H. (1984). Sports and the political movement of disabled persons: Examining nondisabled social values. *ARENA Review, 8*, 1-15.

Hale, S. (1988). *Dynamic analysis of the above the knee amputee swing phase during speed walking under varying prosthetic conditions.* Unpublished master's thesis, Dalhousie University, Halifax.

Hall, M.A. (1985). Knowledge and gender: Epistemological questions in the social analysis of sport. *Sociology of Sport Journal, 2*, 25-42.

Hamilton, E.J., & Anderson, S.C. (1983). Effects of leisure activities on attitudes toward people with disabilities. *Therapeutic Recreation Journal, 17*(3), 50-57.

Hamilton, N., & Adrian, M. (1987). A kinematic analysis of the wheelchair javelin throw. *Abstracts of Research Papers, 1987 AAHPERD Convention.* Reston, VA: American Alliance for Health, Physical Education, Recreation and Dance.

Hanna, R.S. (1986). Effect of exercise on blind persons. *Journal of Visual Impairment and Blindness, 5*(80), 722-725.

Hanrahan, S.J., Grove, J.R., & Lockwood, R.J. (1990). Psychological skills training for the blind athlete: A pilot program. *Adapted Physical Activity Quarterly, 7,* 143-155.

Hansen, R., & Taylor, J. (1987) *Rick Hansen: Man in motion.* Vancouver BC: Douglas & McIntyre.

Hanson, B. (1993). Minnesota Association for Adapted Athletics. In D. Beaver (Ed.), *Proceedings of Achieving a Balance: National Adapted Physical Activity Conference* (pp. 10-15). Macomb, IL: Western Illinois University.

Harrison, C., & Kuric, J. (1987). Community reintegration of spinal cord injured persons: Problems and perceptions. *Abstracts Digest of the Annual Scientific Meeting of the American Spinal Cord Injury Association, 13*, 263-267.

Hedrick, B. (1979, December). A look at disabled sports. *Parks & Recreation,* p. 54.

Hedrick, B. (1984). *The effects of wheelchair tennis participation and mainstreaming upon the perceptions of competence of physically disabled adolescents.* Unpublished doctoral dissertation, University of Illinois at Urbana-Champaign.

Hedrick, B. (1985a). The effect of wheelchair tennis participation on adolescents. *Therapeutic Recreation Journal*, **14**, 34-36.

Hedrick, B. (1985b). Women's wheelchair basketball: A perspective on the U.S. program. *Sports 'n Spokes*, **11**, 14-17.

Hedrick, B., Byrnes, D., & Shaver, L. (1989). *Wheelchair basketball*. Washington, DC: Paralyzed Veterans of America.

Hedrick, B., & Hedrick, S. (1991). Women's wheelchair basketball. In J. Hult & M. Trekell (Eds.), *A century of women's basketball* (pp. 367-378). Reston, VA: American Alliance for Health, Physical Education, Recreation and Dance.

Hedrick, B., & Hedrick, S. (1993). *The undiscovered athlete: A perspective on collegiate sports for persons with disabilities*. Paper presented at CESU Conference, Buffalo, NY, July 1993.

Hedrick B., & Morse M. (1991). Setting goals in wheelchair basketball. *Sports 'n Spokes*, **17**(4), 64-65.

Hedrick B., Morse M., & Figoni, S. (1988). Training practices of elite wheelchair roadracers. *Adapted Physical Activity Quarterly*, **5**, 140-153.

Hedrick, B., Wang, Y.T., Moeinzadeh, M., & Adrian, M. (1990). Aerodynamic positioning and performance in wheelchair racing. *Adapted Physical Activity Quarterly*, **7**, 41-51.

Henderson, C. (1992). *College freshmen with disabilities: A statistical profile*. Washington, DC: Health Resource Center.

Henschen, K., Horvat, M., & French, R. (1984). A visual comparison of psychological profiles between able-bodied and wheelchair athletes. *Adapted Physical Activity Quarterly*, **1**, 118-124.

Hetzler, R.K., Knowlton, R.G., Hammill, J., Noakes, T., & Schneider, T. (1986). A physiological and biomechanical comparison of able-bodied persons to wheelchair-dependent persons during wheelchair ergometry. *Abstracts of Research Papers, 1986 AAHPERD Convention*. Reston, VA: American Alliance for Health, Physical Education, Recreation and Dance.

Hewett, F.M., & Forness, S.R. (1974). *Historical origins*. Boston: Allyn & Bacon.

Heyward, S. (1992). *Access to education for the disabled. A guide to compliance with Section 504 of the Rehabilitation Act of 1973*. Jefferson, NC: McFarland.

Higger, Y. (1984). *Biomechanical analysis of stand-up and wheelchair basketball set shooting*. Unpublished master's thesis, University of Alberta.

Higgs, C. (1983). An analysis of racing wheelchairs used at the 1980 Olympic Games for the Disabled. *Research Quarterly for Exercise and Sport*, **54**, 229-233.

Higgs, C. (1986). Propulsion of racing wheelchairs. In C. Sherrill (Ed.), *Sport and disabled athletes* (pp. 165-172). Champaign, IL: Human Kinetics.

Higgs, C. (1990). Wheelchair racquetball: A preliminary time motion analysis. *Adapted Physical Activity Quarterly*, **7**, 370-384.

Higgs, C. (1992). Wheeling in the wind: The effect of wind velocity and direction on the aerodynamic drag of wheelchairs. *Adapted Physical Activity Quarterly*, **9**(1), 74-87.

Higgs, C., Babstock, P., Buck, J., Parsons, C., & Brewer, J. (1990). Wheelchair clarification for track and field experts: A performance approach. *Adapted Physical Activity Quarterly, 7*(1), 22-40.

Hildebrandt, G., Voigt, E.D., Bahn, D., Berendes, B., & Kroger, J. (1970). Energy cost of propelling a wheelchair at various speeds: Cardiac responses and effect on steering accuracy. *Archives of Physical Medicine and Rehabilitation, 51*, 131-136.

Hoffman, M.D. (1986). Cardiorespiratory fitness and training in quadriplegics and paraplegics. *Sportsmedicine, 5*(3), 312-330.

Holcomb, L.P. (1984). Disabled women: A new issue in education. In M. Nagler (Ed.), *Perspectives on Disability* (pp. 381-388). Palo Alto, CA: Health Markets Research.

Hollands, R.G. (1984). The role of cultural studies and social criticism in sociological study of sports. *Quest, 36*, 66-79.

Hooper, C.A. (1982). Socialization of wheelchair athletes in sport. *Dissertation Abstracts International, 43*, 1976A. (University Microfilms No. 84-235, 7242).

Horvat, M., French, R., & Henschen, K. (1986). A comparison of the psychological characteristics of male and female able-bodied and wheelchair athletes. *Paraplegia, 24*, 115-122.

Horvat, M., French, R., & Henschen, K. (1988). Special Olympics training programs around the world . . . a survey. *Palaestra, 5*, 28-31.

Horvat, M., Golding, L., Beutel-Horvat, T., & McConnell, T. (1984). A treadmill modification for wheelchairs. *Research Quarterly for Exercise and Sport, 55*, 297-301.

Howell, C. (1978). Spinal cord injury. In R.M. Goldenson (Ed.), *Disability and rehabilitation handbook*. The Philippines: McGraw-Hill.

Hoy, M.G., Zernicke, R.F., & Whitting, W.C. (1982). Stride characteristics and knee joint kinetics of child amputee gait. *Archives of Physical Medicine and Rehabilitation, 62*(2), 74-82.

Huber, C.A. (1984). An overview and perspective on international disabled sport: Past, present, future. *Rehabilitation World, 8*, 8-11.

Hughes, E. (1949). Social change and status protest: An essay on the marginal man. *Phylon, 10*, 58-65.

Hullemann, K.D., List, M., Matthes, D., Wiese, G., & Zika, D. (1975). Spiroergometric and telemetric investigations during the XXI International Stoke Mandeville Games. *Paraplegia, 13*, 109-123.

Hult, J.S., & Trekell, M. (1991). *A century of women's basketball: From frailty to Final Four*. Reston, VA: American Alliance for Health, Physical Education, Recreation and Dance.

Hunter, D. (1984). Social constraints on the play behavior of the disabled person. *Journal of Leisurability, 4*(11), 8-12.

Hylbert, K.W., & Hylbert, K.W. (1979). *Medical information for human service workers*. Elizabeth, WV: Counselor Education Press.

International Paralympic Committee Newsletter, 1(1).

International Paralympic Committee Newsletter, **2**(1).

International Paralympic Committee Newsletter, **2**(2).

International Paralympic Committee Newsletter, **3**(1).

International Sports Organization for the Disabled (ISOD). *A Brief Presentation of ISOD.* Pamphlet available from ISOD.

Jackson, R., & Schmader, S.W. (1990). *Special events: Inside and out.* Champaign, IL: Sagamore.

Jackson, R.W., & Davis, G.M. (1983). The value of sports and recreation for the physically disabled. *Orthopedic Clinics of North America,* **14**(2), 301-315.

Jackson, R.W., & Frederickson A. (1979). Sports for the physically disabled: The 1976 Olympiad (Toronto). *American Journal of Sports Medicine,* **7**, 293-296.

Jochheim, K.A., & Strohkendl, H. (1973). Value of particular sports of the wheel-chair-disabled in maintaining health of the paraplegic. *Paraplegia,* **11**, 173-178.

Johansson, J.O., & DePauw, K.P. (1991). *Sport socialization of Swedish disabled athletes.* Paper presented at 1991 ISAPA, Miami, FL.

Johnson, R.E., Sundheim, R., & Santos, J. (1989). An outcome study of Special Olympics training techniques on athletes in track and field. *Palaestra,* **5**, 9-11, 62.

Johnston, B. (1992). *Innovator of Disability Equipment and Adaptations.* Pewaukee, WI: IDEA.

Jones, J. (1988). *Training guide to cerebral palsy sports* (3rd ed.). Champaign, IL: Human Kinetics.

Jones, J. (Ed.). (1990). Focus on training. *Palaestra,* **6**(4), 57-58.

Jones, J. (Ed.). (1991). Focus on training. *Palaestra,* **7**(4), 56-57.

Jones, J. (Ed.). (1992). Focus on training. *Palaestra,* **8**(1), 60-61.

Karwas, M.R., & DePauw, K.P. (1990). Parallels between the women's and disabled sport movements. *Abstracts of Research Papers, 1990 AAHPERD Convention.* Reston, VA: American Alliance for Health, Physical Education, Recreation and Dance.

Katz, S., Shurks, E., & Florian, V. (1978). The relationship between physical disability, social perception, and psychological stress. *Scandinavian Journal of Rehabilitation Medicine,* **10**, 109-113.

Kegel, B. (1985). Sports and recreation for those with lower limb impairment. *Journal of Rehabilitation Research and Development* (Suppl. 1), Washington, DC: Veterans Administration.

Kegel, B., Burgess, E.M., Starr, T.W., & Daley, W.K. (1981). Effects of isometric muscle training on residual limb volume, strength, and gait of below-knee amputees. *Physical Therapy,* **61**, 1419-1426.

Kelly, J., & Frieden, L. (1989). *Go for it: A book on sport and recreation for persons with disabilities.* Orlando, FL: Jovanovich.

Kennedy, M.J. (1980). *Sport role socialization and attitudes toward physical activity of wheelchair athletes.* Unpublished master's thesis, University of Oregon, Eugene.

Kennedy, S.O. (1988). Flexibility training for wheelchair athletes. *Sports 'n Spokes*, **13**, 43-46.

Kenyon, G., & McPherson, B. (1973). Becoming involved in physical activity and sport: A process of socialization. In G.L. Rarick (Ed.), *Physical activity: Human growth and development* (pp. 303-332). New York: Academic Press.

Kenyon, G.S. (1968). A conceptual model of characterising physical activity. *Research Quarterly*, **39**, 96-105.

Kisabeth, K.L., & Richardson, D.B. (1985). Changing attitudes toward disabled individuals: The effect on one disabled person. *Therapeutic Recreation Journal*, **19**, 24-33.

Knaus, R.L. (1987). Physiological and psychological benefits of exercise for athletes with disabilities: An interview with George Murray. *Journal of Osteopathic Sports Medicine*, **4**(1), 7-9.

Knoppers, A. (1987). Gender and the coaching profession. *Quest*, **39**, 9-22.

Knowlton, R.G., Fitzgerald, P.L., & Sedlock, D.A. (1981). Mechanical efficiency of wheelchair-dependent women during wheelchair ergometry. *Canadian Journal of Applied Sport Sciences*, **6**, 187-190.

Kobberling, G., Jankowski, L.W., & Leger, L. (1989). Energy cost of locomotion in blind athletes. *Adapted Physical Activity Quarterly*, **6**, 58-67.

Kofsky, P.R., Davis, G.M., Shephard, R.J., Jackson, R.W., & Keene, G.C.R. (1983). Field testing assessment of physical fitness of disabled adults. *European Journal of Applied Physiology and Occupational Physiology*, **5**, 109-120.

Koivumaki, K. (1987). Sports and physical activities for special groups. In *Sports and Physical Education in Finland*. Helsinki: Finnish Society for Research in Sport and Physical Education.

Kowalski, E., & McCann, H. (1991). The Victory Games: Milestone on the road to Barcelona. *Palaestra*, **8**(1), 24-29.

Kruimer, A., Hoeberigs, J.H., & Vorteveld, H. (1985). Classification system for wheelchair basketball (pp. 111-117). *Workshop on Sport for Disabled* (*Proceedings*), Amersfoot, The Netherlands.

Labanowich, S. (1978). Psychology of wheelchair sports. *Therapeutic Recreation Journal*, **12**, 11-17.

Labanowich, S. (1980). *NCAA proposed statement of policy and recommendations for the implementation of Section 504 of the Rehabilitation Act of 1973*. Unpublished manuscript.

Labanowich, S. (1988). A case for the integration of the disabled into the Olympic Games. *Adapted Physical Activity Quarterly*, **5**, 264-272.

Labanowich, S., Karman, P., Veal, L.E., & Wiley, B.D. (1984). Principles and foundations for the organization of wheelchair sports. *Sports 'n Spokes*, **2**, 26-32.

Lakomy, H.K.A., Campbell, I., & Williams, C. (1987). Treadmill performance and selected physiological characteristics of wheelchair athletes. *British Journal of Sports Medicine*, **21**, 130-133.

LaMere, T., & Labanowich, S. (1984a). The history of sport wheelchairs: 1. Background of wheelchair basketball. *Sports 'n Spokes*, **2**, 6-11.

LaMere, T., & Labanowich, S. (1984b). The history of sport wheelchairs: 2. The racing wheelchair. *Sports 'n Spokes*, **2**, 12-16.

Landry, F. (1992). *Olympism, Olympics, Paralympism, Paralympics: Converging or diverging notions and courses on the eve of the third millennium?* Paper presented at the 1st Paralympic Congress, August 31, 1992, Barcelona.

Le, C.T., & Price, M. (1982). Survival from spinal cord injury. *Journal of Chronic Disease*, **35**, 487-492.

Lee, M., Ward, G., & Shephard, R.J. (1985). Physical capacities of sightless adolescents. *Developmental Medicine and Child Neurology*, **27**, 767-774.

Lenskyj, H. (1991). *Women, sport and physical activity: Research and bibliography.* Ottawa, Canada: Minister of Supply and Services Canada.

Leonard, J. (1980). *A sociological perspective of sport.* Minneapolis: Burgess.

Lewallen, R., Quanbury, A.O., Ross, K., & Letts, R.M. (1985). A biomechanical study of normal and amputee gait. In D.A. Winter, R.W. Norman, R.P. Wells, K.C. Hayes, & A.E. Patla (Eds.), *Biomechanics IX-A* (pp. 587-593). Champaign, IL: Human Kinetics.

Lewis, S., Higam, L., & Cherry, D. (1985). Development of an exercise program to improve the static and dynamic balance of profoundly hearing impaired children. *American Annals of the Deaf*, **4**(130), 278-283.

Lewko, J. (1979). Significant others and sport socialization of the handicapped child. In F. Smoll & R. Smith (Eds.), *Psychological perspectives in youth sports* (pp. 249-277). New York: Wiley.

Lilly, M.S. (1983). *Divestiture in special education: An alternative model for resource and support services.* Unpublished manuscript.

Lindstrom, H. (1984). Sports for disabled: Alive and well. *Rehabilitation World*, **8**, 12-16.

Lindstrom, H. (1985). An integrated classification system. *Palaestra*, **2**(1), 47-49.

Lindstrom, H. (1986). Sports classification for locomotor disabilities: Integrated versus diagnostic systems. In C. Sherrill (Ed.), *Sport and disabled athletes* (pp. 131-136). Champaign, IL: Human Kinetics.

Lindstrom, H. (1990). The dramatic birth of a new international body for the disabled. *Palaestra*, **6**, 12-15.

Lipton, B.H. (1970). Role of wheelchair sports in rehabilitation. *International Rehabilitation Review*, **21**(2), 25-27.

Lugo, A., Sherrill, C., & Pizarro, A. (1992). Use of a sport socialization inventory with cerebral palsied youth. *Perception and Motor Skills*, **74**, 203-208.

Lundberg, A. (1980). Wheelchair driving evaluation of a new training outfit. *Scandinavian Journal of Rehabilitation Medicine*, **12**, 67-72.

Lussier, L., Knight, J., Bell, G., Lohmann, T., & Morris, A.F. (1983). Body composition in two elite female wheelchair athletes. *Paraplegia*, **21**, 16-22.

MacGowan, H.E. (1983). The kinematic analysis of the walking gait of sighted and congenitally blind and sighted children. *Dissertation Abstracts International,* **44,** 703a.

Madorsky, J.B., & Curtis, K.A. (1984). Wheelchair sports medicine. *American Journal of Sports Medicine,* **12,** 128-132.

Madorsky, J.B., & Kiley, D.P. (1984). Wheelchair mountaineering. *Archives of Physical Medicine and Rehabilitation,* **65,** 490-492.

Madorsky, J.B., & Madorsky, A. (1983). Wheelchair racing: An important modality in acute rehabilitation after paraplegia. *Archives of Physical Medicine and Rehabilitation,* **64,** 186-187.

Maki, B.E., Rosen, J.H., & Simon, R. (1985). Modification of spastic gait through mechanical damping. *Journal of Biomechanics,* **18,** 431-443.

Mangus, B. (1987). Sports injuries, the disabled athlete, and the athletic trainer. *Athletic Training,* **22**(4), 305-308.

Marti, B., Abelin, T., & Minder, C. (1988). Relationship of training and lifestyle to 16km running time of 4,000 joggers. *International Journal of Sports Medicine,* **9,** 85-91.

Martinez, R. (1991). Catastrophes at sporting events. *Physician and Sportsmedicine,* **19**(11), 40, 43-44.

Mastenbroek, A.C. (1979). *Delta and net muscular efficiency in wheelchair athletes during steady rate exercise in two types of wheelchairs.* Unpublished master's thesis, University of Oregon, Eugene.

Mastro, J.V., Canabal, M., & French, R. (1986). Mood profiles of visually impaired and sighted beep baseball players. *Abstracts of Research Papers, 1986 AAHPERD Convention.* Reston, VA: American Alliance for Health, Physical Education, Recreation and Dance.

Mastro, J.V., & French, R. (1986). Sport anxiety and elite blind athletes. In C. Sherrill (Ed.), *Sport and disabled athletes* (pp. 203-208). Champaign, IL: Human Kinetics.

Mastro, J.V., French, R., Henschen, K., & Horvat, M. (1985). Use of the State-Trait anxiety inventory for visually impaired athletes. *Perceptual and Motor Skills,* **61,** 775-778.

Mastro, J.V., French, R., Henschen, K., & Horvat, M. (1986). Selected psychological characteristics of blind golfers and their coaches. *American Corrective Therapy Journal,* **40,** 111-114.

Mastro, J.V., Hall, M.M., & Canabal, M.Y. (1988). Cultural and attitudinal similarities: Female and disabled individuals in sport and athletics. *Journal of Physical Education, Recreation and Dance,* **59,** 80-83.

Mastro, J.V., Sherrill, C., Gench, B., & French, R. (1987). Psychological characteristics of elite visually impaired athletes: The iceberg profile. *Journal of Sport Behavior,* **10,** 39-46.

Mayberry, R.P. (1978). The mystique of the horse is strong medicine: Riding as therapeutic recreation. *Rehabilitation Literature,* **39,** 192-196.

McCann, C.B. (1979). Wheelchair medical classification system. *Proceedings of the First International Conference on Sport and Training of the Physically Disabled Athlete*, University of Alberta, Edmonton, 25-35.

McCann, C.B. (1980). Medical classification: Art, science, or instinct? *Sports 'n Spokes*, **5**, 12-14.

McCann, C.B. (1981). Does the track athlete need medical classification? A possible effect of wheelchair design. *Sports 'n Spokes*, **7**, 22-24.

McCann, C.B. (1984). Classification of the locomotor disabled for competitive sports: Theory and practice. *International Journal of Sports Medicine*, (Suppl. 5), 167-170.

McCann, C.B. (1987). The structure and future of sport for the disabled: The Arnheim seminar. *Palaestra*, **3**, 9-40.

McCormick, D. (1985). Injuries in handicapped alpine ski racers. *Physician and Sportsmedicine*, **13**, 93-97.

McCubbin, J.A., & Shasby, G.B. (1985). Effects of isokinetic exercise on adolescents with cerebral palsy. *Adapted Physical Activity Quarterly*, **2**, 56-64.

McPherson, B.D., Curtis, J.E., & Loy, J.W. (1989). *The social significance of sport*. Champaign, IL: Human Kinetics.

Merklinger, A. (1991). Committee on integration of athletes with a disability. *International Paralympic Committee Newsletter*, **2**, 8-9.

Miles, D.S., Sawka, M.N., Wilde, S.W., Durbin, R.J., & Gotshall, R.W. (1982). Pulmonary function changes in wheelchair athletes subsequent to exercise training. *Ergonomics*, **25**, 239-246.

Miller, D.I. (1981). Biomechanical considerations in lower extremity amputee running and sports performance. *Australian Journal of Sport Medicine*, **13**(3), 55-87.

Monnazzi, G. (1982). Paraplegics and sports: A psychological survey. *International Journal of Sports Psychology*, **13**, 85-95.

Morgan, W.P. (1982). Psychological effects of exercise. *Behavioral Medicine Update*, **4**, 25-30.

Morris, A.F. (1984). A philosophy of sports and recreation at a comprehensive rehabilitation center. *Rehabilitation World*, **8**, 30-31, 60-61.

Morris, A.F. (1986). A case study of a female ultramarathon wheelchair road racer. *Paraplegia*, **24**, 260-264.

Munson, A.L., & Comodeca, J.A. (1993). The act of inclusion. *Athletic Management*, **5**(4), 14-17.

Murphy-Howe, R., & Charboneau, B. (1987). *Therapeutic recreation intervention: An ecological perspective*. Englewood Cliffs, NJ: Prentice-Hall.

Myers, K. (1991). Pushing a wheelchair . . . fast! *Sports 'n Spokes*, **16**, 51-54.

Nesbitt, J.A. (1986). *The international directory of recreation-oriented assistive diver's sources*. Marina del Rey, CA: Lifeboat Press.

Nilsen, R., Nygaard, P., & Bjorholt, P.G. (1985). Complications that may occur in those with spinal cord injuries who participate in sport. *Paraplegia*, **23**, 52-58.

Nilsson, S. (1975). Physical work capacity and the effect of training on subjects with longstanding paraplegia. *Scandinavian Journal of Rehabilitation Medicine,* **7,** 51-56.

Nixon, H. (1988). Getting over the worry hurdle: Parental encouragement and sports involvement of visually impaired children and youths. *Adapted Physical Activity Quarterly,* **5**(1), 29-43.

Nixon, H.L. (1989). Integration of disabled people in mainstream sports: Case study of a partially sighted child. *Adapted Physical Activity Quarterly,* **6**(1), 17-31.

Nugent, T.J. (1964). Let's look beyond. *Recreation in Treatment Centers,* **3,** 3-42.

Ogilvie, B.C. (1985). Sports psychologists and the disabled athlete. *Palaestra,* **4**(1), 36-40, 43.

O'Leary, H. (1987). *Bold tracks: Skiing for the disabled.* Evergreen, CO: Cordillera Press.

Orr, R. (1979). Sport, myth and the handicapped athlete. *Journal of Physical Education, Recreation and Dance,* **50,** 33-34.

Owen, E. (1982). *Playing and coaching wheelchair basketball.* Urbana: University of Illinois Press.

Pachner, J.L. (1993-94). *Products to assist the disabled sportsman.* Laguna Niguel, CA: Author.

Paciorek, M.J. (1993). Technology only a part of the story as world records fall. *Palaestra,* **9,** 14-19.

Paciorek, M.J., & Jones, J.A. (1989). *Sports and recreation for the disabled: A resource handbook.* Indianapolis: Benchmark Press.

Pardine, P., Napoli, A., & Eustace, A. (1985). Personality profiles of world-class disabled athletes. *Abstracts of Research Papers, 1985 AAHPERD Convention.* Reston, VA: American Alliance for Health, Physical Education, Recreation and Dance.

Park, R. (1928). Human migration and the marginal man. *American Journal of Sociology,* **33,** 881-893.

Parks, W. (1986). A model program: The journal wheelchair sports camp program. *Palaestra,* **3**(2), 16-19.

Patrick, G.D. (1986). The effects of wheelchair competition on self-concept and acceptance of disability in novice athletes. *Therapeutic Recreation Journal,* **4**(20), 61-71.

Patrick, G.D. (1987). Improving attitudes towards disabled persons. *Adapted Physical Activity Quarterly,* **4,** 316-325.

Pender, R.H., & Patterson, P.E. (1982). A comparison of selected motor fitness items between congenitally deaf and hearing children. *Journal for Special Education,* **4**(18), 71-75.

Physical activity and women with disabilities: A national survey. (n.d.). Ottawa, ON: Fitness Canada.

Pitetti, K.H., Jackson, J.A., Stubbs, N.B., Campbell, K.D., & Battar, S.S. (1989). Fitness levels of adult Special Olympic participants. *Adapted Physical Activity Quarterly*, **6**, 354-370.

Pollock, M.L., Miller, H.S., Linnerud, A.C., Laughridge, E., & Coleman, E. (1974). Arm pedaling as an endurance training regimen for the disabled. *Archives of Physical Medicine and Rehabilitation*, **55**, 418-424.

Pope, C.J., McGrain, P., & Arnhold, R.W. (1986). Running gait of the blind: A kinematic analysis. In C. Sherrill (Ed.), *Sport and disabled athletes* (pp. 173-179). Champaign, IL: Human Kinetics.

Pope, C.J., Sherrill, C., Wilkerson, J., & Pyfer, J. (1993). Biomechanical variables in sprint running of athletes with cerebral palsy. *Adapted Physical Activity Quarterly*, **10**, 226-254.

Price, R. (1983). *Spinal cord injury, life stage and leisure satisfaction*. Unpublished doctoral dissertation, University of Illinois at Urbana-Champaign.

Pyfer, J.L. (1986). Early research concerns in adapted physical education. *Adapted Physical Activity Quarterly*, **3**, 95-103.

Raiborn, M.H. (1990). *Revenues and expenses of intercollegiate athletics programs: Analysis of financial trends and relationships, 1985-1989*. Overland Park, KS: National Collegiate Athletic Association.

Rarick, G.L., Dobbins, D.A., & Broadhead, G.D. (1976). *The motor domain and its correlates in educationally handicapped children*. Englewood Cliffs, NJ: Prentice-Hall.

Reid, G. (1986). Ideas about motor behavior research with special populations. *Adapted Physical Activity Quarterly*, **3**, 1-10.

Rich, S. (1990). Factors influencing the learning process. In J. Winnick (Ed.), *Adapted physical education and sport* (pp. 121-130). Champaign, IL: Human Kinetics.

Richardson, D.B. (1986). Movement purpose values among wheelchair athletes. *Abstracts of Research Papers, 1986 AAHPERD Convention*. Reston, VA: American Alliance of Health, Physical Education, Recreation and Dance.

Richter, K.J., Adams-Mushett, C., Ferrara, M.S., & McCann, B.C. (1992). Integrated swimming classification: A faulted system. *Adapted Physical Activity Quarterly*, **9**(1), 5-13.

Ridgeway, M., Pope, C., & Wilkerson, J. (1988). A kinematic analysis of 800-meter wheelchair racing techniques. *Adapted Physical Activity Quarterly*, **5**, 96-107.

Riggen, K., & Ulrich, D. (1993). The effects of sport participation on individuals with mental retardation, *Adapted Physical Activity Quarterly*, **10**(1), 42-51.

Rimmer, J.H., & Kelly, L.E. (1991). Effects of a resistance training program on adults with mental retardation. *Adapted Physical Activity Quarterly*, **8**(2), 146-153.

Road racing training. (1986, Spring). *National Wheelchair Athletic Association Newsletter*, 18-19.

Roeder, L.K., & Aufsesser, P.M. (1986). Selected attentional and interpersonal characteristics of wheelchair athletes. *Palaestra*, **2**, 28-32.

Roper, P.A., & Silver, C. (1989). Regular track competition for athletes with mental retardation. *Palaestra*, **5**, 14-16, 42-43, 58-59.

Roswal, G.M. (1988). Coaches' training the Special Olympics way. *Palaestra*, **5**, 36-37, 41.

Roswell, G., Jacobs, D., & Horvat, M. (1986). Psychological make-up and self-concept of the junior wheelchair athlete. *NCPERH Newsletter*, **15**, 6.

Rothschild, C.S. (1968). Prejudice against the disabled and the means to combat it. In J. Stebbins (Ed.), *Social and psychological aspects of disability: A handbook for practitioners* (pp. 261-267). Baltimore: University Park Press.

Ryser, D.K., Erickson, R.P., & Calahan, T. (1988). Isometric and isokinetic hip abductor strength in persons with above-knee amputations. *Archives of Physical Medicine and Rehabilitation*, **10**(69), 840-845.

Sage, G.H. (1987). Pursuit of knowledge in sociology of sport: Issues and prospects. *Quest*, **39**, 255-281.

Sanderson, D.J., & Sommer, H.J. (1985). Kinematic features of wheelchair propulsion. *Journal of Biomechanics*, **18**, 423-429.

Schuman, S. (1979). Wheelchair frame modification. *Sports 'n Spokes*, **4**, 5-6.

Seymour, R.J., & Lacefield, W.E. (1985). Wheelchair cushion effect on pressure and skin temperature. *Archives of Physical Medicine and Rehabilitation*, **66**, 103-108.

Shephard, R.J. (1990). *Fitness in special populations*. Champaign, IL: Human Kinetics.

Sherrill, C. (1986). Social and psychological dimensions of sports for disabled athletes. In C. Sherrill (Ed.), *Sport and disabled athletes* (pp. 21-33). Champaign, IL: Human Kinetics.

Sherrill, C. (1990). Psychosocial status of disabled athletes. In G. Reid (Ed.), *Problems in motor control* (pp. 339-364). Amsterdam: North-Holland.

Sherrill, C. (1993). Paralympics 1992: Excellence and challenge. *Palaestra*, **9**, 25-42.

Sherrill, C., Adams-Mushett, C., & Jones, J. (1986). Classification and other issues in sports for blind, cerebral palsied, les autres, and amputee athletes. In C. Sherrill (Ed.), *Sport and disabled athletes* (pp. 113-130). Champaign, IL: Human Kinetics.

Sherrill, C., Pope, C., & Arnhold, R. (1986). Sport socialization of blind athletes. *Journal of Visual Impairment and Blindness*, **80**(5), 740-744.

Sherrill, C., & Rainbolt, W.J. (1986). Sociological perspectives of cerebral palsy sports. *Palaestra*, **4**(2), 21-26, 50.

Sherrill, C., & Rainbolt, W.J. (1987). Self-actualization profiles and able-bodied and cerebral palsied female athletes. *Abstracts of research papers presented at the 1987 AAHPERD Convention*. Reston, VA: American Alliance for Health, Physical Education, Recreation and Dance.

Sherrill, C., Rainbolt, W.J, Montelione, T., & Pope, C. (1986). Sport socialization of blind and cerebral palsied elite athletes. In C. Sherrill (Ed.), *Sport and disabled athletes* (pp. 189-196). Champaign, IL: Human Kinetics.

Shontz, F.C. (1978). Psychological adjustment to physical disability: Trends in theories. *Archives of Physical Medicine and Rehabilitation*, **59**, 251-254.

Siller, J.S. (1960). Psychological concomitants of amputation in children. *Child Development*, **31**, 109-120.

Silliman, L.M., Annabelle, M.L., & French, R. (1989). Integrating profoundly mentally retarded children and youth into the community through physical recreation activities. *Palaestra*, **5**, 13-15, 36.

Skrinar, G.S., Evans, W.J., Ornstein, L.J., & Brown, D.A. (1982). Glycogen utilization in wheelchair-dependent athletes. *International Journal of Sports Medicine*, **3**, 215-219.

Skrotsky, K. (1983). Gait analysis in cerebral palsied and nonhandicapped children. *Archives of Physical Medicine and Rehabilitation*, **64**, 291-295.

Smith, A.W. (1990). A biomechanical analysis of amputee athlete gait. *International Journal of Sport Biomechanics*, **6**, 262-282.

Smith, A.W., Smith, L., Fraser, C., & Grebert, J. (1988). Biomechanical analyses of amputee athlete gait. In M. Torode (Ed.), *The athlete maximising participation and minimising risk* (pp. 123-132). Sydney: Cumberland College of Health Sciences, Australian Sports Federation.

Snyder, E.E. (1984). Sport involvement for the handicapped: Some analytical and sensitizing concepts. *ARENA Review*, **8**, 16-26.

Songster, T. (1986). The Special Olympics sport program: An international sport program for mentally retarded athletes. In C. Sherrill (Ed.), *Sport and disabled athletes* (pp. 73-80). Champaign, IL: Human Kinetics.

Sparling P., Wilson G., & Pate R. (1987). Project overview and description of performance, training, and physical characteristics in elite women distance runners. *International Journal of Sports Medicine*, **2**, 73-76.

Squires, J. (1987). Classification: Can the best means to the fairest end be found? *Palaestra*, **3**(4), 45-48.

Staros, A. (1981). Testing manually propelled wheelchairs. *Prosthetics and Orthotics International*, **5**, 75-84.

Steadward, R.D. (1980). Analysis of wheelchair sport events. In H. Navtig (Ed.), *Proceedings of the First International Medical Congress on Sports for the Disabled* (pp. 184-192). Oslo, Norway: Royal Ministry of Church and Education, State Office for Youth and Sports.

Steadward, R.D. (1987). Advance in knowledge related to disabled athletes. *CAHPER/ACSEPL Journal*, **5**(53), 36-38.

Steadward, R.D. (1990). International Paralympic Committee. *IFAPA Newsletter*. Berlin: International Federation of Adapted Physical Activity.

Steadward, R.D., & Walsh, C. (1986). Training and fitness programs for disabled athletes: Past, present and future. In C. Sherrill (Ed.), *Sport and disabled athletes* (pp. 3-19). Champaign, IL: Human Kinetics.

Stein, J.U. (1983). Bridge over troubled waters—Research and recommendations for relevance. In R.L. Eason, T.L. Smith, & F. Caron (Eds.), *Adapted physical activity* (pp. 189-198). Champaign, IL: Human Kinetics.

Stein, J.U. (1986). International perspectives: Physical education and sport for participants with handicapping conditions. In C. Sherrill (Ed.), *Sport and disabled athletes* (pp. 51-64). Champaign, IL: Human Kinetics.

Stewart, D.A. (1985). Silently succeeding: How to become a better coach of deaf athletes. *Coaching Review*, **8**, 30-33.

Stewart, D.A. (1987). Social factors influencing participation in sport for the deaf. *Palaestra*, **4**(3), 22-28, 50.

Stewart, D.A. (1990). Global dimensions of World Games for the Deaf. *Palaestra*, **6**, 32-35, 43.

Stewart, D.A. (1991). *Deaf sport: The impact of sports within the Deaf community.* Washington, DC: Gallaudet University Press.

Stewart, D.A. (1993). Participating in deaf sport: Characteristics of deaf spectators. *Adapted Physical Activity Quarterly*, **10**, 146-156.

Stewart, D.A., McCarthy, D., & Robinson, J. (1988). Participation in deaf sport: characteristics of deaf sport directors. *Adapted Physical Activity Quarterly*, **5**, 233-244.

Stewart, D.A., Robinson, J., & McCarthy, D. (1991). Participation in deaf sport: Characteristics of elite deaf athletes. *Adapted Physical Activity Quarterly*, **8**(2), 136-145.

Stewart, N. (1981). The value of sport in the rehabilitation of the physically disabled. *Canadian Journal of Applied Sport Sciences*, **6**(4), 166-167.

Stoboy, H., & Wilson-Rich, B. (1971). Muscle strength and electrical activity, heart rate and energy cost during isometric contractions in disabled and nondisabled. *Paraplegia*, **8**(4), 217-222.

Stotts, K.M. (1985). Health maintenance: Paraplegic athletes and nonathletes. *Archives of Physical Medicine and Rehabilitation*, **67**, 109-114.

Strohkendl, H. (1986). The new classification for wheelchair basketball. In C. Sherrill (Ed.), *Sport and disabled athletes* (pp. 101-112). Champaign, IL: Human Kinetics.

Surburg, P.R. (1985). Basic problems in motor learning research. *Adapted Physical Activity Quarterly*, **2**(2), 98-106.

Szyman, R. (1980). *The effect of participation in wheelchair sports.* Unpublished doctoral dissertation, University of Illinois at Urbana-Champaign.

Taylor, A.W., McDonnell, E., Royer, D., Loiselle, R., Luch, N., & Steadward, R. (1979). Skeletal muscle analysis of wheelchair athletes. *Paraplegia*, **17**, 456-460.

Taylor, A.W., McDonnell, E., & Brassard, L. (1986). The effect of an arm ergometer training programme on wheelchair subjects. *Paraplegia*, **24**, 105-114.

Tesch, A., & Karlsson, J. (1983). Muscle fiber type characteristics of M. Deltoideus in wheelchair users. *American Journal of Physical Medicine*, **62**, 239-243.

Theberge, N. (1985). Toward a feminist alternative to sport as a male perspective. *Quest*, **37**, 193-202.

Thiboutot, A., Smith, R.W., & Labanowich, S. (1992). Examining the concept of reverse integration: A response to Brasile's new perspective on integration. *Adapted Physical Activity Quarterly*, **9**, 283-292.

Thiboutot, T. (1986). Classification: Time for change. *Sports 'n Spokes*, **11**, 42-44.

United States Department of Health and Human Services Public Health Service. (1991). *Healthy people 2000: National health promotion and disease prevention objectives*. Washington, DC: Author.

United States Olympic Committee. (1989). *USOC constitution and by-laws*. Colorado Springs, CO: Author.

United States Olympic Committee. (1993). *1993 United States Olympic Committee fact book*. Colorado Springs, CO: Author.

United we stand. (1988). International Fund Sports Disabled. Arnhern, The Netherlands: Author.

Valliant, P.M., Bezzubyk, I., Daley, L., & Asu, M.E. (1985). Psychological impact of sport on disabled athletes. *Psychological Reports*, **3**(56), 923-929.

van Alste, J.A., Cruts, H.E., Huisman, K., & de Vries, J. (1985). Exercise testing of leg amputees and the result of prosthetic training. *International Rehabilitation Medicine*, **3**(7), 93-98.

van Hal, L., Rarick, G.L., & Vermeer, A. (1984). *Sport for the mentally handicapped*. Haarlem, The Netherlands: Uitgeverij de Vrisesborch.

Vargo, J.W. (1978). Some psychological effects of physical disability. *American Journal of Occupational Therapy*, **32**, 32-34.

Vermeer, A. (1986). *Sports for the disabled*. Haarlem, The Netherlands: Uitgeverij de Vrisesborch.

Vermeer, A. (1988). *European Association for Research in Adapted Physical Activity Newsletter*. Amsterdam: Faculty of Human Movement Sciences.

Vinton, D.A., Hawkins, D.E., Pantzer, B.D., & Farley, E.M. (1978). *Camping and environmental education for handicapped children and youth*. Washington, DC: Hawkins.

Voeltz, L.M. (1982). Social validation of leisure activities training with severely handicapped youths. *Journal of the Association for the Severely Handicapped*, **4**(7), 3-13.

Voigt, E.D., & Bahn, D. (1969). Metabolism and pulse rate in physically handicapped when propelling a wheelchair up an incline. *Scandinavian Journal of Rehabilitation Medicine*, **1**, 101-106.

Wall, A.E. (1990). Fostering physical activity among Canadians with disabilities. *Journal of Physical Education, Recreation and Dance*, **61**, 52, 54, 56.

Walsh, C.M. (1986). *The effect of pushing frequency on the kinematics of wheelchair sprinting*. Unpublished master's thesis, University of Alberta.

Walsh, C.M., Holland, L.J., & Steadward, R.D. (1985). *Get fit: Aerobic exercises for the wheelchair user*. Edmonton, Alberta: University of Alberta (Research and Training Centre for the Physically Disabled).

Walsh, C.M., Hoy, D.J., & Holland, L.J. (1982). *Get fit: Flexibility exercises for the wheelchair user.* Edmonton, Alberta: University of Alberta (Research and Training Centre for the Physically Disabled).

Walsh, C.M., Marchiori, G.E., & Steadward, R.D. (1986). Effect of seat position on maximal linear velocity in wheelchair sprinting. *Canadian Journal of Applied Sport Sciences,* **11,** 186-190.

Walsh, C.M., & Steadward, R.D. (1984). *Get fit: Muscular exercises for the wheelchair user.* Edmonton, Alberta: University of Alberta (Research and Training Centre for the Physically Disabled).

Wang, W., & DePauw, K.P. (1991). *Early sport socialization of Chinese disabled athletes.* Paper presented at 1991 International Symposium on Adapted Physical Activity, Miami, FL.

Wantanabe, K.T., Cooper, R.A., Vosse, A.J., Baldini, F.D., & Robertson, R.N. (1992). Training practices of athletes who participated in the National Wheelchair Athletic Association training camps. *Adapted Physical Activity Quarterly,* **9**(3), 249-260.

Weiss, M., & Curtis, K. (1986). Controversies in medical classification of wheelchair athletes. In C. Sherrill (Ed.), *Sport and disabled athletes* (pp. 93-100). Champaign, IL: Human Kinetics.

Weller, R.B., & Truex, W.O. (1985). Assessing the effects of experimental studies on the self-concept of preadolescent physically handicapped. *American Corrective Therapy Journal,* **6**(39), 134-140.

Wells, C.L., & Hooker, S.P. (1990). The spinal injured athlete. *Adapted Physical Activity Quarterly,* **7,** 265-285.

West, J. (Ed.) (1991). *The Americans with Disabilities Act: From policy to practice.* New York: Milbank Memorial Fund.

Whitaker, G., & Molstead, S. (1988). Role modeling and female coaches. *Sex Roles,* **18,** 555-566.

White, A.S., & Duda, J.L. (1993). Dimensions of goals and beliefs among adolescent athletes with physical disabilities. *Adapted Physical Activity Quarterly,* **10**(2), 125-136.

Wicks, J.R., Oldridge, N.G., Cameron, B.J., & Jones, N.L. (1983). Arm cranking and wheelchair ergometry in elite spinal cord–injured athletes. *Medicine and Science in Sports and Exercise,* **15,** 224-231.

Williams, T. (1994). Disability sport socialization and identity construction. *Adapted Physical Activity Quarterly,* **11,** 14-31.

Winnick, J.P. (1988). Classification of individuals with handicapping conditions for testing. *Journal of Physical Education, Recreation and Dance,* **59**(1), 34-37.

Wirta, R.W., Golbranson, F.L., Manson, R., & Calvo, K. (1990). Analysis of below-knee suspension systems: Effect on gait. *Journal of Rehabilitation Research,* **27**(4), 385-396.

Wolfensberger, W. (1983). Social role valorization: A proposed new term for the principle of normalization. *Mental Retardation,* **21**(6), 234-239.

Woodman, L. (1988). Coaching advances for athletes with disabilities. *NICAN Networking,* **1**(2), 1-2.

Wright, B.A. (1960. *Physical disability: A psychological approach.* New York: Harper & Brothers.

Wright, J., & Cowden, J. (1986). Changes in self-concept and cardiovascular endurance of mentally retarded youths in a Special Olympics swim training program. *Adapted Physical Activity Quarterly,* **3**, 177-183.

Wyness, G.B. (1984). Strategic reminders for effective event management. *Athletic Business,* **8**, 72-77.

York, S., & Kimura, I. (1986). An analysis of basic construction variables of racing wheelchairs used in the 1984 International Games for the Disabled. *Research Quarterly for Exercise and Sports,* **58**, 16-20.

Zwiren, L., & Bar-Or, O. (1975). Responses to exercise of paraplegics who differ in conditioning level. *Medicine and Science in Sports and Exercise,* **7**, 94-98.

Zwiren, L., Huberman, G., & Bar-Or, O. (1973). Cardiopulmonary functions of sedentary and highly active paraplegics. *Medicine and Science in Sport,* **5**, 683-686.

INDEX

Karen DePauw   Susan Gavron

About the Authors

Karen P. DePauw, PhD, is associate dean of the Graduate School and professor in the Department of Kinesiology and Leisure Studies at Washington State University. She received her doctorate in adapted physical education at Texas Woman's University in 1980. She has been involved in adapted physical activity and disability sport as an educator, author, and researcher since 1970.

From 1981 to 1993, Dr. DePauw served on the United States Olympic Committee (USOC) Committee on Sports for the Disabled, USOC Task Force on Disability, and USOC Task Force on Women. She is also a member of the Organizing Committee for the 1996 Paralympic Congress in Atlanta, GA.

Dr. DePauw is president of the International Federation on Adapted Physical Activity (IFAPA). She is also a member of the American Alliance for Health, Physical Education, Recreation and Dance (AAHPERD); American College of Sports Medicine; National Association for Physical Education in Higher Education (NAPEHE); National Consortium on Physical Education and Recreation for Handicapped (NCPERH); and North American Federation for Adapted Physical Activity. She also serves on the editorial board of *Adapted Physical Activity Quarterly*.

Susan J. Gavron, PED, is associate professor and graduate program coordinator in the School of Health, Physical Education, and Recreation at Bowling Green State University in Ohio. She received her doctorate in adapted secondary special education at Indiana University in 1976.

Dr. Gavron has more than 20 years' experience working with individuals with disabilities from age 6 months through adult—including work as a volunteer for Special Olympics. She participated in the research advisory group for the USOC Committee on Sports for the Disabled and has been involved in research of elite athletes with disabilities at the national and international levels. Dr. Gavron also has extensive programming experience in physical education and leisure for individuals with disabilities. She is a member of IFAPA, AAHPERD, NCPERH, NAPEHE, and NAFAPA.

You'll find other outstanding adapted physical activity resources at

www.humankinetics.com

In the U.S. call
1-800-747-4457

Australia .... (08) 8277-1555
Canada .... (800) 465-7301
Europe .... +44 (0) 113-278-1708
New Zealand .... (09) 309-1890